Ancient Greek Religion

Blackwell Ancient Religions

Ancient religious practice and belief are at once fascinating and alien for twenty-first century readers. There was no Bible, no creed, no fixed set of beliefs. Rather, ancient religion was characterized by extraordinary diversity in belief and ritual.

This distance means that modern readers need a guide to ancient religious experience. Written by experts, the books in this series provide accessible introductions to this central aspect of the ancient world.

Published

Ancient Greek Religion
Jon D. Mikalson

Forthcoming

Religion of the Roman Republic
Christopher McDonough

Religion in the Roman Empire
James Rives

Death, Burial and the Afterlife in Ancient Egypt
Steven Snape

Ancient Greek Religion

Jon D. Mikalson

Blackwell
Publishing

© 2005 by Jon D. Mikalson

BLACKWELL PUBLISHING
350 Main Street, Malden, MA 02148-5020, USA
9600 Garsington Road, Oxford OX4 2DQ, UK
550 Swanston Street, Carlton, Victoria 3053, Australia

First published 2005 by Blackwell Publishing Ltd

2   2005

Library of Congress Cataloging-in-Publication Data

Mikalson, Jon D., 1943–
   Ancient Greek religion / Jon D. Mikalson.
      p. cm. – (Blackwell ancient religions)
   Includes bibliographical references and index.
      ISBN 0-631-23222-2 (alk. paper) ISBN 0-631-23223-0 (pbk. : alk. paper)
   1. Greece–Religion.   2. Religion–History.   I. Title.   II. Series.

   BL783.M55 2004
   292.08–dc22   2003021518

ISBN-13: 978-0-631-23222-3 (alk. paper) ISBN-13: 978-0-631-23223-0 (pbk. : alk. paper)

A catalogue record for this title is available from the British Library.

Set in 9.75/12.5 pt Utopia
by Graphicraft Limited, Hong Kong
Printed and bound in the United Kingdom
by TJ International, Padstow, Cornwall

The publisher's policy is to use permanent paper from mills that operate a sustainable
forestry policy, and which has been manufactured from pulp processed using acid-free and
elementary chlorine-free practices. Furthermore, the publisher ensures that the text paper
and cover board used have met acceptable environmental accreditation standards.

For further information on
Blackwell Publishing, visit our website:
www.blackwellpublishing.com

Contents

Figures

Maps

Preface

This book is intended to serve as a first introduction to the fascinating subject of ancient Greek religion. It will be, I hope, a place to begin but certainly not to end. The study of Greek religion is wondrously complex, involving hundreds of deities of several different types who were worshiped over a period of nearly two thousand years in hundreds of ancient Greek city-states. The deities, their myths and rituals, and even the beliefs about them varied, in greater or smaller degrees, from city to city and from century to century. The complexity of Greek religion is understandably daunting for those first approaching it, and I attempt here to make the subject more intelligible initially by a variety of strategies. First I limit my descriptions largely to Greek religion as it was practiced in the Classical period, from about 500 to 323 B.C.E. I do not attempt to describe the developments over many preceding centuries that led to its form at this time, and I devote only Chapter VIII to distinctive features of religion in the Hellenistic period (323–30 B.C.E.). Secondly, I center much of the discussion on Athens because the evidence – literary, artistic, archaeological, and epigraphical – is many, many times more abundant for Athens than for any other one Greek city-state and this allows us to see better the coherency of the Greek religious system. But even a full account of religion in classical Athens would require several volumes, and for this introduction I have chosen to direct attention first to some basic concepts, then to a select group of deities and cults which, each in its own way, represent important aspects of Greek religious life, then to the religion as practiced in the context of the family, the village, and the city-state, and, finally, to the religious life of the individual. For each deity, ritual, belief, and myth I have attempted to concentrate on what seems to me essential for the purpose at hand, leaving aside many of the questions and uncertainties, variant ancient accounts, and details that accompany many of these topics. Also, we intend to give a general account, and to virtually any general statement about Greek religion some exceptions may be found. In addition, readers should be forewarned that many of the statements made on every page have been challenged one time or another by one modern scholar or another. And, finally, this book is largely descriptive, based on the ancient evidence that survives, and it limits discussion of modern theoretical interpretations of these complex subjects. Over the last hundred and fifty years a number of theoretical systems to explain major elements of Greek religion have come and sometimes gone. These theoretical approaches hold great interest in themselves, but one needs to know what the Greeks themselves did and said about their religion before one can adequately apply or evaluate the various theoretical systems to explain it all. The books and essays suggested in Further Reading at the end of each chapter will begin to open up for readers the full complexity of these subjects, but we need a place for those interested in the subject to begin, and I hope that this book offers that.

An excellent place to pursue further the topics, deities, and religious practices introduced in this study is the third edition of *The Oxford Classical Dictionary* (Oxford, 1996) which offers concise discussions by experts along with some basic bibliography. For more advanced study I offer, at the end of each chapter, suggestions for Further Reading. In most cases these suggestions are given in two tiers. The first includes references to other general accounts of Greek religion, and they include especially J. N. Bremmer, *Greek Religion* (*GR*) (Oxford, 1994), W. Burkert, *Greek Religion* (*GR*) (Cambridge, MA, 1985), S. Price, *Religions of the Ancient Greeks* (*RAG*) (Cambridge, 1999), and L. B. Zaidman and P. S. Pantel, *Religion in the Ancient Greek City* (*RAGC*) (Cambridge, 1992). Each of these books is valuable in quite different ways, and in the first tier of Further Reading I give references to them when they offer a fuller account or a different interpretation of the topic at hand. In the second tier I offer references to more detailed accounts of the individual topics to be found in scholarly articles, books, and collections of essays. These suggestions for Further Reading form in no sense a complete bibliography for each topic, but each item will lead the reader to many further treatments of the topic.

Some discussion in the text is based on quotations or summaries of important ancient writings, and I strongly suggest that some of these be read in their entirety. These include the *Homeric Hymns* to Demeter and to Apollo, Euripides' *Bacchae* and *Ion*, Aristophanes' *Thesmophoriazusae*, and Pausanias' descriptions of Olympia in Books 5 and 6 of his *Description of Greece*. For the *Iliad*, *Odyssey*, and the poems of Hesiod and Pindar I use the translations of Richmond Lattimore (*The Iliad of Homer*, Chicago, 1951; *The Odyssey of Homer*, New York, 1965; *Hesiod*, Ann Arbor, 1959; *The Odes of Pindar*, Chicago, 1947); for the *Homeric Hymns*, the translations of Apostolos N. Athanassakis (*The Homeric Hymns*, Baltimore, 1976). All other translations are my own.

I throughout offer what would seem proximate equivalents in dollars for the ancient Greek monetary sums, at the rate of one drachma to $100. In fifth-century Athens one drachma was roughly the average daily wage, and by our conversion a lower- to middle-class Athenian would earn approximately $30,000 a year. For the English spelling of ancient Greek names I follow, with the exception primarily of epithets of the gods, the conventions of *The Oxford Classical Dictionary*[3].

Alfred Bertrand at Blackwell Publishing first suggested this book to me, and he and his colleagues Angela Cohen and Simon Alexander have contributed much to making it a reality. Robert Garland read the whole of this manuscript and offered many valuable suggestions and corrections, as did the anonymous reader for Blackwell Publishing. Kevin Clinton kindly commented on the Eleusinian material. I am especially indebted to my colleague Tyler Jo Smith who helped me find, select, acquire, and properly describe the many illustrations which Blackwell Publishing so generously granted. Finally, I would like to dedicate this book to the many undergraduate and graduate students of the University of Virginia who over the years have, quite unbeknownst to them, shaped the form of this book even before it was thought of as a book.

Abbreviations

Bremmer, *GR*	Bremmer, J.N., *Greek Religion* (Oxford, 1994)
Burkert, *GR*	Burkert, W., *Greek Religion* (Cambridge, MA, 1985)
Hansen	Hansen, P.A., *Carmina Epigraphica Graeca* (Berlin, 1983)
IE	Engelmann, H. and R. Merkelbach, *Die Inschriften von Erythrai und Klazomenai*, 2 vols. (Bonn, 1972–3)
IG	*Inscriptiones Graecae*
Price, *RAG*	Price, S., *Religions of the Ancient Greeks* (Cambridge, 1999)
Zaidman and Pantel, *RAGC*	Zaidman, L.B. and P.S. Pantel, *Religion in the Ancient Greek City* (Cambridge, 1992)

An Overview: Greek Sanctuaries and Worship

ᒣᒧᒣᒧᒣᒧᒣᒧ

Greeks most often prayed and made offerings to a deity in that deity's own sanctuary. In this chapter we begin by constructing such a sanctuary, first introducing the essential elements and then adding features found in many sanctuaries. In its simpler form, with an altar and a surrounding fence, our sanctuary will be typical of thousands of sanctuaries in the city-state of Athens alone and of many more thousands elsewhere in the Greek world; in its developed state, with a temple and monumental statue of the deity, it will be similar to only about twenty major sanctuaries even in Athens, the richest of the Greek city-states at this time.

Ours will be a sanctuary of Poseidon, the god who, for all Greeks, was, among other roles, the master of the sea. For Athenians in the fifth century Poseidon was particularly important because their navy was instrumental in establishing and maintaining their empire and because trade by sea, especially the importation of the grain necessary to feed their people, was central to their economy. The Athenians were the most sea-oriented of all Greeks in this period, and for them Poseidon assumed a special importance.

Our sanctuary of Poseidon will be located at Sunium, on the summit of a promontory on the southernmost tip of the Athenian coastline. This promontory overlooks a large expanse of the Aegean Sea which Athenian warships and freighters regularly traversed as they made their way to and from the Athenian harbor at Piraeus. We have chosen this cult site for our Poseidon because the Athenians chose it for theirs. By the middle of the fifth century the Athenians had at Sunium a fully developed sanctuary of Poseidon, with a temple visible still today from many miles out at sea. We re-create, hypothetically, the beginnings and development of this sanctuary,

Figure I.1   Head of a bronze statue of a god, usually identified as Poseidon or Zeus and dated to about 460 B.C.E. For a photograph of the complete statue, see Figure I.7. It was recovered from the sea near Cape Artemisium off the east coast of Greece in the 1920s and is now in the National Museum, Athens. Courtesy of the Deutsches Archäologisches Institut, Athens, neg. no. Hege 850.

not in an attempt to describe and explain the features of the real cult of Poseidon there but to establish a model for the nature and development of Greek sanctuaries in general. We shall later see many modifications to this model as we examine the cults of Athena on the Athenian Acropolis, of Demeter at Eleusis, of Apollo at Delphi, and several others, but it will be useful to have a model of typical sanctuaries in mind before we turn to the exceptions.

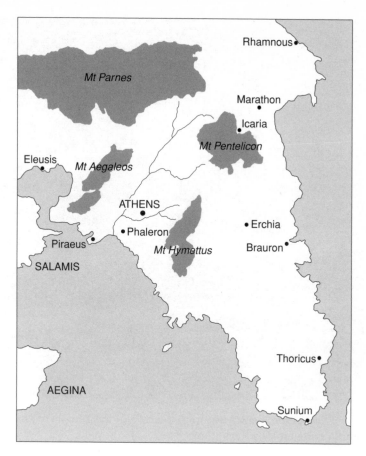

Map I.1   Map of Attica.

Location

Why did the Athenians locate a cult of Poseidon at just this spot on the Athenian coast? How were cult sites in general selected? Some sites apparently had a natural mystique. Mountain tops were often sacred to Zeus, the god of the sky and the weather. Springs, the source of the water always in short supply in Greece, and caves almost always attracted cults. Springs and caves were often assigned to the Nymphs. The god Pan, himself often associated with Nymphs, was given a cave on the north slope of the Acropolis when his cult was established in Athens about 490. Artemis preferred rural sanctuaries, also often associated with sources of water. A water source, necessary for medicinal purposes, may have played a

Figure I.2   View of the Aegean Sea from the *cella* of the Temple of Poseidon at Sunium. Photograph by the author.

role in locating Asclepius' sanctuary on the south slope of the Acropolis in 420/19. Places touched by the gods themselves, as by Zeus with his lightning or by Poseidon with his trident on the Athenian Acropolis, also became sacred. By contrast to these naturally numinous places many cult sites, especially in urban areas, seem to have been selected based on the deity's function. Athena, the armed patroness and protectress of Athens, had her major sanctuaries on the Acropolis, the city's fortified citadel. The cult sites of Zeus Boulaios (of the Council), Zeus Eleutherios (of Freedom), and Apollo Patroös (Ancestral) were clustered on the west side of the Agora (marketplace), in the Classical period the governmental and archival center of Athens. Similarly Hephaestus, the god of fire, shared a temple with Athena in an area of Athens that housed foundries and blacksmiths. The siting of these sanctuaries as well as of many in new cities founded as colonies suggests that often the Greeks were willing to locate sanctuaries, as we do churches, on the basis of land available and to fit them into a larger urban design. These sanctuaries were built in places appropriate to the gods' activities in civic affairs, not in a place sacred, as it were, by nature. In these cases the site was made sacred by the establishment of the sanctuary. The reasons for choices of sites for cults surely varied widely, and we can see patterns but no one pattern. Myths, as we shall later see for the cult of Apollo at Delphi, sometimes explained that the deity selected the location of a cult site. Many of the smaller cult sites throughout the Greek world also had myths explaining their origins, but these myths do not survive, and we now have no way of knowing why they were where they were.

For our cult of Poseidon, the site of Sunium seems an obvious choice, with its commanding view over one of the major sea lanes to and from Piraeus, the last such vantage point before the ships disappear from view on the open sea and the first point from which hostile ships would be sighted. It may also be that this site was initially chosen or later developed especially because of its frontier location, with the intent of laying permanent claim to this remote spot and establishing Poseidon as a potent defender against the form of attack most likely at this border. In the late fifth century, in fact, the Poseidon sanctuary at Sunium was enclosed within a large military fort with considerable naval installations.

The Altar

The altar serves to receive offerings to the deity, and since giving offerings was a fundamental form of worship for the Greeks, the altar was the one essential physical component of cult. An altar may, in fact, serve as the litmus test for religious cult: if a deity had one, we can be sure that he or she was worshiped and was a part of practiced Greek religion. If a deity did not have an altar, that deity was most probably a creation of the literary tradition or of folklore, not of the religious tradition, and did not receive sacrifice, prayer, or dedications. A few figures such as the personifications Eirene (Peace) and Agathe Tyche (Good Fortune) made the transition from literary to religious figures in the fourth century, and we recognize that transformation in Athens when altars are built and dedicated to them.

Some altars were simple pits (*bothroi*) or low-lying structures with openings to the bare earth (*escharai*). Liquid offerings such as water, milk, and honey were poured into these. These altars were for deities and divine figures thought to dwell *in* or *beneath* the earth, and, presumably, the offerings were thought to seep down into the earth to their recipients. Poseidon is, however, an *ouranic* ("of the sky") deity who dwelled and moved about above ground, in the sky. The offerings to these deities are directed upwards, towards the sky. Their altars (*bômoi*) needed to have a flat surface on top to hold the offerings, but otherwise could assume a variety of shapes – usually rectangular but sometimes square or cylindrical. Altars ranged greatly in size, often in proportion to the size of the sanctuary itself. Simple altars might be waist high, a block of stone a meter square or a cylinder equally tall. Monumental altars were often features of panhellenic sanctuaries. The altar of Zeus at Nemea, for example, was a rectangular structure over 41.5 meters long and 2.42 meters wide and that of Zeus at Olympia was 38.1 meters in circumference at its base and 6.7 meters high. Such were, however, very much the exception.

Since the ouranic deities were in the sky, for the offerings to be visible to them and for the savor of the burnt offerings to reach them their altars had to be outdoors, not within a building and covered by a roof, and so altars within a temple were a rarity. And, finally, altars of the ouranic deities were oriented to the east. The priest, as he made the offerings or sacrifice, stood on the west side of the altar, facing east. Offerings to ouranic deities were made before noon, often at dawn, and as he performed his rituals the priest would be looking towards the rising sun.

The altar will be the first element of our sanctuary of Poseidon. Let us make it a block of stone. In other cities we might well use limestone, but in Athens, with its mountains of marble, we can make it of this beautiful and durable stone. Let us make it of Pentelic marble, about $1^1/_4$ meters high and wide, two meters long, and with a molding around the top edge. We are obliged to carve Poseidon's name on it, so that both the god and visitors know it is his. Each altar is so designated with the god's name or with the name of a specific group of gods because there were no "common" altars to serve all the gods. If one wished to make an offering to Athena, one must offer on her altar. If, as in our case, the offering is to Poseidon, it must be made on his altar. An offering to Poseidon on an altar of Athena would be received by and would influence neither deity. Our altar is of stone because it must endure the elements. On occasion we will want to burn offerings on it, and then we will put on the altar a metal pan to protect its surface from the fire and ashes. We will orient our altar, as always, to the east, but, by chance, in our sanctuary at Sunium it will appropriately also face the open sea. We have inscribed on it Poseidon's name in large letters, perhaps painted for ease of reading.

And so our sanctuary of Poseidon is founded. The one essential element, the altar, is in place, inscribed with Poseidon's name. The altar is oriented to the east and overlooks the Aegean. Since it is of marble and has sculpted moldings, it is a bit more elaborate than altars found in the simplest sanctuaries, and this betokens future development of the sanctuary.

Figure I.3 A marble altar, dedicated by the Athenians to Aphrodite and the Charites in 194/3 B.C.E. It was discovered by the Agora in Athens and is now on display in the National Museum. Photograph courtesy of the National Museum, Athens, inv. no. 1495.

The Temenos

As was very commonly done, we will mark off an area around our altar. We might use boundary stones (*horoi*) at the corners or a surrounding fence (*peribolos*), thereby establishing the enclosed area as a separate precinct. We are "cutting off" (for which the Greek is *temnein*) an area from the surrounding land, and the Greek term for such an enclosed area is *temenos*. Our *temenos* is to be dedicated to a god and hence is "sacred" (*hieron*), and the two terms together, *temenos* and *hieron*, mark the two aspects of our sanctuary: a *temenos* as a separate precinct, and a *hieron* as a sacred place, the god's property. Let us use a low fence, quite probably of mud brick or field stone, which will serve more to demarcate the sacred area than to protect it. It might deter the wandering cow or sheep, but its gate would not be locked and the *temenos* would be readily accessible to human visitors. Everything within the *temenos* is "sacred," that is, the property of the deity, and the deity, not the fence, will protect it. *Sylân* is the Greek word for "to steal," and property and persons in Greek sanctuaries enjoyed *asylia*, the right "not to be stolen." Individuals seeking refuge in these sanctuaries had *asylum*. They were under the protection of the god of the sanctuary and could not be removed against their will. They might be tricked out or starved out, but under no circumstances could they be forcibly dragged out. To steal property of the god from a *temenos* was both a civil and a religious crime. In Athens such malefactors if caught would be prosecuted in the courts, but an even greater danger faced them, caught or not, from the wrath of the offended deity.

> The abode of the gods is a protection shared by all men.
>
> Euripides, *Heraclidae* 260
>
> The altar is an unbreakable shield, stronger than a fortification tower.
>
> Aeschylus, *Suppliant Women* 190

Most cults of Poseidon had open access and were not, like some Greek cults, limited to either men or women worshipers. Let us assume that men, women, and children of Athens could enter the *temenos* of our Poseidon cult at will – unless they were "polluted." Those polluted were ritually impure and were denied access to virtually all sanctuaries in the Greek world. One "polluted" from sexual intercourse must bathe to remove the pollution before entering the sanctuary. Those who had entered the home of a woman just having given birth could not enter a sanctuary for three days, and new mothers and midwives probably had to wait longer. Men and women who were "polluted" from attending a funeral or being in the presence of a corpse were excluded from sanctuaries for a time. Sexual intercourse, childbirth, and attendance at funerals are, of course, normal events of life and were not in moral terms "polluting" or reproachable, but they made one ritually impure, repulsive to the divine. Those who had killed another, except in battle, voluntarily or not, were also polluted, and they were forbidden entrance until they had undergone formal rites of purification, rituals distinct from any legal proceedings that might be involved. An individual recently engaged in these various activities "did not belong in" and was "out of place" in a sanctuary, and the concept of "pollution" was a marker for that. He or she was, while polluted, excluded from the worshiping community. If a polluted person was in the sanctuary, the deity would not come, and prayers and offerings would be in vain. Pollution in the classical Greek religious tradition is a quasi-physical state – in the sense that pollution is a real or symbolic "dirt" that can be passed on by contact –, not a moral state. One rids oneself of such pollution by washing, by the gradually cleansing passage of time, or by appropriate rituals. The impure "dirt" from sexual intercourse, childbirth, and murder are physical and, perhaps, obvious. Funerals and the aversion to the dead may be explained by the nature of the ouranic gods themselves. They were by nature deathless, the gods of the living, and in the Greek tradition these gods abhorred death and withdrew from anything (except their own sacrificial victims) tainted by it. For this reason the dead, those who had recently attended the dead, and murderers were excluded from the gods' sanctuaries. As the whole of the island of Delos gradually became thought of as the sanctuary of Apollo, the Athenian tyrant Pisistratus in the sixth century removed from the surrounding hills all tombs which even overlooked Apollo's *temenos*, and then in 426/5 the Athenians had all the remaining tombs removed from the island.

The same acts that pollute individuals and prevent them from entering sanctuaries are all the greater dangers if they occur *in* a sanctuary, and therefore every effort was made to prevent sexual intercourse, child-birth, or a death from occurring there. Those caught trysting in a sanc-tuary could even be put to death, and on Delos it became the practice to remove both those who were dying and women in childbirth to a nearby island before they "polluted" Apollo's sacred island. And, of course, to kill someone in a sanctuary was a heinous sacrilege which would be punished by the god.

> Never, from dawn forward, pour a shining libation
> of wine to Zeus or the other immortals, without washing your hands first.
> When you do, they do not hear your prayers; they spit them back at you.
> Hesiod, *Works and Days* 724–26 (Lattimore translation)

Pollution can be imagined as a form of real "dirt" or "filth" and in its most minor forms could simply be washed away. Greeks wished to be physic-ally clean when they approached their deities – morally clean was not the issue. Often, just at the gate of a sanctuary, stood a basin (*perirrhanterion*) of water with which the worshiper sprinkled himself, symbolically cleans-ing himself before approaching the divine. A Hippocratic author (*On the Sacred Disease* 4.55–60) describes the act as follows:

> We ourselves establish boundaries of the sanctuaries and precincts for the god so that no one may pass over them unless he is pure. When we go in, we sprinkle water around ourselves, not as though we were polluted but to purify an uncleanliness we had before.

Sprinkling the water from the *perirrhanterion* around oneself would not eliminate the more serious pollutions of association with the dead and of murder, but it would suffice for the accumulated "dirt" of the day.

For our cult of Poseidon let the first *temenos* fence be of mud brick, low, perhaps a meter high, and with a single gate. For most sanctuaries the area

Figure I.4 Drawing of the sanctuary of the Twelve Gods, founded in Athens by the grandson of the tyrant Pisistratus in 522 / 1 B.C.E. It served also as the official central milestone from which all distances in Attica were measured. It has the typical form of a sacred *temenos* with an altar facing east, a *peribolos* wall, and a *perirrhanterion* at the main gate. Courtesy of the American School of Classical Studies, Athens: Agora Excavations.

enclosed was probably quite small, with land enough just for the altar and for the priest to perform the necessary rituals. Poseidon, however, is a major deity, and even as we establish his cult at Sunium we foresee expansion and development of the sanctuary. Therefore we make his initial *temenos* rather large, 10 × 20 meters. Let us have also a *perirrhanterion* at the gate for the worshipers' final "cleansing" before they enter the sanctuary. With the altar, its surrounding fence, and the *perirrhanterion* we now have the basic elements of a Greek sanctuary – the altar being required, the fence and *perirrhanterion* being very common. Our *temenos* is somewhat larger and our altar a bit more elaborate than most, but together they represent the most common form of a Greek sanctuary.

Priests and Priestesses

For Poseidon and his sanctuary we need a priest (*hiereus*) since our deity is male. If our deity were female, Athena or Artemis, we would have a priestess (*hiereia*). The priest will probably be an elder of the family that has tended Poseidon on this site for decades or even centuries. We have been imagining that "we" are founding this cult of Poseidon, but in fact such a cult would probably have been originally founded, perhaps in the eighth century B.C.E. or earlier, by an aristocratic family who owned the property, and the priest is quite likely a descendant of the family of the original founders. He is chosen by the family and will hold his priesthood for life or until he cedes it to another member of the family. The foundation of our cult predates the establishment of Athenian democratic institutions in 508/7. For state cults established after this date priests and priestesses were often, in the tradition of Athenian democracy, selected by lot for annual terms. The priest's prime responsibility as *hiereus* is to manage the *hiera*: the offerings, sacrifices, and the sanctuary itself and its property, all of which were *hiera* ("sacred"). The priest would surely know much of the traditions and rituals of the cult, but for a cult of Poseidon, unlike, for example, that of Demeter at Eleusis, this would not be esoteric, closely held, secret knowledge. Even the rituals of sacrifice would be, as it were, generic, common to the cults of many deities, but with, perhaps, one or two local idiosyncracies. The priest's role was not that of a rabbi or pastor – he tended not the worshipers but the deity. He would serve only the cult of one deity, and his authority as priest was limited to the cult of that deity. There were no "colleges" of priests whereby individual priests might combine their authority or knowledge and make pronouncements on matters of religion in general. In a small cult such as ours the priest's duties would occupy only a few days each year, and he would be, if not retired, a farmer, sailor, merchant, stone mason, or engaged in some other occupation. While holding his priesthood he could serve in the military and hold government office. His income from his priesthood would be minimal, probably only portions, often the skins, of the animals sacrificed on the altar or of other food offerings left there. Our priest would live in his own home away from the sanctuary and would have no special restrictions on his dress and behavior. Except on festival days, when he might wear special robes, he would be indistinguishable from his fellow citizens. The priesthood would, however, bring him a certain respect in the community, perhaps even a reserved seat in the theater for the tragedies and comedies in the annual festival of Dionysos.

Priests, as tradition says, are expert in giving gifts through sacrifices from us to the gods as the gods wish them and in asking for us from the gods in prayers the acquisition of good things.

Plato, *Politicus* 290c8–d2

Figure I.5   The tombstone (.62 m. high) of the Athenian priest Simos of the deme Myrrhinous, dating from 370–360 B.C.E. His priesthood is indicated by the sacrificial knife he carries and by his long, unbelted garment. Courtesy of National Museum, Athens, inv. no. 772.

Sacred Days

Virtually every one of the hundreds or even thousands of deities with cult sites in a Greek city-state had one day each year that was specially his or hers. The day might be celebrated by only the family that tended the cult, by the people of the neighborhood, or by all the citizens of the state. Worship on this day was intended, in general terms, to keep the deity happy with his devotees throughout the year. It was, as it were, routine religious maintenance and might be thought of, in crude terms, as an annual auto or home insurance payment. For a cult tended by one family, it might well involve just a simple prayer and offering by the priest in the morning. The family might also sacrifice a goat or sheep and have a feast for family members and friends. The deity's festival day might also include the whole neighborhood or village that participated in this cult.

Let us imagine at this early stage a rather simple festival day for Poseidon at Sunium. For all Athenians the eighth day of each month was sacred to Poseidon, and let us put his annual festival day on the eighth day of the month Posideon. This, the sixth month of the Athenian year, fell in mid-winter and was named, like most Greek months, after a festival held in it – here the Posidea of Poseidon. And so, on Posideon 8, the priest, members of his family, and some neighbors will gather at the sanctuary at dawn to celebrate the Posidea. They will offer a prayer to Poseidon to come to their sanctuary – since Greek gods were not omnipresent –, to receive their offering, and to protect them and their friends as they venture out to sea, and then they will make an offering. This might well be the end of it, and they then would turn to other business of the day. If they sacrifice an animal, however, they will probably make a day of it, butchering and cooking the animal and settling down for a feast in the afternoon. The prayer and sacrifice will offer moments of great religious solemnity, but they will occur in the context of the pleasures of family, friends, neighbors, and good food.

Months of the Athenian Year

Hekatombaion	June–July
Metageitnion	July–August
Boedromion	August–September
Pyanopsion	September–October
Maimakterion	October–November
Posideon	November–December
Gamelion	December–January
Anthesterion	January–February
Elaphebolion	February–March
Mounichion	March–April
Thargelion	April–May
Skirophorion	May–June

Figure I.6   An Athenian red-figure *crater* (mixing bowl for wine) from about
425 B.C.E., by the Cleophon painter or a member of his circle; 42.3 cm.
high and 47 cm. in diameter. In the lower center stands the altar over which
the bearded sacrificer washes his hands in a bowl held by a young man.
In his left hand the young man holds a container for the sacrificial knife.
The victim, a sheep, is depicted on the left. Note the double-flute player
on the far left and the garlands worn by all. Courtesy of the Museum of
Fine Arts, Boston, 95.25. Photograph © Museum of Fine Arts, Boston.

Dedications

There were also occasions of worship apart from the annual festival days,
and these often arose in times of personal need. We might imagine that
Apollodorus is about to make a business trip, sailing with a cargo of wine
to Byzantium and planning, with the proceeds of the sale, to buy grain,
sail back to Athens, and sell the grain there for another profit. Apollodorus
might well come to our sanctuary and promise Poseidon one-tenth of
his profits if he returns safely from this long and dangerous voyage. He
makes a *vow* to Poseidon in a prayer, and, if all goes as he wishes, he must
give to Poseidon what he promised. The gift he gives to Poseidon as a
result of such a *vow* is a *votive offering*, and, in the Greek tradition, he
would most likely not give the cash but would have made from the cash

a beautiful object (*agalma*) such as a small statuette or a sculpted or painted plaque which would *adorn* the sanctuary. He would, of course, wish to memorialize his gift, to let his friends and the god know who gave it, and so he would inscribe his name on it, perhaps in a text like this:

> "Apollodorus, son of Diopeithes, after having made a vow,
> Erects this for you, Poseidon, as a tithe."

Similarly Diocles, after a long and successful career as a sailor, might present the sanctuary with a *thank-offering* – perhaps some tools of his trade or a terracotta plaque inscribed simply,

> "With thanks, to Poseidon, from Diocles, son of Hermias, a sailor."

We call such gifts, both votive offerings and thank-offerings, *dedications*, and we find them today in museum cases throughout the world. They include vases of all types, often in miniature; statues and statuettes of deities and of the animals commonly sacrificed to them; stone, wooden, and terracotta plaques representing the deity or the worshipers praying and sacrificing to the deity; clothing and tools; and inscriptions describing the deity's services to the individual. When these gifts have been dedicated in a sanctuary, they become the god's property and are sacred. Some might be used for processions and other religious purposes, but they otherwise cannot be removed from the *temenos*. We should imagine them set on pedestals or benches, hung from the *temenos* wall, nailed to or hung from trees within the sanctuary, perhaps set on the altar, and displayed in various other ways.

After a few decades, there would be dozens of such dedications in our sanctuary of Poseidon. They are now his property, but more importantly they demonstrate to all visitors the power of the deity. Each represents, in its own way, an individual who thought he was helped by Poseidon, who thought his prayers to Poseidon were answered. This is well illustrated by an anecdote set on the island Samothrace at the sanctuary of the Great Gods who, like Poseidon, protected sailors at sea. A friend is trying to convince the notoriously impious Diagoras of Melos that the gods are concerned with human affairs. He points to the many dedications in the sanctuary and asks, "Do you not see from so many painted votive tablets how many men by their vows escaped the violence of storms and arrived safely into port?" His argument did not impress Diagoras, but the anecdote serves to record how most Greeks would view the collection of dedications in a Greek sanctuary.[1] Taken as a group, dedications are tangible evidence of the deity's existence, power, and the range of that power, and they show the *honor* in which the deity is held by his worshipers.

These dedications are durable goods, unlike the food of offerings and sacrifices on the altar. They were probably meant to survive in the sanctuary forever, but, of course, some were more durable than others. Silver statuettes, for example, might suffer from the elements and from pigeon droppings, and we will soon want to erect in our sanctuary a small building to protect them. In major panhellenic sanctuaries like Delphi and Olympia there were many such *treasury buildings*, finely built, often of marble with elaborate sculptural dedication, often given by prosperous city-states to house their dedications in the sanctuary. But for our Poseidon sanctuary we imagine in a corner of the *temenos* a rather simple wooden building, roofed, with shelves on the interior walls to hold the dedications. It might have a locked door, but perhaps not. Again, the prime protection for these and all dedications is their location in a sanctuary and the god's concern for his own property. It is most important that our treasury building be *within* the sanctuary. We are not to remove any of the god's property from his *temenos*. If some of the vase or terracotta dedications are accidentally broken and become unsightly, we will bury them in a *votive pit* within the sanctuary. Even when old and broken, they must still be respected as the god's property. Once buried, these *votive deposits* may survive through the centuries and millennia, and when discovered by archaeologists they are a prime source for the many Greek dedications we see in the museums today.

Now, before we undertake a major expansion of our sanctuary, let us review what we have: an altar, inscribed with Poseidon's name, oriented to the east; a *peribolos* enclosing the altar in a *temenos* about 10 × 20 meters; dozens of dedications, both votive and thank-offerings, displayed throughout the sanctuary; and a treasury building housing the more perishable and perhaps more precious dedications. All of this is superintended by the priest of Poseidon.

Statue and Temple

Let us imagine that we are in now 479 B.C.E. The Greeks have in the past year successfully repelled a massive invasion of their lands by the Persian king Xerxes with, as Herodotus (7.184–185) claims, his 1,000 warships and 2,500,000 soldiers of many eastern nationalities. Decisive in the Greek success was their total victory in the sea battle in the Bay of Salamis, off the coast of southern Attica and a mere two hours' voyage from Sunium. After this victory the Persian navy fled to Asia Minor, and Xerxes himself retreated north with the bulk of his army. More battles on land at Plataea and on land and sea at Mycale on the coast of Asia Minor would follow, but the victory at Salamis seriously crippled the Persian invasion and marked the turning point of the war for the Greeks. It was their first major victory in this war, and from it they went from victory to victory.

The Persians during their occupation of Attica had impiously and sacrilegiously pillaged and burned all the sanctuaries, including our sanctuary of Poseidon, and we will first have to rebuild it. But in the rebuilding we will have to expand the sanctuary because from the spoils of the victory at Salamis the Greeks dedicated Phoenician warships captured in the battle to Poseidon of the Isthmus of Corinth, to Ajax of Salamis, and to our Poseidon (Herodotus 8.121). The Phoenicians had the best navy of those serving under the Persians, and these dedicated warships, one in each sanctuary, represent the Greek victory over the very best that the Persians had to put up against them.

At the war's end the Greeks made further dedications: a magnificent gold tripod with snake-stand for Apollo at Delphi; a four-and-one-half-meter tall bronze statue of Zeus at Olympia; and a similar, three-meter statue of Poseidon at the Isthmus. Each of these panhellenic dedications was made at a panhellenic sanctuary (Herodotus 9.81.1). Since individual Greek cities also honored deities of their homelands for the victory, let us have the Athenians at this time give Poseidon of Sunium a new title, "Soter" (Savior), for the help he gave them at Salamis, and let us hypothesize – since there is no evidence to support this – that the Athenians also promised on this occasion a statue to our Poseidon, now Poseidon Soter, a specifically Athenian dedication to join the captured Phoenician warship dedicated by the Greeks as a group. This statue of Poseidon is to be made of bronze, two meters tall, bearded, wielding in his right hand a trident.

The Persian destruction and burning of our sanctuary, the victories at Salamis and elsewhere over the Persians, and the resulting major dedications of the captured Phoenician ship and the new bronze statue of Poseidon will require major repairs and expansion of the sanctuary. We must repair or replace the altar – but on the same exact site as the original one. Most of the pre-war dedications that survived the Persian pillaging have been damaged, and they must be buried in votive pits within the sanctuary. If some dedications of silver or bronze survive in pieces, we will melt them down and cast from them new vases or statuettes, taking care that all the precious metal is returned to the god and that the names of the original donors are kept on record. We need to restore the *temenos* wall, but it seems just the right time to expand the sanctuary so that it can include the Phoenician ship and the statue. A neighbor might donate additional land – itself a form of dedication to Poseidon –, or the state, flush with the spoils of the war, might simply purchase it. In either case, let us expand the size of our sanctuary now to be 60 × 80 meters, a size appropriate for a deity who has become – after the victories at sea and the beginnings of the Athenian naval empire – one of the most important patrons of the Athenian people. Let us also replace the mudbrick *peribolos* with one built of rectangular blocks of poros stone, a substantial wall which will also serve as a terrace wall to allow us to level the land of the hill top. We can now make an impressive gateway of marble, with several doorways. The gate will be on one of the long north–south sides of the *peribolos*, giving direct access to the sacrificial area at the altar. But, however large and impressive, the *peribolos* and the gateway are still both designed not so much to protect as to mark the sacred area.

After the devastation of all Athens and Attica by the Persians, the restoration and expansion of our sanctuary will take time. Soon after the retreat of the Persians in 479 the sanctuary would be cleaned, the debris buried, and a temporary altar erected. Within a decade or so we may have a new marble altar, a stone *peribolos* with its marble gateway, and, off at one end of the sanctuary, the Phoenician warship – probably now on temporary wooden supports. By the 440s our long-promised bronze statue of Poseidon Soter is being constructed, at state expense. Until now we have had in our sanctuary statuettes of Poseidon dedicated by individual worshipers, but no single, larger than life-size, dominating statue of the god. Most cults in the Greek world, like our original simple sanctuary, would never have had such a statue. Of those few that did, some, like that of Athena Polias on the Acropolis, had statues of great antiquity and veneration, some reputedly having appeared in miraculous circumstances. Most others, like our cult of Poseidon, had specially made statues, often, as for us, thank-offerings financed by the state with booty from victory in war. Such a statue, as a dedication to the deity, was of course sacred. A finely wrought statue by a great artist would also be widely admired for its beauty – an *agalma*, and this, too, has a religious aspect because the Greeks always wished to adorn the sanctuaries of their deities. Greek deities, like Greek people, appreciated fine art. The statue, in the Greek tradition, represented but did not embody the deity. It usually has the attributes described in epic poetry – armor for Athena, for example, or the bow for Apollo, or, as for us, the trident for Poseidon. The statue would certainly make a strong impression on the worshiper by its size and appearance, but it would not be given a special, distinct sanctity as if it were the deity. It is a welcome addition to our cult, but unlike the altar it is not essential. If stolen or destroyed, it could be, like any other dedication, replaced.

Our new two-meter tall bronze statue of Poseidon Soter will become a second focal point of the sanctuary – the first being, of course, the altar.

Figure I.7 Bronze statue of a god, 2.09 m. high, usually identified as Poseidon or Zeus, from about 460 B.C.E. It was recovered from the sea near Cape Artemisium off the east coast of Greece and is now in the National Museum, Athens. For a close view of the head, see Figure I.1. It is this statue we use as a model for the statue of Poseidon Soter in his sanctuary at Sunium. Courtesy of the Deutsches Archäologisches Institut, Athens, neg. no. Wagner N.M. 4533.

We must plan where to place it and how to shelter it, and this introduces the most familiar but perhaps least common element of a Greek sanctuary, the temple. The temple is, in essence, a large rectangular room, oriented to the east, with a door on the short, eastern side. It may, but not necessarily, have a front porch, a back porch, and a detached colonnade supporting the superstructure of the roof. The Greek term for the whole building is *naos*, for the central interior room *megaron*, but for both we most commonly use Latin-based terms, for the building *temple*, for the inner room *cella*. The columns are usually fluted, the entablature above the architrave and the pediments may be decorated with sculpture appropriate to the deity, and the roof may be surmounted with ornaments. But the central room, the *cella*, is our concern now, because it will house the new statue of Poseidon. He will stand on a base near the west end of this room, facing toward the door of the *cella*. It is often said that Greek temples are oriented to the east. That is true, but the matter can be better stated. In a sanctuary the altar – which almost always preexists the temple – is oriented to the east, and the temple is oriented to the altar. Both thus face east, but the altar determines the orientation of the temple. As a result, we will have aligned, facing the east, our monumental statue of Poseidon Soter, the building in which he stands, and the altar. We should imagine that on his festival day, the Posidea of Posideon 8, when the *cella's* doors are opened in early morning, the light of the sun rising in the east flows in upon Poseidon, illuminating him and bringing the bronze to life in an otherwise rather dark room. Poseidon's gaze, in turn, is directed through the open doors and falls upon the activities around his own altar. Our bronze Poseidon will observe the acts of worship directed to the real Poseidon at his altar on his festival day.

The temple itself is a dedication to the deity, albeit a very expensive one, paid for by the state often from the booty of war or, as at this time by the Athenians, from revenues from their empire. Like other dedications it may be a thank-offering for victory in war, a votive offering fulfilling a vow made by the state in unusually desperate circumstances, or even a gift to appease an angry deity. Unlike a Christian church, the temple does not house the altar and is not the central place of worship. In the Greek sanctuary the outdoor altar remains the religious center, the place of offering and prayer. The temple functions rather as an elaborate treasury building, sheltering the statue and other particularly precious or fragile dedications made to the deity.

Our sanctuary of Poseidon at Sunium has now undergone repair, expansion, and elaboration, and for our purposes is complete. Let us survey the results and imagine the sanctuary as it appeared in about 440 B.C.E. The altar is very much like the original, a rectangular block of marble, $1^1/_2$ meters high and wide, 2 meters long, inscribed with Poseidon's name and epithet (Poseidon Soter). It is surrounded by a stone *temenos* wall, 2 meters high, enclosing a level area of 60 × 80 meters, with an ornate, marble gateway. Beside the gate now stands a handsome marble *perirrhanterion*, inscribed with Poseidon's name. To the west of the altar and oriented on it stands the temple, and let it be the one the Athenians themselves built at Sunium in just these years. It is a Doric temple of white marble from a local quarry, about 31 meters long and 13 meters wide, with 34 exterior columns (6 on the front and back, 13 on each long side) supporting an entablature of marble and a roof of wood. It has both a front porch and a back porch. A sculptured frieze represents the battle of the Centaurs against the Lapiths, that of the gods against the giants, and the labors of Theseus, Poseidon's son – all symbolizing the victory of the forces of civilization over those of violence and disorder. Inside the *cella*, at its west end, stands on a marble base the bronze Poseidon Soter wielding his trident. Also inside the *cella*, probably on shelves and pedestals, are precious dedications accumulated in recent years. The whole sanctuary is gradually being filled by statuettes, plaques, inscriptions, and other private dedications, but most prominent among them, perhaps along one long side of the *temenos* wall, is the Phoenician ship, now on a marble base, with an inscription in large letters reading,

"To Poseidon Soter of Sunium, from the ships of the Phoenicians and Persians in the glorious victory of the Athenians around divine Salamis."

Our sanctuary is now large, elaborate, and quite wealthy, and a single priest can no longer assume all the responsibilities for it. He may well appoint a lay assistant, a *neokoros*, who will tend to the maintenance of the buildings and grounds. The Athenian state, which has invested heavily in our sanctuary, may also appoint, annually, a lay committee of *hierotamiai* (sacred treasurers) or *epimeletai* (overseers) to superintend the finances of our sanctuary, both of its property and its expenditures for festivals and other activities. The state thereby establishes jurisdiction over financial matters, but the purely religious matters of worship – sacrifice, prayer, and dedication – are still under the authority of our priest. And, in our cult, the priest is still selected by his family, largely free from any state authority.

As we have completed our sanctuary, we caution again here that it is not intended to represent precisely the actual sanctuary at Sunium that one can trace on the ground at the site or in the plans of books describing it.[2] Our sanctuary has most of the elements actually found there, but is intended primarily as a model of a typical, fully developed Greek sanctuary, and each real sanctuary, including that of Poseidon at Sunium, had some distinct, idiosyncratic features of buildings, dedications, priesthoods, and ritual. The same is true of the activities of worship we now attribute to our cult of Poseidon Soter at Sunium. Most are not expressly attested for this sanctuary by historical sources, but all are typical of such activities at other sanctuaries and thus, like the sanctuary itself, form a standard model for comparison with religious activities we describe in later chapters.

Figure I.8   A reconstruction of the sanctuary of Poseidon Soter at Sunium and of the fort which enclosed it in the late fifth century B.C.E. 1. The temple of Poseidon Soter. 2. The gateway to the sanctuary. 3. The quarters of the soldiers and sailors manning the fort. 4. The naval installations of the fort. Courtesy of EKDOTIKE ATHENON S.A.

Worship

With our sanctuary complete, we can now turn to the worship of Poseidon. But what is worship in the Greek religious tradition? Greek religious worship is fundamentally the doing of deeds and the giving of gifts that show honor (*tîmê*) to the deity. Worshipers wanted to honor the deity for the power the deity had and for the good things that deity provided. Greek gods wanted from their devotees "honor" and "respect," not "love." Unlike in the Christian tradition, the Greek god, even Zeus, is not "our father," and we are not "his children." We are not expected to love a Greek deity as a child would his parent. It is "honor" and "respect" that the Greek gods want from humans. But what kind of "honor" is this to be? It is not the honor that children owe their parents, nor the honor that a slave owes to his master. The Greeks, who themselves had slaves and thought slavish honor unworthy of a freeman and typical of barbarian societies like the Persian, would not subject themselves to it, even for their gods. Rather it is, I think, the kind of "honor" a subject owes his king, the kind of honor a *good* subject owes to a *good* king. That in highly democratic Athens of the fifth century Athenian worshipers thought themselves subjects of a good, divine royalty may seem paradoxical, but fundamental Greek conceptions of the relationship of god to man had been established centuries before, in the Mycenaean (*ca.* 2200–1100 B.C.E.) and Dark (ca. 1100–750 B.C.E.) Ages, and those conceptions of the relationship, because of the strong conservatism in Greek religious tradition, maintained themselves through the various changes of the political systems of Athens and other Greek city-states.

The Greeks honored their gods because these gods had the power to help them and did help them in matters which the Greeks thought lay beyond their control. These matters included, in the most general terms, 1) fertility of crops, animals, and human beings, 2) economic prosperity, 3) good health, and 4) safety in the dangers of war and seafaring. Most Greek gods contributed to human life in one or more of these areas. The rites of Demeter, for example, were very much directed to fertility of crops and probably aided the fertility of animals and humans as well. Aphrodite had her role in human fertility, Hera in marriage. Zeus gave the rain necessary for abundant harvests, promoting both fertility of crops and economic prosperity to this farming society. Artisans turned to Hephaestus and Athena in their work, and merchant sailors to, of course, our Poseidon. For good health in the mid-fifth century the Athenians turned to local heroes, to Apollo, and even to a cult of Athena Hygieia (Of Health) on the Acropolis, but in 420, after a devastating plague, they imported Asclepius from Epidaurus and established major sanctuaries and healing centers for him in both Piraeus and Athens itself. The Athenians faced constant, annual dangers from war

> As far as you have the power, do sacrifice to the immortals,
> innocently and cleanly; burn them the shining thighbones;
> at other times, propitiate them with libations and burnings,
> when you go to bed, and when the holy light goes up in the sky;
> so They may have a complacent feeling and thought about you;
> so you may buy someone else's land, not have someone buy yours.
>
> Hesiod, *Works and Days* 336–41 (Lattimore translation)

> I do not believe that the gods, if they thought they were wronged by me,
> did not punish me when they had me amidst the greatest dangers. For
> what danger is greater for men than to sail the sea in wintertime? When
> they had my person in this situation, when they had control of my life and
> property, then were they saving me? Were they not able even to prevent
> my body from getting proper burial?
>
> Andocides 1.137–38

and seafaring, and for the former they turned especially to their armed
patroness, Athena, and for the latter to Poseidon. In each of these areas
the Greeks recognized the importance of their own efforts, but in each there
was a large element of the uncontrollable, and it was there that they
sought the gods' favor. When they went to war or sailed on their small boats
on the windy, choppy Aegean, they wanted the gods to be happy with them
– hence the annual festivals – and ready to help if need be. They wanted
the gods as an umbrella of protection under which they could exercise
their own human abilities. They looked to the gods' protection as subjects
would look to the protection of a king in matters beyond their control, and,
just as subjects would respect and thank a king for helping in times of need,
so the Greeks "honored" and thanked the gods when they helped them.

Most notably *not* on the list of items the Greeks thought beyond their
control was their own behavior. The Greeks did not have their gods lay down
a code of human behavior or enforce any such code. The Greeks worked
out their standards of ethical behavior in earlier times especially through
their poetic literature and their law codes and later through philosophy. As
we shall see later, Greek gods do occasionally punish human injustice, but
not nearly so often in everyday life as in Greek literature, and usually only
when that behavior impinges on the honor due the gods. By and large, in
practiced religion the Greeks thought that their gods showed little interest
in the ethical behavior of their devotees towards their fellow Greeks.

Piety did, however, concern the gods greatly, and piety in the Greek tradition is the offering of appropriate honors to the gods on appropriate occasions. Piety, for the Greeks, was a matter not so much of emotion as of "commonsense" (*sophrosyne*). It is only "reasonable" to honor someone or some god who helps us in important ways, and therefore piety is largely a matter of *reason*. The impious person – the one who does not repay good services with honor – is not lacking in "faith" (a formulation which the Greeks did not use), but lacks "reason." Impiety is foolishness and is quite often equated with "insanity." And for that the gods would punish a person. The impiety of an individual can also, by alienating the gods, affect the welfare of the community in which he lives, and the citizens through state courts (as some Athenians did Socrates) prosecuted individuals for impiety, for a failure to "believe in the gods worshiped by the state" or "for introducing new gods unsanctioned by the state," or for violating other religious traditions of the state. The legal punishments were usually quite severe for those convicted, either death or exile.

Our worshipers are, however, pious people, and they express appropriate honors to Poseidon on appropriate occasions. The occasions, as we have seen, are Poseidon's annual festivals, times of personal need, and at the successful completion of actions, whether sea battles, voyages, or careers, that benefited from the god's help. His worshipers express their honor by giving the god things that "please" him. They want the god, at all times, to be *pleased*, and if they sense the god is not pleased, they make efforts to *appease* him, to bring themselves back into his good favor.

> If someone knows how to say and do in his prayers and sacrifices what is pleasing to the gods, these things are holy and save private households and the common interests of the city. But the opposites of those pleasing things are impious, and they overthrow and destroy everything.
>
> Euthyphro in Plato, *Euthyphro* 14b

By what are gods *pleased*? They are pleased by gifts given to them in their honor, but they have a rather broad definition of what a gift might be. The gift might well be a beautiful hymn composed in their honor, praising their contributions, and sung by a chorus of young men or women at their festival. Dancing might well accompany the singing of the hymn, and other dances and competitions could also be performed in the god's honor. All these are gifts to the deity. Gods are also pleased by the dedications, another form of gift, which adorn their sanctuaries. The gods are also pleased, as are we humans, by gifts of food and drink, and that brings us to *sacrifice*.

Sacrifice is essentially a process, a ritual, by which a profane, non-sacred object is given as a gift to a deity. It is like a dedication in the sense that the non-sacred object is given to the deity and hence becomes sacred, but unlike a durable dedication a sacrifice is usually taken to mean the giving of food or drink – for example, cakes, fruits, animal meat, milk, and especially wine – all foods and drinks which the Greeks themselves enjoyed. "Sacrifice" is a Latin term, "sacer-facere," to "make sacred," and we tend to use the term rather loosely to indicate the ritual by which the food or drink is given to the deity and hence "made sacred." We should perhaps distinguish between *offering* on the altar cakes, fruits, and vegetables; *pouring* on the altar libations of wine and other beverages; and the *sacrifice* of animals. The common conception that Greek sacrifice was simply the killing of animals for the gods is mistaken in a number of ways. The killing of the animal was only one step, albeit a necessary one, in the ritual of presenting the animal to the god. When a cow was sacrificed, it was first cleansed and decorated, then led to the altar, stunned, killed, bled, butchered, and finally offered to the deity. Usually only portions of the animal were offered, and in a sense the burning of the designated parts of the animal on the deity's altar was the culmination of the sacrificial ritual. Other elements of sacrificial ritual, such as the killing or the feast afterwards, prepared for it or followed from it. The Greek term for "to sacrifice" is *thyein*, and, related to the Latin *fumus*, it means "to make smoke." The designated parts of the animal, or in some cases, in *holocausts*, the whole animal were "made to smoke" on the altar, and it was this savory smoke from the burning meat that rose and "pleased" the ouranic deities in the sky. Virtually all Greek animal sacrifices were also communal rituals, performed in the presence of the family, the village, the state, or other social/political units, and all members of that community would share in the feast that concluded the sacrifice. A Greek sacrifice thus, in addition to honoring the god, would by inclusion mark off and unify the community, bringing it together for a solemn and also festive occasion and thereby reasserting its sense of solidarity.

Sacrifices were, like offerings, libations, songs, dances, and dedications, gifts to the deities, gifts which humans gave them to express their honor toward the deity in return for what the deity offered them. The deity, in turn, was pleased by these gifts. The Greeks expressed this complex of ideas in terms of *charis* (χάρις). A *charis* was a "favor," a favor which was expected

One must sacrifice to the gods for three purposes: to give honor, to show gratitude, or because of one's need of good things.

Theophrastus, *On Piety*, frag. 12 Pötscher, 42–4

to be repaid, and the mutual exchange of "favors" or "gifts" is at the heart of a successful human/divine relationship. This relationship – based on aristocratic rather than mercantile values – is a more subtle and complex one than the formula *do ut des* ("I give so that you may give.") often used to describe it implies. The model for the relationship of a human to a god was, as we suggested, that of a good subject to a beneficent king, a relationship in which "favors" of very different types and monetary values might be exchanged for a variety of purposes. The favors the Greek gods give are, as we saw, successes in fertility, economic prosperity, health, and safety. The favors humans give (or return) to gods are necessarily of a different order and include sanctuaries, offerings, libations, sacrifices, dedications, hymns, and dances. The gods, in turn, "rejoice" (*chairein*, χαίρειν, etymologically related to *charis*) in these gifts of honor. These gifts of humans may be, in addition, "adornment" (*kosmos*) for the deities and their sanctuaries, and much of the finest Greek art, architecture, and poetry results from the inclination of the Greeks to make their gifts to the gods beautiful. In short, humans endeavor, through cult, to establish and maintain with their deities mutually beneficial relationships based on both "honor" and *charis*.

> For of all cities beneath the sun and the starry heaven
> Dwelt in by men who live upon earth, there has never been one
> Honoured nearer to my heart than sacred Ilion
> And Priam, and the people of Priam of the strong ash spear.
> Never yet has my altar gone without fair sacrifice,
> The libation and the savour, since this is our portion of honour.
>
> Zeus to his wife Hera about Priam and Troy, Homer, *Iliad* 4.44–9
> (Lattimore translation)

We now have our sanctuary of Poseidon at Sunium complete. Because of Poseidon's own contributions to the Athenians in the battle of Salamis, his cult now has national attention, interest, and financial support. The Posidea of Posideon 8 is no longer just a day of celebration for the priest's family, friends, and neighbors, but is now a major *state festival*, a holiday financed by the state and celebrated by as many Athenians as can make their way to Sunium on that day. There were a number of such annual state festivals for major deities, some of several days' duration. They might differ significantly in details and tone from one another as we shall later see when we describe other deities' festivals in Chapter IV, but the general pattern is 1) a procession, 2) a hymn to the deity, 3) a prayer, 4) a sacrifice, 5) special events, often competitions, appropriate to the deity, and 6) a communal banquet on the meat of the sacrificed animals.

And so today, Posideon 8, we Athenians will show Poseidon Soter the honor in which we hold him by having a state festival in our newly completed sanctuary. Our procession will begin, of course, down at the seaside at dawn, and will in a stately and leisurely manner make its way to the top of the promontory where the sanctuary is. We are, in essence, escorting Poseidon to his own festival. The priest will lead the way, dressed in his finest robes and, like all present on this day, wearing a wreath. Behind him will come the *neokoros* and the state officials who oversee the festival and the finances of the sanctuary. With them will be top governmental officials, especially those concerned with military affairs and the navy. In the procession will be the three or four bulls, adorned with garlands, which we intend to sacrifice to Poseidon, and bringing up the rear will be a throng of Athenian men, women, and children, also dressed in their festival best. The Panathenaea, which we will describe in Chapter IV, drew tens of thousands of participants, but for our Posidea, way out here in Sunium, let's assume a crowd of several hundred. As they pass through the gates of the sanctuary, each person sprinkles himself with water from the *perirrhanterion*. The bulls are led to the altar, and the priest takes his position at the west side of the altar while the others crowd around it. They will all be under the gaze, through the open doors of the temple, of the magnificent statue of Poseidon. A chorus of young men sing a hymn to Poseidon, inviting him to come, describing his ancestry, his arrival in Athens, and the aid he offered in the great war against the Persians. The priest then faces the altar, raises his hands, palms upwards, and prays that Poseidon receive with a welcoming heart the honors the Athenians are about to give him and that he continue to protect the sailors and ships of the Athenians. Sacrificial attendants then stun the bulls with a blow to the head, slit their throats, and capture the flowing blood in vessels. The animals are then butchered, and the thigh bones wrapped in fat and perhaps the tails are burned on the altar. The savory smoke rises from the altar up to Poseidon. He smells it and is pleased that we have remembered him, that we have shown him this "honor." He feels rewarded for having saved us from the dangers of the sea in the past and feels kindly towards us now, and he will no doubt save us from future dangers when we sail the Aegean. Then the vital organs, the kidneys, hearts, lungs, and spleens of the victims, are cooked on spits over the altar fire and distributed to the officials to eat. All of this is accomplished before midmorning, certainly by noon. What remains of the animals is then cooked, usually by boiling in large cauldrons. While this lengthy process of preparing and cooking of the animals is under way, several teams of young men compete in a regatta, in full view of the festival-goers on the ridge of the promontory. The winning team, which could have won only with the help of Poseidon, is awarded a handsome prize – perhaps a tripod, inscribed with their names, which they in turn will dedicate in the sanctuary as a gift to the god and a memorial of their victory. When the regatta is finished, the meat is ready to be served, and the competitors, the priests, and all in attendance will settle down to a fine communal feast on the meat of the sacrificed animals. That will bring to a close this year's Posidea of Poseidon Soter. As in our much simpler celebration of Poseidon's festival day earlier, there are moments of great religious solemnity, at the hymn, the prayer, and the sacrifice, but there are also times of considerable pleasure and enjoyment of good food, good entertainment, and good company.

Our festival is intended to engender good feelings in Poseidon towards us by showing him honor, and we will attempt to maintain those good feelings and our close relationship with Poseidon in the future by more festivals, more sacrifices, more hymns and prayers, and more dedications. As Greeks, of course, we will be doing much the same at many other sanctuaries throughout the year for the other deities who protect us and sustain us in other areas of our need.

NOTES

1. Diagoras' reply: "It is like that because those who shipwrecked and perished at sea are never painted on votive tablets." (Cicero, *On the Nature of the Gods* 3.89). The same anecdote is associated with the cynic philosopher Diogenes who more wittily responded, "There would be many more dedications if those who were not saved also set up dedications." (Diogenes Laertius, 6.59).
2. For one such book, beautifully illustrated, see A.B. Tataki, *Sunium: The Temple of Poseidon* (Athens, 1994).

FURTHER READING

For general surveys of topics in this chapter:

Bremmer, *GR*, 27–43
Burkert, *GR*, 54–107
Price, *RAG*, 25–70
Zaidman and Pantel, *RAC*, 27–62

On Sunium:

Camp, J.H., *The Archaeology of Athens* (New Haven, 2001), 305–10
Tataki, A.B., *Sunium: The Temple of Poseidon* (Athens, 1994)

On the location and design of sanctuaries:

Bergquist, B., *The Archaic Greek Temenos: A Study of Structure and Function* (Lund, 1967), esp. 108–36

Cole, S., *Landscapes, Gender, and Ritual Space: The Ancient Greek Experience* (Berkeley, forthcoming 2004)

Malkin, I., "Territorial Domination and the Greek Sanctuary," 75–81 in P. Hellström and B. Alroth, eds, *Religion and Power in the Ancient Greek World* (Uppsala, 1996)

Schachter, A., "Policy, Cult, and the Placing of Greek Sanctuaries," 1–64 in A. Schachter, ed., *Le sanctuaire grec* (Entretiens Hardt 37, 1992, Geneva)

On altars:

Yavis, C.G., *Greek Altars* (St. Louis, 1949)

On pollution:

Parker, R., *Miasma: Pollution and Purification in Early Greek Religion* (Oxford, 1983), esp. 32–143

On dedications:

Alroth, B., "The Positioning of Greek Votive Figurines," 195–203 in R. Hägg, N. Marinatos, G.C. Nordquist, eds., *Early Greek Cult Practice* (Stockholm, 1988)

Linders, T., "Gods, Gifts, Society," 115–22 in T. Linders, G. Nordquist, eds., *Gifts of the Gods* (Uppsala, 1987)

Rouse, W.H.D., *Greek Votive Offerings* (Cambridge, UK, 1902; reprinted 1975)

van Straten, F.T., "Gifts for the Gods," 65–151 in H.S. Versnel, *Faith, Hope and Worship* (Leiden, 1981)

Zaidman, L.B., *Le commerce des dieux* (Paris, 2001), 45–51

On priests and priestesses:

Feaver, D., "Historical Development in the Priesthoods of Athens," *Yale Classical Studies* 15 (1957), 123–58

Garland, R., "Priests and Power in Classical Athens," 73–91 in M. Beard and J. North, eds., *Pagan Priests* (London, 1990)

On prayers, hymns, and processions:

Bremer, J.M., "Greek Hymns," 193–215 in H.S. Versnel, *Faith, Hope and Worship* (Leiden, 1981)

Furley, W.D., "Praise and Persuasion in Greek Hymns," *Journal of Hellenic Studies* 115 (1995), 29–46

Pulleyn, S.J., *Prayer in Greek Religion* (Oxford, 1997)

Zaidman, L.B., *Le commerce des dieux*, 27–32

On statues of gods:

Donahue, A.A., "The Greek Images of the Gods: Considerations on Terminology and Methodology," *Hephaistos* 15 (1997), 31–45
Romano, I.B., "Early Greek Cult Images and Cult Practices," 127–34 in R. Hägg, N. Marinatos, G.C. Nordquist, eds., *Early Greek Cult Practice* (Stockholm, 1988)

On temples:

Bergquist, 1967 (above)
Burkert, W., "Greek Temple Builders: Who, Where and Why?" 21–9 in R. Hägg, *The Role of Religion in the Early Greek Polis* (Stockholm, 1996)
Coldstream, J.N., "Greek Temples: Why and Where?" 67–97 in P.E. Easterling and J.V. Muir, eds., *Greek Religion and Society* (Cambridge, UK, 1985)
Corbett, P.E., "Greek Temples and Greek Worshippers: The Literary and Archaeological Evidence," *Bulletin, Institute of Classical Studies* 17 (1970), 149–58

On offerings and sacrifices:

Bowie, A.M., "Greek Sacrifice: Forms and Functions," pp. 463–82 in *The Greek World*, ed. A. Powell (London, 1995)
Peirce, S., "Death, Revelry, and *Thysia*," *Classical Antiquity* 12 (1993), 219–66
van Straten, F., "The God's Portion in Greek Sacrificial Representations: Is the Tail Doing Nicely?" 51–68 in R. Hägg, N. Marinatos, G.C. Nordquist, eds., *Early Greek Cult Practice* (Stockholm, 1988)
Zaidman, L.B., *Le commerce des dieux*, 32–44

On piety, honor, and *charis*:

Mikalson, J.D., *Honor Thy Gods: Popular Religion in Greek Tragedy* (Chapel Hill, 1991), pp. 183–202
Parker, R., "Pleasing Thighs: Reciprocity in Greek Religion," pp. 105–25, in *Reciprocity in Ancient Greece*, C. Gill, N. Postlethwaite, and R. Seaford, eds. (Oxford, 1998)
Zaidman, L.B., *Le commerce des dieux*

On festivals:

Mikalson, J.D., "The *Heorte* of Heortology," *Greek, Roman and Byzantine Studies* 23, 1982, 213–21
Parke, H.W., *Festivals of the Athenians* (Ithaca, 1977)
Zaidman, L.B., *Le commerce des dieux*, 21–5

II

Greek Gods, Heroes, and Polytheism

⌐⌐⌐⌐

When Greeks wanted to express the whole range of deities they worshiped, they put them into two categories: gods and heroes. The laws of the Athenian lawgiver Dracon in the late seventh century bid the Athenians to worship "the gods and heroes," and, after their victory in the Persian Wars in 480/79, the Athenians credited, in addition to themselves, "the gods and heroes." One hundred and fifty years later, when Plato in his *Laws* was devising religious practices for an ideal state, he was concerned that prayers, sacrifices, festivals, and other such rituals be established for "the gods and heroes." The major distinction between the two groups is that gods were born immortal and, of course, remained such. Heroes were real or putative human beings, often, as Plato calls them, "children of the gods," who lived human lives, performed some extraordinarily great or awful deeds, died and were buried, and then, unlike the common dead, received public cult at their tombs because they were thought still able to affect the community for good or ill. There are, however, quite different types of both gods and heroes, and we begin with an analysis of them, with the gods first.

The Gods

> It is proper for a person who is beginning any serious discourse and task to begin first with the gods.
>
> Demosthenes, *Epistula* 1.1

Like most Greek gods our Poseidon Soter of Sunium may be defined in three ways: first, by the *name* Poseidon by which he is associated with the panhellenic deity Poseidon; second, by his *epithet* Soter (Savior), which links him with the protection of sailors and especially with the victory of the Greek navy over the Persians at the battle of Salamis in 480; and, third, by the designation of a *place* – Sunium of Athens – where his cult is located. Each of these elements – name, epithet, and locale – is of critical importance for imagining the conception a Greek worshiper would have of this or any other god.

Let us begin with *locale*. Poseidon Soter of Sunium has strong affinities with a Poseidon Soter worshiped at Isthmia on the Isthmus of Corinth which separates mainland Greece from the Peloponnesus. Both are gods of the sea, both served countries with strong naval forces, and both contributed to the victory at Salamis and, as we saw in Chapter I, were honored for that with dedications by the Greeks. But Poseidon's cult at Sunium and the one at the Isthmus would have had quite different myths explaining how the god came to be at its site and came to be associated with other deities there. The dates and elements of their festivals would also differ, and each may have had local idiosyncracies of ritual. Over time the cult of Poseidon of Sunium remained limited strictly to Athenians whereas that of Poseidon of the Isthmus became panhellenic, with biennial sacrifices, festivals, and games for all Greeks. Here we may think of one Poseidon with one function who, for different reasons given in cult myths, received cult at two places, Sunium and Isthmia, and whose cult at each place either had initially or later developed somewhat different features. And so the same deity with the same function may have quite different types of cult in two different locales.

The *epithet* Soter helps to identify the Poseidons of Sunium and of Isthmia with one another, but differing epithets may indicate very different functions of the deity. Poseidon Hippios (Of Horses), for example, had in Athens a sanctuary with an altar shared with Athena Hippia, a grove of trees, and a temple, situated far inland on "the Hill of Horses" on the northwestern outskirts of the city. Poseidon's epithet Hippios indicates that here his concern was not sailors and the sea, but horses (*hippoi* in Greek). Both Poseidon Soter of Sunium and Poseidon Hippios of the Hill of the Horses are Athenian Poseidons, but they had separate sanctuaries, priests from different families, different myths told about them, probably different festival days and somewhat different rituals, and, most importantly, different roles to play in the lives of the Athenians. Poseidon Soter would protect ships and sailors; Poseidon Hippios would tend horses. One would pray in vain to Poseidon Soter to save his horse or to Poseidon Hippios to save his life at sea. There is a third Poseidon on Delos, that island in the center of the Aegean known even to ancient Greeks for *not* having earthquakes. The Delians had a sanctuary of Poseidon Asphaleios (He who keeps things steady and secure). Poseidon Asphaleios of Delos – again with the three designations of name, epithet, and locale – is that Poseidon who causes earthquakes, and the Delians apparently successfully made prayers and sacrifices, probably annually, to him *not* to cause earthquakes on their island.

In our examples Poseidon's three epithets, Soter, Hippios, and Asphaleios, each represented a distinct activity of Poseidon, and the Poseidon of each sanctuary would concern himself with only that one activity. To us they might appear as three separate gods – one helping with sailing at sea, one with horses, and one with earthquakes –, but the Greeks, for reasons about which we can only speculate, brought all three together under the name Poseidon and viewed the various activities as aspects of the same god. We find distinct functions indicated by different epithets also for virtually all of the Olympian gods. In Athens, for example, Athena had the epithets Polias (Of the City), Nike (Of Victory), Hygieia (Of Health), Boulaia (Of the Boule), Areia (Associated with Ares), Hippia (Of Horses), Phratria (Of the Brotherhoods), Soteira (Protectress), Hephaistia (Associated with Hephaestus), and also a number of epithets which indicated only the location of sanctuaries in Attica (Itonia, Paionia, and Skiras). Each of these epithets reflects an Athena with a separate altar, sanctuary, priesthood, dedications, rituals, and, to a greater or lesser degree, area of concern. And here again we might think of many of these Athenas as essentially different deities offering quite different services, but the Athenians brought them all together under the name Athena.

Homer's *Iliad* and *Odyssey* and Hesiod's *Theogony* described activities of deities with these same *names*, and since these epics were known throughout the Greek world, the epic poets' descriptions of these gods strongly affected their portrayal in later Greek literature. Many today have come to know the Greek gods primarily or solely from this poetic literature and therefore imagine the gods to have been as they are presented in the epics, tragedy, comedy, and the other poetic genres. This raises the fundamental and complex question of the relationship of the gods of Greek literature to those of practiced religion. Because they share the same *names*, many naturally assume that the familiar gods of Greek literature, with their interesting personalities and all too human vices, were the gods actually worshiped by the Greeks, but this leads to a very mistaken conception of the gods to whom real Greeks prayed, sacrificed, and offered their dedications.

One key to understanding the difference between the gods of literature and those of cult is offered by the fifth-century historian Herodotus. He claimed (2.53) that sometime shortly after about 850 B.C.E. Hesiod and Homer "created a divine genealogy, gave their epithets to the gods, distributed to them their 'offices' and their 'skills,' and marked out their

> I think that Hesiod and Homer were older than I by four hundred years
> and no more, and they are the ones who created a divine genealogy for
> Greeks, gave their epithets to the gods, distributed their offices and their
> crafts, and marked out their outward appearances.
>
> Herodotus, *Histories* 2.53

'outward appearances.'" In "creating" the divine genealogy Hesiod and
Homer made, for example, Poseidon the brother of Zeus and made
Athena, Apollo, Artemis, and many others Zeus' sons and daughters.
Hesiod and Homer, in Herodotus' mind, essentially created the divine royal
family as we know it through Greek mythology. The epithets Herodotus
has in mind are those we find in epic poetry, in part those of *function*
("Cloud-Gathering" for Zeus and "Earth-Shaking" for Poseidon) and *locale*
("Argive" for Hera), but also those of *description* ("gray-eyed" for Athena,
"white-armed" for Hera). By "offices" Herodotus means, for example,
Zeus' rule over the sky, Poseidon's rule over the sea, and Hades' rule over
the underworld, and by "skills" the lyre-playing of Apollo or the weaving
of Athena. By "outward appearances" Herodotus means how the gods,
in their usual dress, physically appeared: Athena with her armor and
the aegis or Poseidon a mature man wielding the trident. In Herodotus'
conception, the names of the Greek deities had already long existed, but
Hesiod and Homer arranged these named deities into a family structure
and gave them their distinctive epithets, offices, and skills; that is, they
essentially made them what we think them to be from the Greek literary
and artistic traditions.

Herodotus' claim is exceptionally valuable in pointing us in the right
direction for understanding how the Greek gods of literature came to be
and how they relate to the gods that concern us, the gods of practiced
religion, but we must augment Herodotus' thesis. First, Hesiod and Homer
were the culmination of a very long, probably centuries long, oral poetry
tradition unknown to Herodotus, and the Hesiodic and Homeric deities
were the products of that long tradition, not just of Hesiod's and Homer's
own work. Secondly, this oral tradition did not "create" this picture of the
divine world out of nothing. Some of it was surely the product of poetic
imagination, but that imagination was working with deities, both Greek
and Near Eastern, who were worshiped at the time and were defined
by both function and location. Homer's Poseidon, for example, causes
storms at sea and calms the waters, and two common Homeric epithets
for Poseidon (*enosichthon* and *ennosigaios*, both ("earth-shaker"), indicate
that he also caused earthquakes. Homer's Poseidon thus already has two

> He spoke, and pulled the clouds together, in both hands gripping
> The trident, and staggered the sea, and let loose all the stormblasts
> Of all the winds together, and huddled under the cloud scuds
> Land alike and the great water. Night sprang from heaven.
> East Wind and South Wind clashed together, and the bitter blown
>   West Wind
> And the North Wind born in the bright air rolled up a heavy sea.
>
> Poseidon, stirring up the storm against Odysseus, Homer,
> *Odyssey* 5.291–5 (Lattimore translation)

of the functions of the cultic Poseidons, of Poseidon Soter of Sunium and Poseidon Asphaleios of Delos. Homer's Hera is often called "Argive," and in fact a major cult of Hera was centered in the land of Argos. There are many such elements of practiced religion – in terms of both deities and rituals – throughout the *Iliad*, the *Odyssey*, and the *Theogony*, and the oral poets must have selected among the deities of local cults of the Greek world to create, essentially, composite deities suited to their songs. For each composite deity – Poseidon, or Athena, or Zeus – there were some elements of local, practiced cults, but the oral poets in their songs added or elaborated much themselves, some of it from the mythologies of Near Eastern religions. In effect they probably created much of that with which Herodotus credits them: the gods' genealogies, offices, skills, and physical appearances. These composite deities of epic poetry, brought into a family structure but now largely stripped of local cultic associations, then suited audiences throughout the Greek world, and it was these epic deities who were featured in the later literature of the Greeks and who were also later criticized by the philosophers and the early Christian church fathers. The myths and tales of these epic, composite deities developed in literature along lines quite independent from the local cult myths of the worshiped gods. The myths of the literary deities were open to the invention and interpretation of succeeding poets and took on a life of their own, but the local cult myths, because of the strong Greek sense of religious conservatism in cultic matters, tended to remain static. It is these local cult myths that we examine in Chapter III.

The deities of epic poetry did, however, have a significant influence on their counterparts worshiped in individual, local cults. Athenians would believe that their Poseidon Soter at Sunium was the brother of Zeus and uncle of Athena, just as the epics represented them. And, as they imagined what this Poseidon looked like, they would have in mind the epic portrayal of him: a man of late middle age, bearded, somewhat larger than human,

> So presently he came down from the craggy mountain, striding
> on rapid feet, and the tall mountains trembled and the timber
> under the immortal feet of Poseidon's progress.
> He took three long strides forward, and in the fourth came to his goal,
> Aigai, where his glorious house was built in the water's
> depth, glittering with gold, imperishable forever.
> Going there he harnessed under his chariot his bronze-shod horses,
> flying-footed, with long manes streaming of gold; and he put on
> clothing of gold about his own body, and took up the golden
> lash, carefully compacted, and climbed up into his chariot
> and drove it across the waves. And about him the sea beasts came up
> from their deep places and played in his path, and acknowledged
>   their master,
> and the sea stood apart before him, rejoicing. The horses winged on
> delicately, and the bronze axle beneath was not wetted.
> The fast-running horses carried him to the ships of the Achaians.
>   Poseidon's journey to Troy, Homer, *Iliad* 13.17–31 (Lattimore translation)

wielding a trident. And so the sculptor represented him for the monumental statue in our sanctuary in Chapter I, and so Poseidon would appear in the statuettes dedicated to him there. What is true of Poseidon of Sunium in this regard is true also of the other Olympian deities with cults in Athens or elsewhere. They would usually be imagined and represented physically in the form that epic poetry created for them. The deities of Greek poetry, in a sense, both were (by name, physical appearance, and sometimes function) and were not (by local cult myths, rituals, and sometimes function) the deities whom each Greek personally worshiped. The result is that if we wish to understand the deities of practiced Greek religion, we must begin with the myths, rituals, and functions of the gods at individual sanctuaries – as we do in Chapter IV – and only then see what epic, panhellenic features these same gods exhibited.

There were also some important gods such as Demeter and Dionysus who found only a minor place in the *Iliad* and *Odyssey*. They have their place in the epic genealogy of the gods, but the richest sources for their mythologies are their local cults, and these local mythologies are occasionally elaborated in other poetic forms, in particular in the *Homeric Hymns* and Athenian tragedies. Here the relationship between the poetic and cultic versions of the deity is often quite close, and we shall see examples of this when we describe the cults of Demeter, Dionysus, and Apollo in Chapter IV.

The familiar twelve Olympian deities of Zeus, Hera, Athena, Dionysus, Hermes, Aphrodite, Hephaestus, Demeter, Apollo, Artemis, Ares, and our Poseidon each shared this "dual nature" – a panhellenic type in literature but also, probably in every city-state, a local form, with its own individual cult, myth, ritual, and sometimes even function.

Ouranic and Chthonic Deities

We think of the twelve Olympian gods as *ouranic*, that is "of the sky," and that is generally the case, but some are, in certain cults, termed specifically *chthonic* ("*of* or *in* the earth," *chthon* = "earth"). In some Greek cities, for example, a Hermes Chthonios was represented and named on tombstones, and he has his Homeric counterpart in the Hermes who guides the souls of the dead from the upperworld to the underworld (*Odyssey* 24.1–14). Hermes Chthonios was also the addressee of curses which individuals wrote on tablets against their personal enemies and then buried or deposited in tombs. The tablets were being sent to Hermes "in the earth," but the actions they requested were against enemies living in the upperworld. But, on the ouranic side, the Athenians also worshiped Hermes in their gymnasia and palaestras as a patron of the activities and competitions of male youth, and that worship had all the features of that of our ouranic Poseidon. Purely ouranic deities like Apollo functioned only in the upperworld and concerned themselves only with the living. But deities such as Hermes Chthonios moved between the upperworld and underworld in order to perform their divine functions.

> Let Pherenicus be put under a spell to Hermes Chthonikos and Hecate Chthonia. And I put under a spell to Hermes Chthonikos and Hecate Chthonia Galene, who associates with Pherenicus. And just as this lead is cold and is held in no esteem, so may Pherenicus and his things be cold and held in no esteem, and so may be the things which Pherenicus' collaborators say and plot concerning me.
>
> Wünsch, *Defixionum Tabellae*, no. 107

Offerings and sacrifices to purely ouranic deities were performed in daylight, were directed upwards to the sky, and often resulted in a feast among the participants. Since chthonic deities were "in the earth," offerings and sacrifices to them were directed downwards to the earth, with liquid offerings (*choai*) of milk, blood, or honey poured into low-lying altars (*escharai*) or pits. Such offerings were usually made at night, and animals sacrificed to these deities were to be black, not white as for ouranic deities. Usually the whole victim was offered, as a *holocaust*, with no meat set aside for a banquet of the sacrificers.

There are, however, many exceptions and vagaries in this distinction between ouranic and chthonic deities: some deities who seem purely chthonic have raised altars like the ouranic deities, and banquets are occasionally attested for chthonic cults. Sometimes, too, as we shall see, an ouranic deity like Athena will have a chthonic partner in cult, and the rituals of that cult reflect the two aspects. The exceptions and break-downs of distinctions between chthonic and ouranic deities and rituals are so frequent that some scholars deny that they have any meaning, but the Greeks themselves made these distinctions, and we should accept them, though with caution.

The designations ouranic and chthonic are best understood in terms of the deity's functions. If those functions involved exclusively the upperworld and the living, that deity was ouranic. If the deity's functions included the earth itself (in the production of agricultural crops, for example) or the dead, that deity was chthonic. And, as occasionally happened, if the deity, like Hermes, had some functions that were exclusively of this world and others that involved the underworld, he would be ouranic in the cult featuring the upperlife functions but chthonic in the cult devoted to under-world functions or those involving communication between the two worlds. Again, Hermes might seem to us two separate deities – one serving the youth in purely upperworld ways, the other offering communication with the underworld, and each invoked for different purposes, on different occasions and at different sites, and with different rituals. But the Greeks saw "both" deities as Hermes, and the problems we have categorizing them seem not to have troubled the Greeks.

Deities who promoted agricultural fertility, especially Demeter the giver of grain, also shared in this dual, upper- and underworld nature, as we will see in the description of her cult at Eleusis in Chapter IV. Since seeds were planted *in* the earth, to promote their fertility the deity herself must be *in* the earth, and in several cults Demeter is expressly termed Chthonia. The chthonic aspect of Demeter of Eleusis is also reflected in her rituals and in the myth that makes her both the mother of Persephone, the queen of the underworld, and the giver of secret rites that promise initiates a "blessed afterlife" among the dead.

From our readings of Greek literature and especially the Homeric epics, the ouranic type of ritual, as for our Poseidon Soter of Sunium, seems more familiar, and the chthonic rituals appear often rather bizarre and hard to explain. But we should take care not to think that for the Greeks the ouranic was in some sense "normal" and the various types of chthonic rituals "abnormal." The Greeks performed both sets of rituals commonly and unreservedly, according to the nature of the deity whom they were worshiping at the moment. Both were, as the Greeks would put it, part of their "customary and ancestral practices" in religious matters, and we find both types widely and perhaps almost equally attested in ancient documents which describe actual cult practices.

Heroes and Heroines

The Greeks also distinguished, and more clearly so, between gods and heroes. Heroes as religious deities were real or putative human beings who had lived human lives, had performed some extraordinarily great or awful deeds, had died and been buried, and then, unlike the common dead, received public cult at their tombs. They thus are intermediary figures between gods and humans, and some incline more to the divine side, some more to the human. The focal point of the hero's cult was the tomb. The tomb was often surrounded by a fence, and, like the sanctuary of a god, everything in the *heroön* (hero sanctuary) was "sacred." Offerings, usually of liquids such as milk, honey, and wine, and sacrifices, often holocausts, were made to the hero, and they would be deposited either on the tomb itself or in an adjacent pit or low altar (*eschara*). They would be directed downward, to the hero in his tomb, rather than upward as for the ouranic gods in the sky. Feasts of worshipers were also often held in the *heroa*, probably once annually on the hero's day.

The *heroa* of these heroes and heroines were usually thought to contain their actual remains. Theseus, the king of Athens in olden times who had, apart from his adventures with the Minotaur on Crete, unified all Attica into the city-state Athens, had died on the island of Scyros in the western Aegean Sea. In 476 B.C.E. the Athenians received an oracle to "recover the bones of Theseus," and the general Cimon led an expedition to do just that. Plutarch (*Life of Theseus*, 36.1–2 and *Life of Cimon*, 8.5–6) tells the dramatic story of how Cimon, with miraculous assistance, discovered on Scyros the tomb of "a man of exceptional height, with a bronze spear and a sword lying beside him." The weapons Cimon found with the bones were bronze, and this makes it most likely that what Cimon discovered on Scyros was one of the many large, vaulted Bronze Age tombs scattered over the Greek countryside. The "Theseus" he recovered was quite probably a warrior dating back to the times of the Trojan War. Cimon brought the remains of what he no doubt thought to be Theseus back to Athens, and the Athenians, in their delight, welcomed their hero home and held processions and sacrifices in his honor. They installed the remains in a

Figure II.1 An Athenian red-figure cup by the Codrus Painter, of about 440–430 B.C.E. In the center Theseus drags the dead Minotaur from the labyrinth. In the other scenes, clockwise from the top, Theseus 1) wrestles Cercyon, 2) attacks Procrustes with an ax, 3) attacks Sciron, 4) controls the Marathonian bull, 5) holds Sinis, and 6) wards off the sow of Crommyon. Courtesy of the Trustees of the British Museum, inv. no. BM E 84.

Theseion, the *heroön* for the founder of their city-state. After that they made offerings to Theseus on the eighth day of each month, a day he shared with his father Poseidon,[1] and annually on Pyanopsion 8, in the autumn, they held his major festival, the Theseia, with sacrifices and games.

Because a hero's cult was centered on his real or imagined tomb, the hero was bound, unlike a god, to one locality. He usually would have only one sanctuary, in only one city-state, unless two or more states laid claim to his bones. Because his *heroön* was accessible to the offerings of only the residents of that state, the hero's activity and influence would affect, at most, only that state and perhaps only the immediate neighborhood in which his *heroön* was located. For Athens we know by their names *and* cults over 160 such heroes and heroines, and there were many more of whose cults we know nothing, who were nameless (just "the hero" or "the heroine") or who otherwise have left no record. The Athenian heroes with known cults are a diverse group, including the Homeric hero Ajax and his son Eurysaces; Heracles and his mother Alcmene and various children; early kings of Athens such as Cecrops and his daughters Aglaurus, Pandrosus, and Herse; Theseus, his father Aegeus and son Demophon; Academus who lent his name to the Academy, the gymnasium near which Plato established his school; and even Helen whom Theseus reputedly carried off as a young girl from Sparta.

Heroes, unlike gods, continued to "come into being" in the historical period. Shortly after 514 Harmodius and Aristogiton, who assassinated a son of Pisistratus, became for democratic Athens the "tyrant-slayer" heroes, received offerings and the statues common in hero cult, and became a popular subject for drinking songs. The 192 Athenian soldiers who died in the victory over the Persians at Marathon in 490 were buried on the battlefield. They received hero cult for centuries afterwards, and one may still today visit their funeral mound on the plain of Marathon. All of these heroes and heroines worshiped in Athens were either Athenians themselves or, like Heracles, had myths which linked them to Athens and explained the origins of their cults there.

Figure II.2   Tomb (Soros) in plain of Marathon of the 192 Athenian soldiers who fought the Persians and died there in 490 B.C.E. Ten meters high and about 180 m. in circumference. Excavations have confirmed the burials and the date. It became the site of hero cult for the Marathonian dead for centuries afterwards. Photograph by the author.

What these heroes provided their worshipers was as varied as the heroes themselves. Amphiaraus' large sanctuary at Oropus, on the northeastern border of Attica, was a virtual hospital where patients came in hopes, no doubt, of miraculous cures. In addition there were scattered throughout Attica cults of at least four other "healers," nameless figures known only as Physician Heroes. Theseus as well as the local hero Marathon were imagined by the Athenians to have personally been present at the battle of Marathon and to have contributed to that victory. Theseus played many roles in Athenian cult and myth, but particularly important was his role as founder of the state. Just as the founder of a colony in historical times would be honored after his death with a hero cult in that new city's center, so Theseus, the unifier of Attica and founder of the Athenian state, was worshiped by all Athenians. The cult was probably both a marker of the respect for the hero's accomplishments as well as a means to secure his help in the future.

The residents of Marathon considered Marathon, a son of Apollo, their *eponymous* hero, that is, the hero who *gave his name* to their district. Gods often gave their names to city-states, as Athena did to Athens or Poseidon to Potidaea, but hundreds, probably thousands of heroes throughout Greece were thought, like Marathon, to have been early ancestors who lent their names to prominent families (as Eumolpus to the Eumolpidae of Eleusis), to districts (as Marathon to Marathon), or even to large regions of Greece itself (as Pelops to the Peloponnesus, "the Island of Pelops"). Such heroes would be worshiped by the group named after them, perhaps just as prominent ancestors or perhaps as deities who could still provide assistance. When Cleisthenes in 508/7 B.C.E. restructured the Athenian political institutions and divided the Athenian citizenry into ten new tribes, he had the Delphic Oracle select from a list of 100 Athenian heroes ten who would give their names to the new tribes. Cecrops was among the select ten eponymous heroes, and the members of his tribe, Cecropis, would meet and make offerings annually at his *heroön*. Cleisthenes was clearly manipulating preexisting hero cults for political purposes, and we know little of how Cecrops' new role as the eponymous hero of a political unit of the state affected or changed distinctive features of his cult. A new set of citizens would, however, have felt particular allegiance to his cult and may have thought that he not only in some sense "represented" their tribe but also furthered its interests. In inter-tribal athletic contests at religious festivals winners from the Cecropis tribe would dedicate their prizes to him in his sanctuary on the Acropolis. Because of their local affiliations it is the heroes of Greek religion even more than the Olympian gods that give a distinctive character to the cults, the rituals, and, as we will see in Chapter III, the mythology of the individual Greek city-states.

Many heroes and heroines were beneficent deities, helping individuals especially in matters of health, wealth, seafaring, and in childbearing and rearing; protecting the state against foreign attacks, on the battlefield or at the gates; and serving as the eponymous patrons of families, demes, and tribes. But heroes were still from the realm of the dead, and some had a dark side. Worship was intended to *appease* them and prevent them from causing harm. Herodotus tells the story of how the Agyllaei of Italy stoned some Greek refugees from the city of Phocaea in Asia Minor. When men and animals passing by the place of the stoning became lame and deranged, the Agyllaei were ordered by the Delphic Oracle to make offerings and hold games for the dead Phocaeans, and they were still continuing the practice in Herodotus' time (1.167.1–2). In this case the Phocaeans had suffered a terrible wrong, were filled with wrath, punished their killers, and had to be *appeased*. One can imagine that if the Agyllaei neglected this cult, the Phocaean heroes would again vent their wrath. Among the heroes of the Greek pantheon were several such whose cult was intended not to acquire benefits from the hero but to avert the evils he might cause.

Some heroes provided benefits to their worshipers very much as the gods did and even ranged around the Greek world like the gods. A few of them, most notably Asclepius and Heracles, crossed the border from hero to god. In Homer's *Iliad* Asclepius is completely mortal, the "blameless physician" (*Iliad* 4.194 and 11.518); in his Thessalian homeland of Tricca he seems to have been worshiped as a hero; but at Epidaurus, which became in the Classical period his major cult center, and in cults like those at Athens founded as colonies of the Epidaurian cult, Asclepius is designated a "god" and is worshiped in the manner of ouranic deities. About Heracles even the Greeks of the time held divided opinions. Some worshiped him as a hero, with the rituals befitting such a cult; others treated him as a god. Herodotus speaks approvingly of those Greeks who have in their cities *two* kinds of sanctuaries of Heracles and sacrifice to one Heracles as an immortal with the epithet "Olympios" and make offerings to the other as a hero (2.44.5). Mythology offered a bridge between the hero and the god, with both Heracles and Asclepius being "apotheosized," that is, "made a god."

We see, then, that the distinctions we draw among the deities of the Greek pantheon are subject to many vagaries. The Greeks distinguished between ouranic and chthonic deities, but some ouranic deities had their chthonic counterparts and some had chthonic elements in their cults, and vice versa. Likewise heroes and gods are distinct, but often heroes have a role to play in a god's cult and mythology, and vice versa. A few heroes even become gods. If we attempt to understand these differences in the

Figure II.3   Drawing from a red-figure Athenian *amphora*, of about 475–450 B.C.E. Heracles is depicted as being received on Mount Olympus by a winged Nike (Victory) and being escorted by a scepter- and thunderbolt-bearing Zeus. With permission, from J. Swaddling, *The Ancient Olympic Games*, 1999, p. 9. Inv. no. British Museum, E 262.

abstract, the difficulties and exceptions seem overwhelming, but if, as we will do in Chapter IV, we examine how they played out in individual cults, we will find them little troubling, as apparently the Greeks themselves thought them to be.

Gods and Heroes in Combinations

In cult, major deities seldom stood alone. They were often associated with "family" members, as Apollo on Delos where, according to his myth, he and his sister Artemis were born. Inside his sanctuary there, in addition to the statues, temples, dedications, and altar of Apollo, there were smaller sanctuaries of his mother Leto, of his sister Artemis, and even of the goddess Eileithyia who assisted in the twins' birth. There, too, was the date-palm tree to which Leto clung during her labor. At Olympia Zeus had his magnificent fifth-century temple and statue and his monumental altar, but Hera, too, had a temple there, and adjoining Zeus' sanctuary was the Hill of Cronus, Zeus' father. Around Asclepius at Epidaurus were ranged his father Apollo, his wife Epione, and his daughters Aceso, Iaso, Panacea, and Hygieia, whose names all refer to aspects of healing and health. The daughters may be mere personifications of Asclepius' activity, but all were eventually integrated into Asclepius' cult and could be included in hymns, dedications, and sacrifices in the god's honor. This divine family of Asclepius seems to have taken shape in the fifth century, but those of Delian Apollo and Olympian Zeus date much further back, at least to the seventh century and probably earlier. To what extent they are the source or the product of the epic genealogies of these gods we do not know.

Deities might also be associated in cult by *function*, as we have seen with Poseidon Hippios and Athena Hippia. In their joint cult in Athens Poseidon seems more concerned with the breeding and riding of horses, and the Athenian cavalrymen made dedications particularly to him. His partner Athena Hippia, who had taught men to make horse-drawn wagons and chariots, would oversee activities involving those. Together they would cover Athenians' concerns about horses. So too Zeus Boulaios and Athena Boulaia shared a cult with an altar in the Athenian Bouleuterion where the 500 members of the Boule met, sacrificed, and deliberated every non-holiday day of the year. At Erythrae in Asia Minor at the city's gate Heracles Kallinikos (Victor), Poseidon Asphaleios, Apollo, and Artemis – all here to be associated with various aspects of the protection of gates and fortification walls – received, probably one day each month, a joint sacrifice from the Erythraeans. In these cases it was not the family connections but the shared or related functions that united the deities in cult.

Heroes, too, drew family members into their cults. In Athens, Cecrops and his daughters Aglaurus, Pandrosus, and Herse were all worshiped, and with the cult of Heracles came also the worship of his mother Alcmene, of several of his children, and even of his loyal follower Iolaus. Plato designates heroes "the children of gods," but this is usually not the relationship that is emphasized when a god and hero are united in cult. The relationship between hero and god in cult is often more complex. The hero, for example, might receive a place in a god's sanctuary because he originated the festival or worship of that deity, as Erechtheus had the Panathenaea at Athens for Athena Polias. Aglaurus was Athena's first priestess, and as heroine could serve as the model for all later human priestesses of Athena. A quite different situation occurs at Amyclae in Sparta where, according to local myth, the young man Hyacinthus was accidentally killed by Apollo. Hyacinthus then, as a hero, shared a sanctuary with Apollo, and Apollo's statue even stood over his grave. Hyacinthus was integrated into the cult to the extent that the festival was called the Hyacinthia and one of Apollo's epithets there was Hyacinthios (Pausanias 3.19.1–5). In Athens, as we shall see in Chapters III and IV, Erechtheus was a close partner of Athena in the cult on the Acropolis. The building they shared was for most of the Classical period called the "Temple of Athena" but eventually became known, and remains widely known today, as the Erechtheum, named after the hero, not the goddess. There is even the possibility that Hyacinthus and Erechtheus held prior possession of these cult sites and that their divine "partners" were relative late-comers. Myths and cults, then, may reflect the eventual accommodation between god and hero. Such, apparently, was the case at Olympia, where the famous Olympic Games may have been originally held in honor of the hero Pelops. They soon, however, became associated with the quadrennial festival of Zeus, and the accommodation reached between the hero and the god is reflected by the large *heroön* of Pelops inside Zeus' sanctuary there. We will explore these hero/god relationships more when we treat individual cults in following chapters, but we stress here that heroes and gods did not inhabit mutually exclusive realms. They could be, and often were, united in cult and myth.

Sometimes the reasons for associating one god with another or with a hero are less clear and are suggested only by the proximity of their sanctuaries. Sunium offers a good example of this. About 500 meters north-east of our sanctuary of Poseidon Soter there was a large sanctuary of Athena Sounias with an Ionic temple, a statue of Athena, and an altar. The temple, like Poseidon's, was built in mid-fifth century and was perhaps, again like Poseidon's, a dedication from the victory over the Persians in 479 B.C.E. We can only guess at why Poseidon and Athena had neighboring sanctuaries at Sunium, but it may be because Sunium was an important border area to be defended, and Poseidon would provide the protection by sea, Athena by land. Integrated into Athena's sanctuary was a large *heroön*. The identity of the hero is not certain.[2] It was obviously a hero directly associated with Athena, and in Chapters III and IV we will see Athena, Poseidon, and a hero all united in Athens' most central and most important cult on the Acropolis. A myth explains the complex of associations among these three deities on the Acropolis, and a similar myth, now lost, may have explained the links between the two gods and the hero at Sunium.

We can add to the Greek "deities" figures such as the Nymphs and Satyrs who were viewed as groups. These groups were distinguished by gender and age – the Nymphs, for example, being young women –, but individuals within the group were usually not named. Nymphs had altars throughout the Greek world, often in association with Pan and particularly at springs and caves. Such Nymphs were clearly worshiped, but other such young female groups as the Oreads of the mountains and the Nereids of the sea seem merely companions of major deities without cults of their own.

Figure II.4　A reconstruction of the sanctuary of Athena Sounias at Sunium, near the sanctuary of Poseidon Soter. The sanctuary has a temple, treasury building, gateway, and various dedications. The area between the northern *temenos* wall (on the left) and the pathway was probably a *heroön*. Courtesy of EKDOTIKE ATHENON S.A.

So, too, the wild and lascivious Satyrs (half-man, half-beast) in art and literature form part of the retinue of Dionysus, but do not receive offerings either with him or independently. Because of their association with poetry and their long and continuing role in literature and education, the Muses are a particularly interesting example of this type of deity. In the Archaic and Classical periods they apparently had cult centers in Macedonia, at Pieria and on Mount Olympus, and on Mount Helicon between Delphi and Thebes. The early poets appealed to these goddesses for inspiration, often referring to their specific cult sites, as Hesiod does to his neighboring Muses of Helicon in the opening of his *Theogony*. The Muses of Helicon had, at least from the third century B.C.E. on, a full-scale sanctuary with an altar, theater, statues of the goddesses and poets, and a quadrennial festival with contests in tragedy and comedy and, later, music. In some places in the Greek world the Muses become part of the retinue of Apollo Musagetes (Leader of the Muses), but most often they appear only as literary figures, often with individual names and functions, largely divorced from religious cult. In the fourth century Plato's Academy and other philosophical schools adopted the Muses as their patrons and gave them a new type of cultic life. For the Muses, as for the Nymphs and for so many other deities of all types, local circumstances determined what type of "deities" they were and whether or not they received worship, and the poetic tradition, strongly influenced by Hesiod, eventually developed a fairly uniform literary and artistic type of them for all Greeks.

Gods and Heroes as a Unified Collective

The Greeks commonly also spoke of their gods or gods and heroes together as a unified group. The Athenian general Themistocles claimed that "the gods and heroes" punished the Persian king Xerxes for his impieties and that this contributed to the victory of the Greeks over the Persians (Herodotus 8.109.3). A plaintiff in a law-suit in Athens might well claim that "the gods" would punish his opponent. Aeschylus in a tragedy would not hesitate to have a chorus sing that "the gods" reward piety and punish impiety, and similar statements may be found throughout tragedy and other poetry and the writings of Plato and Aristotle. Such statements of the unified views and actions of all the gods are a product of generalizing thought about the gods, a tendency apparent already in Homer and Hesiod and then increasingly common in later literature and philosophy. These statements about "the gods" are abstracted from and override the many distinctions between gods and their epithets, locales, and functions that prevail in practiced religion. Thought about "the gods" as a single, unified group was critically important to the development of Greek theology and ethics, but it is also another example of the parting of ways between the religion practiced in cult by the Greeks and the religion represented in their literature.

A Human in a Polytheistic World

If we were to survey all the gods and heroes cultically worshiped in the Greek world, and if we distinguished among them, as we should, by name, epithet, and locale, they would come to several thousands in number. Each would have his or her own altar, sanctuary, priest or priestess, annual remembrance, and function. To understand how a single individual dealt with the many deities of the Greek world, we need to put him into a specific location in Greece and we must keep in mind, from Chapter I, the areas of life in which he sought help from his deities. These areas were, in the most general terms, 1) fertility of crops, animals, and human beings; 2) economic prosperity; 3) good health; and 4) safety, particularly in the dangers of war and seafaring. By prayers and offerings to the gods of his family cult, to those who had sanctuaries in his village, and, finally, to those of statewide importance, the individual would attempt to secure divine help in those areas of need.

A few Greeks might, once or twice in their lifetimes, visit the sanctuary of one of the truly panhellenic deities of Greece, such as Apollo of Delphi or Zeus of Olympia. But in his everyday religious life the largest pantheon of interest to a Greek would be the gods and heroes of his own city-state. An Athenian, for example, would be concerned only with gods and heroes of Athens. Those of Sparta or Corinth would hold no interest for him, and, not being a citizen of those states, he could not participate in their cults even if he had wished to. It is characteristic of the Greek religious temperament in the Classical period that citizens of one state respected the power of deities of other city-states and even of foreign peoples, but they would not participate in others' cults, not out of disrespect or disbelief, but because they were not members of those communities and had the gods of their own community to fulfill their needs.

Within the city-state there were some gods and heroes worshiped by all the residents, often in annual statewide festivals. At Athens Theseus was such a hero, and Athena Polias and Demeter Eleusinia, whose cults we will describe in Chapter IV, were such gods. But we must imagine also that many or even most of the individual cults in a large city-state such as Athens had little relevance to the individual citizen.

Since 508/7 B.C.E. the 10,000 square miles of Attica had been divided into 139 demes (townships) which were both geographical and administrative units. Most demes were centered on preexisting villages. Each had within its borders a number of sanctuaries, and it was to these that the residents of the deme would on most occasions turn. If his deme deity could provide what was needed, an Athenian would hardly trek 30 miles to a distant deme to accomplish the same purpose. Also, the deme was a closed community, the deities of that deme were part of that community, and worship of those deities was a marker of membership in that community. A resident of one deme would be, as it were, entering somewhat alien territory and a somewhat alien sanctuary if he went to the god of another deme. The individual's family and ancestors had worshiped for centuries at their village's sanctuaries, and he would not find in another deme people, deities, and priests as familiar to him as those of his own deme.

The next and smallest social unit in which an individual would worship was that of his household. We devote Chapter V to family cult and the religious activities of the individual members of the family, but, to round out our picture of the gods worshiped by one Greek, we need to introduce those gods such as Zeus Herkeios (Of the Fence), Zeus Ktesios (Of the Stores), and Apollo Agyieus (Of the Street). Each family in their own home would

Check Out Receipt

Livingston Public Library
973-992-4600

Monday, March 27, 2017 5:17:51 PM

Item: 31792002774607
Title: The complete dream dictionary : a p
ractical guide to interpreting dreams
Due: 04/24/2017

Item: 31792003651028
Title: Unchosen : the hidden lives of Hasi
dic rebels
Due: 04/24/2017

Item: 31792003601148
Title: Ancient Greek religion
Due: 04/24/2017

Total items: 3

You just saved $80.00 by using your librar
y. You have saved $80.00 this past year an
d $80.00 since you began using the library

Thank you for visiting the
Livingston Public Library!

livingston.bccls.org
(973) 992-4600

render worship privately to these deities who gave prosperity and protection to their house and its property and inhabitants.

Let us try now to reconstruct, however hypothetically, the deities of family, deme, and city-state that a typical Athenian of the fifth century would worship. First, and probably daily, he would attend to the gods of his household, Zeus Herkeios, Zeus Ktesios, and Apollo Apotropaios. At the next level he would honor the deities of his deme, usually just on their annual festival days but also occasionally in times of special need. A complete calendar of the annual sacrifices made by the deme Erchia in the fourth century gives us some idea of the number and variety of deities worshiped in these demes. Erchia was located in the midlands of Attica, right, in fact, at the site of the new Athens International airport. If we make our Athenian an Erchian, then we can imagine him to be worshiping at Erchia at least thirty-four deities at at least fifteen different cult centers, some of which had several sanctuaries. Among the thirty-four deities are some familiar Olympians: Apollo, Artemis, Athena, Demeter, Dionysus, Hera, Hermes, Poseidon, and Zeus. We should by now, however, realize that simple *names* of deities are insufficient for our purposes, and that we need to look also at the deities' *epithets* and *locales* if we wish to know what deities the Erchians were worshiping. Zeus Teleios (Of Marriage), for example, receives an offering the same day as his wife Hera in her sanctuary in Erchia. Dionysus receives sacrifices, once alone and once on the same day and on the same altar as his mother Semele. Apollo Apotropaios, Apollo Nymphegetes (Leader of the Nymphs), and the Nymphs all receive offerings on the same day, the latter two on the same altar. The Erchians also made sacrifices which linked them with state and even panhellenic deities. On Skirophorion 3, in midsummer, they sacrificed on their own Acropolis to Athena Polias, Zeus Polieus, Poseidon, and Aglaurus, and on Metageitnion 12, in late summer, they sent a delegation to Athens to sacrifice one sheep each to Zeus Polieus and Athena Polias on the Acropolis there and to Demeter Eleusinia at her sanctuary in Athens. As we shall see in Chapters III, IV, and VI, Athena Polias, Zeus Polieus, Poseidon, Aglaurus, and Demeter Eleusinia were all major deities of Athenian state cult. The Erchians also had a local sanctuary and sacrifice for Apollo Pythios, the god worshiped also at the Pythion in state cult. That state cult in turn was linked to the panhellenic Apollo Pythios of Delphi.

Thirty-two of the fifty-nine sacrifices made by the Erchians are to Olympian gods. Many of the rest were made to heroes and heroines, some unknown to us from elsewhere. Heroines (otherwise nameless) twice, in two different locations, are given offerings. So, too, the Tritopatores, mysterious figures representing the ancestral dead, were honored by the Erchians. In summary, our Erchian, through his deme, participated

Sacrificial Calendar for Deme Erchia, Entries for Metageitnion (July/August)

Metageitnion 12
    to Apollo Lykeios, at Athens
        sheep, not to be removed, 12 drachmas ($1200)
    to Demeter, at Athens, in Eleusinion
        sheep, 10 drachmas ($1000)
    to Zeus Polieus, at Athens, on Acropolis
        sheep, not to be removed, 12 drachmas
    to Athena Polias, at Athens, on Acropolis
        sheep, 10 drachmas

Metageitnion 16
    to Artemis Hekate, in Erchia
        goat, 10 drachmas
    to Kourotrophos, in Erchia, in sanctuary of Hekate
        pig, 3 drachmas ($300)

Metageitnion 19
    to Heroinae, in Erchia, at Schoinos
        sheep, not to be removed, skin to priestess, 10 drachmas

Metageitnion 20
    to Hera Thelchinia, at Erchia, on Pagos
        all-black lamb, not to be removed, 7 drachmas ($700)

Metageitnion 25
    to Zeus Epopetes, at Erchia, on Pagos
        pig, completely burned, no wine, 3 drachmas

in sacrifices to a wide, but certainly not infinitely wide, circle of deities, some of whom had sanctuaries in his home, some in Erchia, some on the Acropolis in Athens, and some in nearby districts. Some of these sacrifices seem simply local offerings to statewide deities, some are contributions to the state cult on the Acropolis, and at least one, that to Apollo Pythios, is linked to a panhellenic deity. Others, like those to Epops, Menedeius, and the Heroines, look to be sacrifices to entirely local deities, performed in Attica only by the Erchians.

If we add to the three or four deities of family cult the thirty-four deities our Athenian worships with his fellow demesmen, if we add also Aegeus, the eponymous hero of the tribe Aegeis to which Erchia belonged, and if we add other statewide deities such as Theseus, Athena Nike, our Poseidon

Soter of Sunium, and perhaps a dozen others, we would begin to have an idea of how "polytheistic" our Athenian's religious world was. He would, of course, be aware of many other deities in Attica, and if he knew of him, he would no doubt respect, for example, Thoricus, the eponymous hero of the deme Thoricus, but he would not participate in his worship or expect help from him.

Finally, we must remember that each of these deities, god or hero, would have had a specific function to fulfill in our Athenian's life. The family gods quite clearly protected the home and its property. For many of the others we simply do not know what they promised, but Artemis in the Erchia calendar is linked in sacrifice with Kourotrophos (Nurse of the Young), and Zeus Teleios and Hera oversaw marriages. The statewide role of Athena Polias, Aglaurus, Poseidon, and Demeter Eleusinia we will treat in Chapters III, IV, and VI. The Erchia calendar describes the offerings to these deities throughout the year, and this is a reminder that every deity would receive an offering, or more elaborately a festival, one day each year. But in times of special need, if his marriage was troubled or if his young son was doing poorly, an Athenian of Erchia could go to his local sanctuaries to pray to Zeus Teleios and Hera or to Artemis and Kourotrophos. Another Athenian, in another deme, would likewise go to his own deme sanctuaries for the same purposes, but given the variety of cults and deities even within Attica, he might pray and make offerings to different deities, to, say, Aphrodite for his marriage problems or to a Physician Hero to help his son. The gods and heroes he worshiped would overlap considerably with those of our Erchian, but they would not be identical. The deities differ somewhat from one Athenian deme to another and far more so from one Greek city-state to another, but what seems a constant is the needs for which Greeks turned to their gods. We should assume that the pantheon worshiped by each individual was believed to fulfill those needs, however these gods and heroes might be named and worshiped in his city-state and locality, however their roles might be assigned, and whatever stories were told of them in their cult myths.

NOTES

1. In the early Athenian tradition Aegeus was Theseus' father, but in the nearby city-state of Troizen his father was Poseidon. The mythological tradition offered various attempts to reconcile the differences, and both fathers appear in various Athenian accounts and cults.
2. It may have been Phrontis, the helmsman of Menelaus who died rounding Cape Sunium on the return from the Trojan War and was buried and had a tomb there (Homer, *Odyssey* 3.278–85), but he has no obvious associations with Athena.

FURTHER READING

On gods and heroes in general:

Bremmer, *GR*, 11–26
Burkert, *GR*, 119–25, 173–225

On Homer, Hesiod, and Herodotus and the gods:

Burkert, *GR*, 119–225
Price, *RAG*, 6–7
Kirk, G.S., *The Iliad: A Commentary*, vol. 2 (Cambridge, 1990), 1–14

On ouranic and chthonic deities:

Burkert, *GR*, 199–215
Scullion, S., "Olympian and Chthonian," *Classical Antiquity* 13 (1994), 74–119

On heroes and heroines:

Burkert, *GR*, 203–15
Kearns, E., *The Heroes of Attica, Bulletin of the Institute of Classical Studies*, Supplement 57 (London, 1989) and "Between Gods and Man: Status and Function of Heroes and their Sanctuaries," 65–107 in A. Schachter, ed., *Le sanctuaire grec* (Entretiens Hardt 37, 1992, Geneva)
Nock, A.D., "The Cult of Heroes," *Harvard Theological Review* 37 (1944), 144–74 = *Essays on Religion and the Ancient World*, ed. Z. Stewart (Oxford, 1972), 575–602

On gods and heroes in combinations:

Burkert, *GR*, 173–4
Zaidman and Pantel, *RAGC*, 176–214
Kearns, above

On humans in a polytheistic world:

Daux, G., "La grande démarche: un nouveau calendrier sacrificiel d' Attique (Erchia)," *Bulletin de correspondance hellénique* 87 (1963), 603–34
Zaidman and Pantel, *RAGC*, 176–214

III

Seven Greek Cult Myths

⌐⌐⌐⌐

The "stories" we offer in this chapter are accounts which Athenians and other Greeks told of their very early relations with the gods. We may call them "myths" in the sense that they are, in the most simple terms, "traditional tales relevant to society," or, to give another definition, "on the one hand good stories, on the other hand bearers of important messages about life in general and life-within-society in particular."[1] We must not, however, assume, by calling them myths, that these tales were to their society "untrue." In common parlance "myth" has acquired the connotation of "untrue" or "unreal," as in the statement that "a unicorn is a mythical beast." To the Athenians and other Greeks, however, many such "myths" – as we call them – gave accounts of what they believed to be their national, cultural, and familial histories, and they believed them to be no less "true" than accounts of famous wars and more recent events. We call the myths given here "cultic" because they tell of the origins of the sacred places, of the divine and hero cults and rituals of individual cities, and of the gods' relationship to the humans of those cities. Only the last (Myth #7) tries to explain a panhellenic practice. These myths are cultic but not "sacred" in the sense that it would be impious to change an element of them or to propose a new interpretation. These myths were retold in epic, tragedy, lyric poetry, in sculpture, on pottery, and sometimes even in comedy. For the Greeks with their love for and expertise in story-telling there was no canonical form of a myth to which they had to adhere, and the many variants of the myths that later writers record reflect that. But, as we shall see, these myths were originally told by citizens of one city-state for their fellow citizens, and they concerned their most important national religious concerns and monuments. As long as these myths were being retold, in whatever medium, for a local audience in a local context that involved these national concerns and monuments, they tended to adhere more to the original form.

The myths I have chosen as a representative sample concern primarily
Athens and her gods, heroes, and cults, and because they were originally
for a strictly Athenian audience and addressed primarily Athenian concerns, most never received a panhellenic form in the panhellenic epics
and other poetry. Some became topics of Athenian tragedies, but these
tragedies have been lost. These stories are known to us today largely from
brief retellings in ancient Greek and Roman myth collections or in passing references by ancient scholars, and their versions are largely based
on those lost Athenian tragedies. My "version" of each myth, except for
the last which we owe to Hesiod, is a compilation of details we know from
such sources. Several are told in the ancient sources in variant forms,
and I have chosen for each the one version that seems most likely to have
been current in the fifth century B.C.E.

1. *Athena, Poseidon, and Athens*

In the time of the early Athenian king Cecrops, the gods decided to take
possession of the cities in which each of them would be the patron deity.
Poseidon and Athena, each in a chariot, raced towards Athens, and the one
first to arrive was to claim the land. It was a very close race, but Athena – as
judged by King Cecrops – won, and as "evidence" of her victory planted an
olive tree. Poseidon arrived moments later, struck the Acropolis with his
trident, and thereby created a "salt sea." But Athena had won the race, and
from then on Athens was Athena's city.

As an Athenian in the late fifth century entered the Acropolis through
its monumental gateway, he would see facing him, slightly to his left, a
nine-meter tall bronze statue of Athena, standing, fully armed, holding
a spear. She was Athena Promachos ("Forefighter"), a dedication made
from the spoils of the victories over the Persians in 480–479 B.C.E. As our
Athenian looked slightly to the right, he would see the west front of the
Parthenon, and there, as a sculptural tableau in its pediment, the scene
described in this myth: Athena and Poseidon in the center, with Athena's
olive tree already established between them, with Poseidon just now
striking the rock with his trident, and with both gods flanked by their
chariots. Far to the left, watching, was Cecrops, the judge of the race. The
Athenian would have before him a most impressive and beautiful visual
presentation of the story he had learned from childhood of how Athena
became the eponymous patron of his city. The myth would explain to him,
too, the presence of the olive tree just west of the Erechtheum and why
Athena, as Athena Moria (Of the Sacred Olives), protected the olive trees

Figure III.1 A water color drawing of the Athenian Acropolis and environs by Peter Connolly. A = the Parthenon, B = the Erechtheum, C = the Propylaea (gateway), D = the Pinakotheke (art gallery), E = the Temple of Athena Nike, F = Ramp to Propylaea, and G = the House of the Arrephoroi. Facing the Propylaea is the statue of Athena Promachos. The stoa and other buildings to the right of the Propylaea are in the city sanctuary of Artemis Brauronia. Photograph: AKG London.

of Athens. So, too, would he recognize the significance of the "salt sea" and those three marks on the Acropolis rock, pointed out for centuries to visitors to the Erechtheum as the place where Poseidon cast his trident. The myth was represented on the west pediment of the Parthenon, but the action, those many centuries ago, had played out in the area that was to become Athena's first temple, later to be called the Erechtheum. And, finally, this myth would help to explain why, in Athens, Athena and Poseidon were so often paired as, for example, Poseidon Hippios and Athena Hippia, and Poseidon Soter and Athena at Sunium. Athena was the victor in the race and Athens was hers, but the Athenians needed and found a place for Poseidon too.

Figure III.2   On this Athenian red-figure cup by the Codrus Painter, of
about 440 B.C.E., is represented the birth of Erichthonius (Erechtheus).
In the center Athena receives the earth-born baby Erichthonius from the
arms of Gaia (Earth). Cecrops, half-man, half-snake, observes from the left,
and Hephaestus and Cecrops' daughter Herse watch from the right.
Courtesy of the Antikensammlung, Staatliche Museen zu Berlin, Preussischer
Kulturbesitz, inv. no. F 2537.

2. Erechtheus, Athena, and Athenian Autochthony

A time later Erechtheus was born from the soil of Athens itself, the son of
Hephaestus and the foster son of Athena. Athena had approached Hephaestus
about providing her some weapons. Hephaestus fell into a passion for
Athena and began to pursue her. She fled, but he eventually caught her
and tried to have intercourse with her. She resisted, his semen fell on her
leg, and she wiped it off and threw it to the ground. From it was conceived
Erechtheus. Thus Erechtheus was born from the earth itself. The virgin
Athena adopted Erechtheus as her foster son, installed him in her temple
on the Acropolis, and he eventually became king of Athens. Erechtheus for
his part erected the wooden statue of Athena in her temple and founded
the Panathenaea, Athena's major festival in Athens.[2]

The Athenians were exceptionally proud of the fact that, unlike most
Greeks, they had never migrated to their land from another region of
Greece. They thought themselves *autochthonous*, that is, "born from the
earth itself" in Athens. They thought they had a special relationship to

their land which was, literally, their mother. They were not "newcomers" to Greece, but a people long settled and cultured. In addition, all born Athenians were, in a sense, equal, all tracing their origins to one "earth-born parent," and this, they thought, inclined them to democracy rather than to oligarchy and tyranny. The myth of the birth of Erechtheus from the semen of Hephaestus explained both how this *autochthony* came about and also the very special relationship Athenians had with Athena. Since she was a virgin goddess, they could not be her direct descendants but were the next best thing possible, the descendants, the Erechtheidae, of her favored foster son. And it was Erechtheus as a dutiful foster son who erected the antique olive wood statue, Athena's most sacred statue, that stood in the Erechtheum in the fifth century and for centuries thereafter. He also founded the Panathenaea, the great Panathenian celebration of Athena's birthday which we will describe in Chapter IV. Finally, Hephaestus' role in the myth may explain his pairing, in another temple, with Athena as Athena Hephaistia. Hephaestus, like Poseidon, was necessary to Athenians, and he was given a role in their religious history.

3. Erechtheus, Poseidon, and Athena

Erechtheus later led the Athenians in a war against the neighboring Eleusinians whose champion was the Thracian Eumolpus, a son of Poseidon. Erechtheus received an oracle from Delphi that the Athenians would win the war if he sacrificed one of his daughters. The daughters swore an oath among themselves that, if one were sacrificed, the others would commit suicide. At his wife's patriotic urging, Erechtheus did sacrifice one daughter, and the others killed themselves. Soon afterwards Erechtheus killed Eumolpus, and Poseidon, in his anger, killed Erechtheus with his trident. Athena, in settling this affair, established a heroine cult for the daughters, made Erechtheus' wife her own priestess, and created a cult for Erechtheus and Poseidon in her own temple. Like Hyacinthus and Apollo at Sparta, Erechtheus and Poseidon shared an altar and a priest, and Poseidon was even called "Poseidon Erechtheus." From that time on the Athenians, descendants of Erechtheus and now known also as the Erechtheidae, worshiped Erechtheus every year in the temple of Athena with the sacrifice of bulls and rams.

When the Athenians entered the Theater of Dionysus for their annual drama festival in 423 B.C.E., the building we know as the Erechtheum on the Acropolis was under construction, replacing an earlier Temple of Athena Polias. The Athenians were to see at this festival a new tragedy by Euripides, entitled *Erechtheus*. In this play Euripides offered his version of the myth given above, a myth known to all Athenians as part of their national history. The tragedy survives only in fragments, but fortunately one long fragment has Athena, as *deus ex machina*, settling the Eleusinian–Athenian war and making arrangements for the future cults of Erechtheus' daughters, Erechtheus himself, Poseidon, and herself. The myth, and Euripides' version of it, explained to Athenians why they worshiped the daughters of Erechtheus as heroines with annual sacrifices and dances, Erechtheus and Eumolpus as heroes, and Poseidon; why Erechtheus and Poseidon shared the new Erechtheum with Athena; and why, in this temple at Athens, Poseidon and Erechtheus were united, sharing one altar and one priest, sometimes even merging into one figure, Poseidon Erechtheus. Like the other "myths" we have considered thus far, this story, retold by Euripides and other tragedians in the theater and represented also on vases and probably in other media, set forth for Athenians the "historical" background behind their national cults on the Acropolis. These cults were unique to Athens in some of the deities worshiped, in the relations between these deities, and in some of their rituals.

4. *Dionysus, Icarius, and Erigone*

Dionysus, like Athena and Poseidon, also "arrived" in Athens, but the stories of his arrivals in most cities make him a relative late-comer. For Herodotus (2.145), Dionysus was the last of the Olympian gods to be established in the Greek world, but in fact he was as old as any of the Olympians because his name has been discovered with many of theirs on the Linear B tablets from the Mycenaean Age. It was probably the novelty and disruptive character of the god and his gifts that made him seem "new" to the Greeks, however long he had been with them. The "myth" of Dionysus' arrival in Thebes is the subject of Euripides' *Bacchae* which we will treat at some length in Chapter IV, but the novel character of Dionysus' gifts to men, the initial rejection of him in Thebes, and the resulting suffering are also reflected in this account of his arrival in Athens:

> When Pandion became king, Dionysus came to Attica and was received as a guest by Icarius. Dionysus gave Icarius a branch of a grape vine and taught him wine-making. Icarius produced a batch of wine and, following the god's instructions, wished to share the gift with his fellow citizens. He offered the wine to some shepherds, and, once they tasted it, they found it delightful and began to drink copiously, without mixing it with water.[3] But, as they began to feel its effects, they thought that Icarius had poisoned them, and they killed him. In the morning, when they awoke, they said they had never slept better. They realized their error, gave Icarius a proper burial, and then fled. Erigone, Icarius' daughter, had been searching for her father,

Figure III.3 An Athenian red-figure drinking cup of about 440 B.C.E., probably representing the Aiora ("swinging" ritual) in honor of Erigone, the daughter of Icarius. The satyr symbolizes the Dionysiac context of the ritual and of the larger festival, the Anthesteria, of which the Aiora was a part. Attributed to the Penelope Painter. Courtesy of the Antikensammlung, Staatliche Museen zu Berlin, Preussischer Kulturbesitz, inv. no. F 2589.

and she was led to his burial place by Icarius' faithful dog Maera. Erigone performed a funeral lament over her dead father, called down curses on the Athenians, and then hanged herself from a tree next to Icarius' grave. Soon thereafter Athenian girls began to hang themselves, and finally an oracle bid the Athenians to honor Icarius, Erigone, and the dog every year and to appease Erigone with an annual "swinging" festival.

In 1888 a sanctuary of Dionysus with an altar, a monumental marble statue of Dionysus, and a theater was discovered and excavated about 20 kilometers northwest of Athens in a district now called Dionysou but in antiquity the deme of Icarion. It is in a beautiful wooded dell at the northern foot of the slopes of Mount Pentelicon. The myth, told by a Hellenistic poet and a late mythographer, is obviously the foundation myth of this sanctuary and cult of Dionysus, and it combines, as we have seen before, cults of heroes with that of a god. With the killing and burial of Icarius we have the origins of his cult as the eponymous hero of the deme Icarion. Erigone herself became a heroine, and the myth explains the origins of a "swinging" ritual (the Aiora) which the Athenians celebrated in her honor as part of a larger Dionysiac festival each year. Sacrifices were also made to Icarius, Erigone, and Maera the dog. As with the other "arrival" myths of Dionysus, the drunkenness and the murder in this myth reflect the novelty, potency, and danger of Dionysus' gift to mankind. That there was a theater in Dionysus' sanctuary at Icarion and that Athens' first tragedian Thespis was an Icarian might even suggest that in this sanctuary began, in a seminal form, the Dionysiac dramatic presentations that later flourished in the city at the great Dionysiac festivals.

5. *Artemis Brauronia and the Bears*

In the myths we have seen up to now the gods such as Athena, Poseidon, and Dionysus have encountered struggles in getting established, but they eventually found their place in the Athenian pantheon. This myth concerning the cult of Artemis in the Attic village Brauron explains not Artemis' arrival but rather an unusual feature of her ritual:

> A she-bear once was given to the sanctuary of Artemis and was tamed. Once a maiden was playing with the bear, and the bear scratched out her eyes. The girl's brother(s), in grief for her, killed the bear. And then a famine befell the Athenians. The Athenians inquired at the Oracle of Delphi as to its cause, and Apollo revealed that Artemis was angry at them for the killing of the bear, and as punishment and to appease her every Athenian girl, before marriage, must "play the bear" for Artemis. And so the Athenians voted that an Athenian girl was not to live with a man until she "played the bear" for Artemis in Brauron.

About 32 kilometers southwest of Athens one may still today see the sanctuary of Artemis Brauronia with a Doric temple of Artemis and a large stoa with dining facilities. Once every four years Athenian girls between the ages of, probably, ten and fourteen went to this sanctuary to participate in the festival of Artemis Brauronia. They lived in the sanctuary during the festival, performed sacrifices to Artemis, and, as part of the ritual of the festival, wore saffron-colored dresses and "played the bear," a ritual called the *Arkteia* (*arktos* = "bear" in Greek). This myth is *etiological* in that it gives the "cause" or "reason" (*aition* in Greek) of something, here a distinctive ritual. It explains why Athenian girls of a certain age had to "play the bear" at Artemis' festival, but it also reflects other features of Artemis' cult at Brauron: her association with the animal world – Artemis the huntress is also protectress of wild animals; her attention to young women, especially before the age of puberty; and, lastly, as several other Artemis myths, her rather irascible nature and the need often to "appease" her rather than simply to

Figure III.4   The marble Stoa at Brauron, built in the 420s B.C.E. The Stoa was fitted out with a large courtyard and couches for dining, and here the girls "playing the bear" for Artemis Brauronia may have dined and performed parts of the ritual. Votive reliefs and statues were displayed in the building. Photograph by the author.

"please" her. These aspects of Artemis Brauronia we will discuss further in our account in Chapter V of the religious activities of young women in Athens.

6. *Zeus Polieus, the Bouphonia, and the Ox*

In the kingship of Erechtheus, when Athenians were sacrificing to their gods not animals but vegetable products, a sacrifice was being made to Zeus Polieus (Of the City) on the Acropolis. An ox wandered up to Zeus' altar and ate the cake that had been prepared for the sacrifice. A man named Thaulon in anger then killed the ox with an ax. Thaulon was the first man to kill an ox, and after killing the ox he fled the city, leaving the ax behind. An oracle then came to the Athenians that they should eat the ox in a feast and repeat the "sacrifice" every year.

Every year in Athens, on a day in midsummer, the Athenians performed an unusual ritual called the Bouphonia, the "murder of the ox." Even in the fifth century Athenians thought this an archaic and hoary rite, but they apparently continued to practice it for centuries, well into the second century

C.E. at least. Because it was so odd, the ancient sources recorded many of its details. A group of oxen was led up to the Acropolis, and in the procession were young girls carrying water to sharpen an ax and sacrificial knife. The oxen circled Zeus' altar, and first one to taste the cake on the altar was selected as the victim. He was struck with an ax and killed by the "ox-slayer," a member of the Thaulonidae family. The ox-slayer then threw down the ax and ran away. The other participants in the ritual then butchered and skinned the animal with a sacrificial knife and feasted on the meat. This could not be the end of the ritual, however, because a "crime" had been committed – the ox had been "murdered." A formal trial was held in a special court in Athens, and since the "ox-slayer" himself had fled, the girls who brought the water for sharpening the knife and ax were charged with the "murder." In their defense they claimed that those who actually sharpened the ax and knife were more responsible. The sharpeners in turn charged the man who gave them the ax and knife, and he charged the butcher. But the butcher claimed the knife was the more guilty, and, since the knife could say nothing in its defense, it was found guilty of the murder. The knife was then banished by being thrown into the sea. To conclude this bizarre ritual, back on the Acropolis the skin of the ox was stuffed, stood up, and harnessed to a plow, restoring it, as it were, to its pre-sacrificial condition.

In this case our knowledge of the ritual is much fuller than that of the myth. The myth itself puts the origins of the ritual in the earliest days of Athens' history and gives it an oracular sanction, and the first "ox-slayer" Thaulon is, of course, the eponymous hero of the Thaulonidae family who inherited this ritual role from him. The myth also suggests a time of transition from a vegetarian to a meat-eating way of life. Our best source for the myth is a product of non-Athenian philosophers who imagined an early, golden age when men were vegetarians. They criticized humans' use of meat for food and sacrifice, and this may have inclined them to tell the story in just this way. Most obviously lacking from the myth is the trial resulting in the conviction of the knife, a "comedy of innocence" as it has often been called, and the "reconstruction" of the dead ox. Modern scholars have offered many interpretations of the meaning of this complex ritual, and some of these are summarized in the works listed below in "Further Reading." One such interpretation, most fully elaborated by Walter Burkert, sees in the ritual the anxiety and guilt that arises from any killing and especially when humans in order to sacrifice to their gods and to eat must kill a domestic animal familiar to them and necessary to their livelihoods. The passing of the responsibility in the trial from one person to another and eventually to the knife in a paradoxical way both implicates in and absolves from guilt the whole community. And, of course, the "restoration" of the ox and its plow expresses this same regret, almost a wish that the sacrifice had never happened. There is much more to Burkert's and others' interpretations of this unusual ritual, and I have offered only enough here to indicate that rituals, just as myths, can be "read" for what they reveal about religious beliefs. It is, in fact, such psychological readings of rituals that have attracted the interest of many scholars of Greek religion in recent decades.

7. *Zeus, Prometheus, and the Gods' Portion*

It has always seemed odd that in the sacrifice of a bull or ox to a god or a cow to a goddess the Greeks burned on the altar for the deity some of the worst portions of the animal. Why should the gift to the gods be the thigh bones wrapped in fat and not steaks and meaty ribs? It was an oddity of the cult practice of all Greeks that cried out for explanation, and Hesiod in his *Theogony*, 533–57, offered his explanation, at this early time, of course, in the form of a myth. Hesiod tells how Prometheus, the great champion of mankind, had once offended Zeus. For this offense he had been chained to a mountain and had his liver picked at by Zeus' eagle.

> For Prometheus once had matched wits against the great son of Kronos.
> It was when gods, and mortal men, took their separate positions
> at Mekone,[4] and Prometheus, eager to try his wits, cut up
> a great ox, and set it before Zeus to see if he could outguess him.
> He took the meaty parts and the innards thick with fat, and set them
> before men, hiding them away in an ox's stomach,
> but the white bones of the ox he arranged, with careful deception,
> inside a concealing fold of white fat, and set it before Zeus.
> At last the father of gods and men spoke to him, saying:
> "Son of Iapetos,[5] conspicuous among all Kings,
> old friend, oh how prejudicially you divided the portions."
> So Zeus, who knows imperishable counsels, spoke in displeasure,
> but Prometheus the devious-deviser, lightly smiling,
> answered him again, quite well aware of his artful deception:
> "Zeus most high, most honored among the gods everlasting,
> choose whichever of these the heart within would have you."
> He spoke, with intent to deceive, and Zeus, who knows imperishable
> counsels, saw it, the trick did not escape him, he imagined
> evils for mortal men in his mind, and meant to fulfill them.
> In both his hands he took up the portion of the white fat. Anger
> rose up about his heart and the spite mounted in his spirit
> when he saw the white bones of the ox in deceptive arrangement.
> Ever since that time the races of mortal men on earth have burned
> the white bones to the immortals on the smoky altars.

(Lattimore translation)

In the most simplistic terms, Hesiod's myth has Zeus himself, the greatest of the gods, make the choice of the inferior portion and thereby sanction that offering to the gods by humans for all time. Why Zeus knowingly made this choice, so that he would have reason to punish Prometheus and all mankind, is, of course, quite a different matter, and it reflects Hesiod's perhaps idiosyncratically negative view of the status of human beings and of Zeus' hostility to them. Hesiod's version of this myth may serve as a concluding example of how what is apparently a local myth, perhaps from the city of Sicyon and a cult of Prometheus there, could be taken up and shaped by a skilled poet to fit his narrative and his world view and could become part of the panhellenic tradition. But, at its core, it also serves as an explanation of a common Greek cult practice.

We have already seen how local Athenian myths explained much of the cult of Athenian Athena on the Acropolis: how she came to Athens, why she, and not Poseidon or some other god, became the patron of Athens, and why the olive tree was so important in her cult; how it was the Athenians were autochthonous, "earth-born," the descendants of Erechtheus, and the foster family of Athena; why Poseidon and Erechtheus were both involved in her cult in the Erechtheum; and who it was who created her first statue, who was her first priestess, and who founded her greatest festival, the Panathenaea. In the next chapter we begin with a fuller description of this cult of Athena on the Acropolis reflected in these local myths, and as we move on to the cults of Demeter at Eleusis, Dionysus at Thebes, Apollo at Delphi, and Zeus at Olympia we will have fuller, more coherent local myths telling us of the origins of the cult and rituals of each of them.

NOTES

1. G.S. Kirk, *The Nature of Myths* (Harmondsworth, 1974), 28–9.
2. Often, even in the Athenian mythological tradition, Erechtheus is distinguished from a like-named figure, Erichthonius, and it is claimed that it was Erichthonius who was Athena's "earth-born" foster son and who established the statue in her temple and the Panathenaea. But I have followed the earlier tradition, as old as our text of the *Iliad* (2.546–51), that Erechtheus was this child. For the variants and for additional important elements of Erechtheus' myth, see the sources given in Further Reading.
3. The Greeks usually mixed their wine, with four parts of water to one part wine.
4. Mekone was apparently an earlier name for Sicyon, a city-state on the northern coast of the Peloponnesus.
5. Iapetos was Prometheus' father.

FURTHER READING

On Greek mythology in general:

Burkert, W., *Structure and History in Greek Mythology and Ritual* (Berkeley, 1979)
Graf, F., *Greek Mythology: An Introduction* (Baltimore, 1993)
Gordon, R.L., ed., *Myth, Religion and Society* (Cambridge, 1981)
Kirk, G.S., *The Nature of Greek Myths* (Harmondsworth, 1974)

On Athens, Athena, Poseidon, and Erechtheus:

Binder, J., "The West Pediment of the Parthenon: Poseidon," 15–22 in *Studies Presented to Sterling Dow*, ed. K.J. Rigsby, *Greek, Roman, and Byzantine Monographs* 10 (Durham, 1984)
Kearns, *Heroes of Attica*, esp. 110–15
Parker, R., "Myths of Early Athens," pp. 187–214 in *Interpretations of Greek Mythology* (London and Sydney, 1987), ed. J. Bremmer
Rosivach, V.J., "Autochthony and the Athenians," *Classical Quarterly* 37 (1987), 294–306
Tyrrell, W.B. and F.S. Brown, *Athenian Myths and Institutions* (Oxford, 1991), 138–43, 180–1

On Dionysus, Icarius, and Erigone:

Camp, J.M., *The Archaeology of Athens* (New Haven, 2001), 289–91
Gantz, T., *Early Greek Myth* (Baltimore, 1993), vol. 1, 112–19
Kearns, *Heroes of Attica*, 167, 172

On Artemis Brauronia and the Bears:

Kearns, *Heroes of Attica*, 27–33
Osborne, R., *Demos: The Discovery of Classical Attica* (Cambridge, UK, 1985), 154–72
Sale, W., "The Temple-Legends of the Arkteia," *Rheinische Museum* 118 (1975), 265–84

On Zeus Polieus, the Bouphonia, and the Ox:

Burkert, W., *Homo Necans* (Berkeley, 1983), especially 136–43

On Zeus, Prometheus, and the Gods' Portion:

Vernant, J.-P., "At Man's Table: Hesiod's Foundation Myth of Sacrifice," pp. 21–86 in *The Cuisine of Sacrifice among the Greeks*, ed. M. Detienne and J.-P. Vernant (Chicago, 1989)

IV

Five Major Greek Cults

⌐⌐⌐⌐

In this chapter we describe major features of the cults of five gods: Athena Polias and Demeter Eleusinia of Athens, Dionysus of Thebes, Apollo Pythios of Delphi, and Zeus Olympios of Olympia. Many other deities could, of course, have been selected, but each of these five is quite different, and together they suggest some of the variety of cult, ritual, and function that gods had in Greek religion. They also are among those deities for whom we have the most and best evidence. There are cult myths for each, and for all but the Dionysus of Thebes we have, in addition to literary evidence, sanctuaries which have been excavated and have yielded an abundance of archaeological evidence.

Athena Polias of Athens

The Acropolis of Athens was enclosed by a large fortification wall with one major gateway on the west side. It was thus a *temenos*, and it was viewed, as a whole, as the sanctuary of Athena. If one had any doubt of this, he needed only look before him as he passed through the gateway. There stood squarely facing him, about forty meters away, a nine-meter tall bronze statue of a fully armed Athena.

For our visitor Athena's Great Altar, which was the religious center of her cult, lay at the far, east end of Acropolis. It was perhaps 15 meters in width and 8.5 meters in depth, and it was there that prayers would be made and offerings would be burned in the goddess' honor at her festival of the Panathenaea and on other occasions. In the early fifth century this altar stood directly east of the Temple of Athena, but this "old" temple of Athena was at least partially destroyed by the Persians in 480 B.C.E. In the fifth-century rebuilding of the Acropolis, the old temple was replaced

Figure IV.1 A "new-style" four-drachma ($400) Athenian silver coin from the late second century B.C.E. The head of Athena is probably modeled on that of Phidias' statue of Athena Parthenos in the Parthenon. With permission of the Royal Ontario Museum, ©ROM.

Figure IV.2 View through the Propylaea (gateway) of the Athenian Acropolis, with the Parthenon on the right, the Erechtheum on the left, the Athena Promachos statue by Phidias in the center left, and smoke rising from the Altar of Athenian Polias in the far distance. Courtesy of the American School of Classical Studies at Athens: Agora Excavations.

by a new temple, the building which we for convenience will call the Erechtheum. The Erechtheum was built just to the north of the old temple, and so, uncharacteristically, did not align perfectly with the Great Altar. The plan of the Erechtheum was unusual. The east end, facing the Altar, is usual, but what should be the west end has been swung around as a porch at a lower level facing north, and another porch, supported by columns in the form of women (Caryatids, hence the Caryatid Porch), was added to the south side. These peculiarities of design can be explained only by requirements of cult, and, though we do not know the specific arrangements, the building encompassed some sacred marks and tokens and artifacts of three deities: Athena Polias, Poseidon, and the hero Erechtheus.[1] In the east section of the building, facing the Altar, was the very old olive-wood statue of Athena Polias herself. Adjoining the west end of the Erechtheum was a special precinct of Pandrosus, a daughter of Cecrops, and in this precinct grew the olive tree sacred to Athena, the symbol of her possession of and devotion to Athens.

The Great Altar, the Erechtheum, and the precinct with the sacred olive tree on the north side of the Acropolis made up the core of the cult of Athena Polias, the center of Athenian state cult in general. Much that concerned the mythology and cult of this complex, however, was represented in the

Figure IV.3　View of Erechtheum from the south, with east façade of the cella and, to the west, the projecting Caryatid Porch. Built in the years 421–406 B.C.E. Photograph by the author.

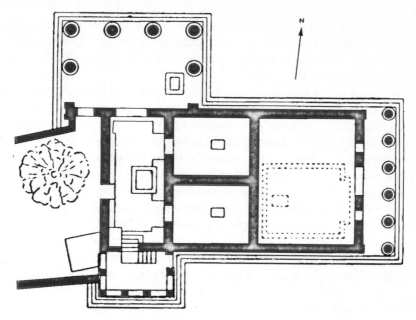

Figure IV.4 Plan of Erechtheum, with cella of Athena Polias to the east, Caryatid porch to the south, and the North Porch. To the west are the sanctuary of Pandrosus and the sacred olive tree of Athena.

sculpture of the Parthenon on the south side of the Acropolis: on the east pediment the birth of Athena; on the west pediment the competition of Poseidon and Athena for patronage of Athens; and, on the frieze, the procession of the Panathenaea and the presentation of the sacred robe, the *peplos*, that was to be worn by the Athena Polias of the Erechtheum. This raises the question of the function of the Parthenon in this sanctuary complex. It, too, had a statue of Athena, the ten-meter tall gold and ivory Athena Parthenos (Virgin) sculpted by Phidias. The Parthenon also housed precious gold and silver dedications to Athena, and its west room served as the treasury of Athens. But, unlike the Erechtheum, it had no altar to its east nor did it shelter, like the Erechtheum, ancient marks or tokens of special religious reverence. Scholars have established, in fact, that Athena Parthenos was not a deity distinct from Athena Polias – she did not have, for example, her own priestess or altar – but that Parthenos was an added, descriptive (not functional) epithet for Athena Polias. That makes it most probable that the Parthenon was, as it were, a treasury building of the Athena Polias cult – one exceptionally large and beautiful, and possessing an exceptionally beautiful dedication in Phidias' statue, but still, in terms of sanctuary design, more a building for storage than for worship. The cult that the Parthenon "supported," both physically and by its sculpture, was that of Athena Polias with her Great Altar, Erechtheum, and sacred olive tree.

The statue of Athena Polias in the Erechtheum was probably life-sized and seated, of olive wood, and very ancient, so ancient and crudely shaped that some thought it had fallen from the sky, others that Cecrops or Erechtheus had had it made. She wore the saffron-colored *peplos*, a dress woven and decorated with scenes of the battle between the gods and the Giants. A new *peplos* was presented to her each year at the Panathenaea, and the presentation of the *peplos* is the central scene amidst the gathering of gods and ten heroes, perhaps Athens' ten eponymous heroes, on the east frieze of the Parthenon.[2] Athena Polias wore, in addition, a crown, earrings, a neckband, a gold owl, and an *aegis* with the image of the Gorgon. She held in one hand a type of bowl commonly used in offerings to the gods. The goddess might thus seem to be in domestic garb, but the *aegis*, a goatskin fringed with snakes and worn over her *peplos* and with the Gorgon's head in the center, served as an almost magical breastplate. It was with the *aegis* that Athena armed herself for battle in the *Iliad* (5.733–47), and the similarity between the dress of Polias and the Athena of the *Iliad* is so great that one might be inclined to assume that the Athenians used Homer's description to design the "clothing" for their most sacred statue.

Now in turn Athene, daughter of Zeus of the aegis,
beside the threshold of her father slipped off her elaborate
dress which she herself had wrought with her hands' patience,
and now assuming the war tunic of Zeus who gathers
the clouds, she armed in her gear for the dismal fighting.
And across her shoulders she threw the betasselled, terrible
aegis, all about which Terror hangs like a garland,
and Hatred is there, and Battle Strength, and heart-freezing Onslaught
and thereon is set the head of the grim gigantic Gorgon,
a thing of fear and horror, portent of Zeus of the aegis.
Upon her head she set the golden helm with its four sheets
and two horns, wrought with the fighting men of a hundred cities.
She set her feet in the blazing chariot and took up a spear
heavy, huge, thick, wherewith she beats down the battalions of fighting
men, against whom she of the mighty father is angered.

Homer, *Iliad* 5.733–47 (Lattimore translation)

Figure IV.5   The *peplos* and how it was worn by Greek women. Drawing courtesy of Susan Bird.

Figure IV.6   This central scene of the east side of the Parthenon frieze apparently represents the presentation of Athena's new *peplos* (folded, on right), a distinctive and core element of the Panathenaia, Athena's major festival in Athens. The female figure (center right) may be the priestess of Athena, and the male figure to her right a state official, but the identity of all figures and of the objects represented are much disputed. Courtesy of the Trustees of the British Museum.

Athena Promachos was the armed goddess facing the entrance of the Acropolis, known to the Athenians as the "bronze Athena." She was a dedication from the victory over the Persians and was erected in the 450s. The ivory and gold Athena Parthenos was completed in 438 B.C.E. Both were much more overtly militaristic than Polias herself. Both goddesses, monumental in size, were represented by Phidias as fully armed, with helmets, breastplates, spears, and with shields resting on the ground at their sides. Both are the warrior goddess "at ease, but vigilant." The upright spear and helmet of Promachos could be seen from out at sea by those sailing into Piraeus harbor. The Parthenos held in her right hand a life-sized statue of a winged Nike (Victory). Inside her shield was coiled a large snake. In the Erechtheum the Athenians tended a real snake, perhaps embodying or symbolizing the hero Erechtheus, and, when the Persian attack on Athens was imminent in 480, the Athenians discovered that the food they left out each month for the snake had gone uneaten. They concluded that the goddess had evacuated the Acropolis and that they should take their statue of Athena Polias and do the same.

We may view both Athena Promachos and Athena Parthenos as monumental dedications to Athena Polias, and therefore in attempting to understand the cult of Athena on the Acropolis, we should focus our attention on Athena Polias. She, a goddess, was appropriately served by a priestess. Her first priestess may have been Cecrops' daughter Aglaurus, and we saw in Myth #3 of Chapter III that Euripides had Athena herself name Erechtheus' wife to be her priestess. In the historical period the priestess of Athena Polias was chosen from the family of the Eteobutadae, and the same family provided the priest for the cult of Poseidon-Erechtheus who was also, for reasons we saw in Myth #3 of Chapter III, worshiped in the Erechtheum. One old, aristocratic family thus provided the priest and priestess of this core state cult, and they would do so for centuries to come. The priest's and priestess' main duties were to make the prayers and offerings to their respective deities, and the priestess no doubt presented the *peplos* to Athena as one of the culminating acts of the Panathenaea. Athena Polias was also served each year by four girls aged 7–10, who, under adult supervision, wove and embroidered Athena's *peplos*. Athena's cult was also very wealthy, with hundreds of dedications, many of gold and silver, and with many precious statues. The gold of the Parthenos statue alone weighed about 1,000 kilos (Thucydides 2.13). During the prosperous times of the Athenian empire Athena received 1/60 of the tribute being paid by subject states, and Athena's share of this tribute could amount to as much as ten talents ($6,000,000) in some years. To record, inventory, and account for these considerable assets the Athenians elected, each year, a civilian board of four treasurers.

A civilian board of ten (the *athlothetai*) was also selected to oversee important aspects of Athena's festival, the Panathenaea. They superintended the making of the *peplos*, the procession, the athletic, equestrian, and musical contests, and the making and awarding of the prizes for the victors. The

Figure IV.7 The Royal Ontario Museum model of Athena Parthenos in the *cella* of the Parthenon. Phidias' original of Athena had garments and armor made of gold, and her exposed skin was of ivory. The statue of the winged Nike she holds in her right hand was approximately 1.85 m. high, and the goddess herself may have stood about 10 m. high. She wears her *aegis* with the snakes and the gorgon head in the center. Beneath her left hand is her shield, on the inside of which curls a large gold snake associated with the cult of Erechtheus. On the base is represented the birth of Pandora, the first human woman. For scale, note the human figures in the lower right. With permission of the Royal Ontario Museum, ©ROM.

Panathenaea celebrated Athena's birthday (represented on the east pediment of the Parthenon) on Hekatombaion 28, in midsummer, but events spilled over to days before and after Hekatombaion 28 and probably encompassed a full week. Once every four years there was an especially elaborate celebration, with an extended program of competitions for international competitors. The core events of the festival were, however, the sacrifices to Athena at the Great Altar and the presentation of the *peplos* to Athena in her temple, and these were performed every year, on her birthday. This day was preceded by a *pannychis*, an all-night celebration held on the Acropolis which featured a torch race and choruses of young men and women.[3] At dawn the following morning, on Hecatombaion 28, the Athenians, emancipated slaves, and even foreign residents would gather, dressed in holiday finery, some holding boughs of olive, at the city's main gate. They would go in a large procession from there one kilometer along the Panathenaic Way, through the Agora, and up to the Acropolis to Athena's Great Altar. The priestess of Athena and the priest of Poseidon-Erechtheus would no doubt lead the way. They would be followed by others who served Athena's cult, and then by a host of religious and government officials. Prominent in the procession would be one hundred Athenian girls carrying baskets. This festival was the only one in Athens intended to include not just citizens but all the residents of Attica. It was to be truly "Panathenian." Emancipated slaves were included, carrying oak boughs. Resident foreigners participated, wearing purple robes and holding silver trays of cakes and honeycombs, and their daughters carried water pitchers. In the procession were led the sacrificial animals. We know that in 410/9 B.C.E., in financially difficult times for Athens, 100 animals were sacrificed at the Greater Panathenaea, at a cost of 5114 drachmas ($511,400) (*IG* I[3] 375, line 7). In better times the Athenians may have sacrificed as many as 300 animals for this festival. We have a unique opportunity to visualize this procession in the frieze on the south and north sides of the Parthenon. There we see priests walking, other men walking and on horseback, parade marshals, young women carrying bowls, competitors in the chariot contests, and a number of sacrificial victims being led along.

The destination of the Panathenaic procession was the Great Altar of Athena, and there, before noon, the assembled worshipers would watch the priestess of Athena officiate over the sacrifices. The horns of the cattle had been gilded, and, after some preliminary offerings, each was struck a heavy blow on the head. It was then apparently lifted up by attendants, its throat was cut, and the blood was caught in bowls. The animals were then butchered, and the thigh pieces were placed on the Great Altar as an offering to Athena. This moment of offering to the god was accompanied by flute music, by hymns sung by choruses, and by the prayers of the

Figure IV.8 The Panathenaic procession on the Acropolis, through the Propylaea, past Athena Promachos, the Erechtheum, and the Parthenon to the Great Altar of Athena in the background. Watercolor by Peter Connolly. Photograph: AKG London.

priestess. If the sacrifice followed Homeric procedures, bits of the victims' vital organs such as the heart, liver, and kidneys were placed on spits, roasted over the altar fire, and then served to the religious and governmental officials. In addition to the sacrifice to Athena Polias, individual cattle were sacrificed to Athena Nike on her altar and to Athena Hygieia (Of Health) who also had a sanctuary and altar on the Acropolis. For a good part of the rest of the day, the beef was boiled in large cauldrons. In the late afternoon the cooked meat was distributed. Religious and governmental officials received special portions, and the rest of the meat provided a feast for all participants, either on the Acropolis or else back at the Dipylon Gate from

Now Nestor, the aged horseman,
gave the smith the gold, and he gilded the cow's horns with it
carefully, so the god might take pleasure seeing her offering.
Stratios and the noble Echephron led the cow by
the horns, and Aretos came from the inner chamber carrying
lustral water in a flowered bowl, and in the other hand
scattering barley in a basket. Steadfast Thrasymedes
stood by with the sharp ax in his hand, to strike down the heifer.
Perseus held the dish for the blood, and the aged horseman
Nestor began with the water and barley, making long prayers
to Athene, in dedication, and threw the head hairs in the fire.
Now when all had made prayer and flung down the scattering barley,
Thrasymedes, the high-hearted son of Nestor, standing
close up, struck, and the ax chopped its way through the tendons
of the neck and unstrung the strength of the cow, and now the daughters
and daughters-in-law of Nestor and his grave wife Eurydike,
eldest of the daughters of Klymenos, raised the outcry.
They lifted the cow from earth of the wide ways, and held her
fast in place, and Peisistratos, leader of men, slaughtered her.
Now, when the black blood had run out, and the spirit went from
the bones, they divided her into parts, and cut out the thigh bones
all according to due order, and wrapped them in fat,
making a double fold, and laid shreds of flesh upon them.
The old man burned these on cleft sticks, and poured the gleaming
wine over, while the young men with forks in their hands stood about him.
But when they had burned the thigh pieces and tasted the vitals,
they cut all the remainder into pieces and spitted them,
and roasted all carefully and took off the pieces.

> Nestor and his family sacrifice to Athena, Homer, *Odyssey* 3.436–63
> (Lattimore translation)

which the procession had begun. In simple terms we have the usual sacrifice of an animal, the burning of parts of it on the altar for the deity, and a later feast for the participants. The program is the same for the Panathenaea, but the scale is greatly larger, with a hundred or more animals in the fifth century, thousands of participants, and a large roster of religious and governmental personnel. It was probably at the sacrifice, just before or after the offering on the Great Altar, that her priestess received the newly woven *peplos* and presented it to Athena Polias in the Erechtheum.

It was common for Greeks at festivals to participate in or watch competitions while the meat of the sacrifice was cooking, and we can imagine that in the very early Panathenaea games were held only on the afternoon of Hecatombaion 28 and that it was a one-day festival. It is even possible that, initially, the games were to honor Erechtheus, but then, as for Pelops and Zeus at Olympia, the honor of the games shifted from the hero to the Olympian god. Such games became very popular throughout the Greek world, and at the Panathenaea, as at the modern Olympics, the program was constantly being expanded to the point that competitions had to be placed on days before and after Hecatombaion 28. In the annual Panathenaea the competitions may have been limited to Athenian participants, with, as examples, a team torch race, a team competition by tribes in an armed dance that formed a mock battle (the *pyrrhic* dance), a regatta with tribal teams, and various equestrian and chariot competitions.[4] The Greater Panathenaea, celebrated quadrennially, included these events specifically for Athenians but had a very large additional program for both Athenian and international competitors. These included athletic events (footraces of 200, 400, and 4800 meters, wrestling, boxing, a pentathlon of running, wrestling, long jump, discus and javelin throws, and the *pancration*, a combination of boxing, wrestling, and kicking); equestrian events (a horse race, two- and four-horse chariot races, a mule cart-race, and javelin throw from horseback); musical contests (solo flute, solo lyre, singing to flute accompaniment, and singing and playing the lyre); and, finally, a contest among rhapsodes reciting episodes from the *Iliad* and *Odyssey*. For many of these competitions there were two or three age divisions, and in the Greater Panathenaea the competition was at the highest levels, rivaling that of the Olympic Games.

Some of these competitions were military in nature, especially those held every year and reserved for Athenians, and the Athena Polias worshiped in this festival was primarily the warrior goddess. Athena as Parthenos and Promachos were both armed, and on their shields, as on the *peplos* of Athena Polias, were represented mythical battles in which the forces of order and civilization (the gods or Greeks) overcame the forces of violence and disorder (the Giants or Amazons). On the Acropolis dedications were made to Athena by the state for military victories over various foes, but those from the Persian Wars were the grandest. Athena Promachos was a dedication from the victory at Marathon in 490, and the Parthenon itself and Athena Parthenos might have been a dedication, several years later, for the ultimate victory over the Persians. Athena brought Athens "victory" in war, and Parthenos surely and Promachos perhaps each held in her hand a life-size statue of a Nike (Victory). On the bastion projecting west from the Acropolis Athena herself, as Athena Nike, had an altar and a small, elegant Ionic temple, and the south frieze of that temple represented the Athenians defeating the Persians in battle.

The same Athena, however, had also given Athenians the olive tree, the source of the oil critical to both the ancient and modern Greek life and economy. She thus had a role in the agricultural life of the community too, and this also was reflected in the Panathenaea. Winners in the musical competitions were given gold crowns and cash prizes, with, for example, the man who won playing and singing to the lyre receiving prizes worth 150 drachmas ($15,000). But the victors in athletic and equestrian competitions of the Greater Panathenaea were awarded large vases (*amphoras*) filled with olive oil pressed from the olives of trees sacred to Athena. The winner of the 200 meter footrace, for example, received 100 such vases, each holding 35–40 liters of oil. It has been estimated that 1,400 Panathenaic amphoras were required as prizes for each Greater Panathenaea, and because they were so highly prized by their owners and because they were often buried with them, about 300 have survived. They portray on one side the competition for which they were won and, on the other, a powerful image of an armed Athena Polias. The olive oil they contained, the competition they show, the "victory" they represent as prizes, and the figure of the armed Athena nicely symbolize the various aspects of Athena Polias celebrated at the Panathenaea.

Aeschylus in the *Eumenides*, the third play of his trilogy *Oresteia*, has the Athena of the Acropolis create for Athenians the first law court among men, a court administered by humans to judge the case of Orestes. In a series of vendettas Clytemnestra had killed her husband Agamemnon, and their son Orestes killed Clytemnestra. Athena brings this chain of vengeance to an end by creating at Athens a court of men with all proper legal procedures to try (and eventually acquit) Orestes. It is to be the model for such courts in the future, and it replaces a system of justice by retribution with justice by human law courts. If Aeschylus is reflecting the thoughts of his fellow Athenians in the audience in 458 B.C.E., then Athena of the Acropolis was for Athenians, as well as the giver of victory in battle and of the olive tree, the giver of justice as administered by the Athenian legal system. Aeschylus, however, was deeply concerned with

Figure IV.9 An Athenian black-figure Panathenaic vase by the Cleophrades Painter, from about 490 B.C.E. Athena wears the *aegis* and bears a shield with the winged horse Pegasus as an emblem. The Doric columns to the left and right are surmounted by cocks. On the reverse of the vase is represented a wrestling contest. The inscription running down the side of the left column is, "From the contests at Athens." The vase, 63.5 cm. high, was originally filled with sacred olive oil and was one of several awarded to a victor in one of the contests of the Panathenaia. Courtesy of the Toledo Museum, Toledo, inv. no. 61.24.

theoretical issues of justice and the gods' role in implementing it, and we cannot be sure whether only Aeschylus or all Athenians attributed this role to Athena Polias.

Thus far we have seen the Athenian Athena Polias of the Acropolis primarily as goddess of the state as a whole, giving victory in wars and providing and protecting the precious olive trees, and, perhaps, establishing the model for Athenian law courts. In concluding our description of her we stress that individuals, too, turned to her. Many of the hundreds of dedications to her on the Acropolis and in the Parthenon were made by grateful individuals, and in closing we can let some early fifth-century

B.C.E. Athenians speak for themselves in the texts they had inscribed on these dedications:

> Parthenos, Telesinus of the deme Kettos dedicated this statue to you on the
>   Acropolis.
> May you take pleasure in this and grant that he can dedicate another.
>
> (IG I³ 728, Hansen, #227)

> —— and his children dedicated this statue to Athena.
> May she have a kindly heart towards them.
>
> (IG I³ 722, Hansen, #225)

> Melanthyrus dedicated me, a statue, to you, goddess,
> After vowing a tithe of his work to the daughter of great Zeus.
>
> (IG I³ 608, Hansen, #190)

Demeter Eleusinia and the Eleusinian Mysteries

Twenty-three kilometers west of the city Athens, on the shore of the Bay of Eleusis, lay the deme of Eleusis and the sanctuary of Demeter Eleusinia, where the Eleusinian Mysteries were held each year in the fall.

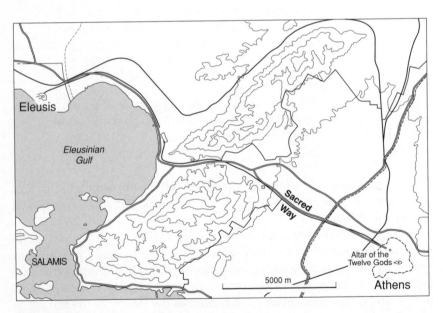

Map IV.1 Map showing the route the initiates of the Eleusinian Mysteries took in the procession from Athens to Eleusis.

Figure IV.10 The "Great Eleusinian Relief" of about 440 B.C.E., found at Eleusis in 1859 and now in the National Museum, Athens. It is 2.20 meters high and 1.55 meters wide. On the left is Demeter holding a scepter, on the right Kore with a torch. The boy in the center has been commonly identified as Triptolemus but is more probably Ploutos (Wealth). Courtesy of National Museum, Athens, inv. no. 126.

A *Hymn to Demeter*, composed probably about 600 B.C.E., gives a version of the foundation myth for Demeter's cult at Eleusis and for the Mysteries themselves. The hymn is 495 lines long, rich in detail and language, and very beautiful. One will want to read the whole poem, but here is a summary of it, with particular attention to those parts concerning Eleusis and the cult of Demeter there.

One spring morning, as Demeter's daughter Persephone was picking wild-flowers in a meadow, the earth gaped open and Hades appeared in his chariot, snatched up Persephone, and carried her off to the underworld to be his queen. Her mother heard her cries and, holding blazing torches in her hand, searched for her nine days long. On the tenth day Demeter learned from the all-seeing Sun what had happened. In grief at the loss of her daughter she withdrew from the gods and in the guise of an old spinster wandered among the cities of men. At Eleusis the daughters of King Celeus found her sitting at a well, treated her nicely, and took her home. One of the daughters, Iambe, cheered her up with jokes. During her search Demeter had been fasting, and the girls offered her wine, but she refused it and asked instead for a special potion, a *kykeon*, of barley, water, and pennyroyal. Demeter, though still grieving for her daughter, became the nurse for Demophon, the infant son of Celeus and his wife Metaneira. Demeter tended the boy "as if he were the child of a god," not giving him human food but anointing him with *ambrosia*, the food of the gods. Each night she laid him like a log in the blazing fire. She would have made him "ageless and immortal," but his mother, finding her child in the fire, was horrified. Demeter, angered, took the child from the fire and stopped the process of deification. Demeter identified herself to Metaneira, announced that Demophon would forever be honored, and ordered the Eleusinians to build her a temple and altar and to perform special rites to appease her. This they did.

Demeter remained in her temple in Eleusis, still grieving for her daughter. She caused the grain crops to fail throughout the world, and was ready to "destroy the whole race of mortal men" and, thereby, to deprive the gods of the gifts they received from humans. Eventually Zeus, who had originally approved Hades' abduction of Persephone, ordered him to return her to the upperworld. But before she left the underworld Hades had forced her to eat a pomegranate seed, and because of that she was bound to spend one-third of the year with him in the underworld. The other two-thirds, spring and summer, she would spend with her mother Demeter in the upperworld. At last, in front of her temple at Eleusis, Demeter was reunited with her daughter in a scene of great joy. Demeter then

> swiftly made the seed sprout out of the fertile fields.
> The whole broad earth teemed with leaves and flowers.[5] (471–2)

After she was reunited with her daughter, Demeter went to Celeus and the other leaders of Eleusis, including Eumolpus and Triptolemus, and explained to all

> the awful mysteries not to be transgressed, violated,
> or divulged, because the tongue is restrained by reverence for the gods.
> Whoever on this earth has seen these is blessed,
> but he who has no part in the holy rites has
> another lot as he wastes away in dank darkness. (478–82)

In addition to a special fate in the afterlife, Demeter and her daughter Persephone also gave Ploutos (Wealth, especially as "agricultural prosperity") and a good livelihood to those they loved among the living.

This *Hymn to Demeter* is not simply the local cult myth of Demeter Eleusinia. It has in places been panhellenized, that is, the myth has been reshaped to suit a wider Greek audience. Most notably, some names have been changed. At Eleusis Kore (Girl) was Persephone's name, and Pluton, not Hades, was the god of the underworld. It is appropriate that the local Eleusinian myth should be made available and intelligible to the wider Greek audience because the Mysteries at Eleusis, unlike virtually all other Athenian cults, were open to all Greeks.

From the *Hymn* we can see the two major domains of Eleusinian Demeter: the fertility of crops, particularly of the wheat and barley which were staples of the Greek diet, and, secondly, the welfare of the dead in the afterlife. Let us begin with her role as goddess of the grain crops. In the *Hymn* grain production is an already established practice, and Demeter can, at will, bring success or failure to these crops. This role of Demeter was recognized throughout the Greek world, and in every Greek city women performed rituals for Demeter, particularly at seeding time, to promote the fertility of the crop. These Thesmophoria[6] were held at Athens and Eleusis too, but at Eleusis there developed, probably in the century after the *Hymn* was composed, the myth that Demeter not only oversaw the grain harvest but also had first taught the cultivation of grain crops to the Eleusinian Triptolemus. In the *Hymn* Triptolemus appears only as one of the Eleusinian royalty, but in Athenian lore he, like Johnny Appleseed or Icarius in the Dionysus myth,[7] spread what Demeter had taught him throughout the world. Through this myth the Eleusinians and Athenians made *their* sanctuary of Demeter and *their* close relationship with the goddess the very origins of the foodstuffs vital to Greek life. In the fifth century, based on their "ancestral practices" and an oracle from Delphi, Athenian farmers gave to Demeter Eleusinia 1/600 of all barley and 1/1200 of all wheat they produced as a "first-fruits" offering – a gift in kind to the goddess in return for the goods she provided them. Silos were built at Demeter's sanctuary to store the grain, and revenue from the sale of this grain brought considerable wealth to the sanctuary. In the 430s the Athenians went so far as to ask all their subject states and to encourage other Greek states to donate to Demeter at Eleusis the same proportions of the grains they produced (*IG* I^3 78). Since other Greeks, however, had their own cults of Demeter and apparently did not accept Eleusinian claims about Triptolemus, they ignored Athens' presumptuous request.

Figure IV.11   An Athenian red-figure cup by Macron, of about 480 B.C.E.
In the center is portrayed Triptolemus in his winged cart and holding ears
of grain. Behind him stands Kore, before him Demeter, each holding a torch.
Courtesy of the Trustees of the British Museum, inv. no. BM E 140.

As we turn now to the Mysteries themselves, we need to remember that
at Eleusis, as elsewhere throughout the Greek world, successful production
of grain crops was the primary domain of Demeter. The *Hymn to Demeter*
squarely puts the founding of the Mysteries at Eleusis, and that claim was
recognized by all Greeks. In the Greek world in the Classical period there
were only a few cults that promised a special relationship with a god through
secret, initiation-type rituals, and the Mysteries at Eleusis held special prominence among them. That is why Greeks and later Romans came from
throughout the Mediterranean world to be initiated into them.

We know far less of the Mysteries than we would like, especially because,
as the *Hymn* says, they were

>   the awful mysteries not to be transgressed, violated,
>   or divulged, because the tongue is restrained by reverence for the gods.

The punishment for revealing the secrets of the Mysteries was death,
and even such a respected figure as Aeschylus faced this danger from an
apparently innocent allusion to the secrets in a tragedy. We must assume
that the *Hymn* itself, which enjoins secrecy, does not reveal any of the secret

rites of the Mysteries but in places reflects public activities and rituals preliminary to the secret rites. We do know that events of the Mysteries occurred during the days Boedromion 15–22, in early autumn, about the time of the planting of grain crops in Athens.[8] The main events included: 1) a procession to the sea coast at Phaleron, where the initiates, perhaps as many as two thousand in number, bathed in seawater piglets they had brought with them; 2) the sacrifice of the piglets, probably at the altar of the Eleusinion in Athens; 3) amidst joyful cries of "Iacche, Iacche," a great procession of initiates – barefoot, wearing myrtle wreaths, and carrying their lunches –, their sponsors, and the Eleusinian priesthood and others, perhaps as many as 30,000 altogether, on the Sacred Road from Athens to Eleusis on Boedromion 19; and 4) both public and secret rituals at Eleusis on the following two days.[9]

We are, of course, most curious about the rituals at Eleusis itself, but about these we can only guess, using the *Hymn* and the Eleusinian priesthood and site as our guides. Demeter, of course, had her priestess, and the goddess, her daughter Kore, and Pluton all received sacrifices as part of the Mysteries. But male priests played the major roles. Demeter had, after all, taught the Eleusinian male royalty her rites. Foremost among these were the Eumolpidae, descendants of the Eumolpus (Of Good Song) of the *Hymn*. The Eumolpidae inherited from generation to generation the role of *Hierophant*, that is, "the one who showed the sacred things." Something was "shown" at a culminating moment in the secret ritual, and the final stage of initiation was called the *epopteia*, the "viewing." The name of a second family prominent at Eleusis, the Ceryces (Heralds), was also derived from the role they played in the rites. They and the Eumolpidae "proclaimed" throughout the Greek world a sacred truce that insured the safety of initiates as they traveled to and from Eleusis for the 55 days surrounding the Mysteries. They also "proclaimed" the ban of murderers and non-Greek speakers from the Mysteries, and they may well also have "announced" something – we are not sure what – in the course of the secret rites. The Ceryces also provided the Dadouchos, the "torch bearer." In the *Hymn*, Demeter carried torches in her search for Persephone, and, as in figure IV.11, Eleusinian Demeter is often represented holding such torches. Many of the Eleusinian rituals were performed at night, and torches figured prominently.

At Eleusis the Eumolpidae and Ceryces together formed a priestly college found in the Greek tradition usually only at international cult centers where cult matters required full-time attention. Besides exercising authority over virtually all cult activities associated with Demeter and Kore, they served as interpreters and enforcers of Eleusinian laws and traditions. But even here the Athenian state, through lay committees, oversaw many aspects of the finances of the cult.

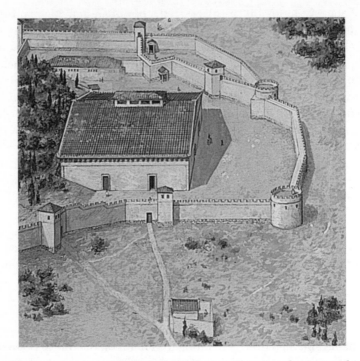

Figure IV.12   Sanctuary of Demeter and Kore at Eleusis as it appeared in the fifth century B.C.E. In the center is the Telesterion, the Hall of Initiation, and in the background the gate by which one entered the sanctuary. Watercolor by Peter Connolly. Photograph: AKG London.

The rituals of the Mysteries were held in and around a large (51 meter square), columned, roofed building which we call the Telesterion (Initiation Hall) but which Eleusinians called both the Temple of Demeter and the *Anaktoron*. It was no doubt that building which, according to the *Hymn*, owed its origins to Demeter's order to the Eleusinians to build her a temple. It was in this building, again according to the *Hymn*, that Demeter waited to be reunited with her daughter and in front of which that reunion occurred.

In the *Hymn* the joyful reunion of Demeter and Kore at Eleusis brought to an end the dearth of crops affecting the world, and the compromise effected among the gods and ratified by Zeus, that Kore spend one-third of the year in the underworld and two-thirds (spring and summer) in the upperworld, seemingly established the Athenian agricultural year. In Attica grain seeds (like Kore?) are placed in the earth in the fall. The plants emerge in the fall, remain dormant for much of the winter, and then, like the flowers, come to fruition in spring (when Kore reemerges from the underworld).

The Mysteries, at least in part, celebrated or perhaps even reenacted the separation and eventual reunion of the goddess and her daughter. The cave of Pluton in the sanctuary at Eleusis would no doubt have figured in any such reenactment, and we know that fasting, jesting, and the drinking of the *kykeon* – all described in the *Hymn* – were parts of the ritual of the Mysteries.

A dream forbade me to write a description of the things within the wall of the sanctuary. It is obvious, I suppose, that the uninitiated have no right to learn of the things which they are prevented from seeing.

Pausanias, 1.38.7, in his description of Eleusis

The reunion of Demeter and Persephone occurred *outside* the Telesterion, and because it is so graphically represented in the *Hymn*, it probably cannot have been part of the secrets of the Mysteries. The secrets would have been "shown" as the culminating ritual *inside* the Telesterion, and the *Hymn* tells us nothing of what was said, shown, or done there. For that we depend on a few comments by Christian church fathers and the educated

Figure IV.13 Interior of the Telesterion, the Hall of Initiation of Demeter's sanctuary at Eleusis. Watercolor by Peter Connolly. Photograph: AKG London.

guesses of modern scholars.[10] The secrets revealed probably concerned both aspects of the Mysteries, both the production of grains and the promise of special status in the underworld. Apparently an ear of grain was shown, lit torches gave off a brilliant light, and the birth of a child, perhaps named Brimus, was announced.[11] Brimus may have been the Ploutos (Wealth) of the *Hymn to Demeter*, and this Ploutos, often represented at Eleusis with a cornucopia, may have been a personification of earth's bountiful produce. In addition, it was through these secret rites in the Telesterion that the initiates were made to believe that, as the *Hymn* states it,

> Whoever on this earth has seen these is blessed,
> but he who has no part in the holy rites has
> another lot as he wastes away in dank darkness.

> Thrice blessed are those mortals
> who after seeing these rites go to Hades.
> They alone live there, but others have all evils.
> Sophocles, fragment 837 (Radt)

Demeter was the giver of grain, and her reunion with her daughter led to the success of human agricultural efforts. But Demeter's daughter Kore was also Queen of the Underworld, and it may be especially through Kore's intervention that this second blessing of the Mysteries was achieved. Kore, uniquely among the major Greek deities, had residences in both the upperworld and the underworld, and hence could, presumably, uniquely establish relationships with humans during their upperworld life which would carry over to their and her underworld life. Those initiated into the Mysteries in their lifetime would establish a valuable bond with the goddess who would rule over them after death. And so Demeter's cult at Eleusis offered, at the least, two great benefits, and the orator Isocrates in 380 B.C.E. nicely summarized how the Athenians viewed them:

Demeter came to our land when she had wandered about after Kore was carried off. Because of their good services, which only the initiates may hear, Demeter was kindly disposed to our ancestors, and she gave them two gifts which are the greatest: the fruits of the field which make it possible for us to live not like animals, and the initiation, and those who partake of the initiation have sweeter hopes about the end of life and all eternity. Our city was not only god-loved but also philanthropic, and so, when it gained control of such good things, it did not begrudge them to others but gave to all a share of what it received.

(*Panegyricus* 28–9)

Dionysus Cadmeios of Thebes

As we saw in Myth #4 of Chapter III, Dionysus came to Athens and taught Icarius the art of wine-making, and Icarius then introduced it to his fellow Athenians. Wine was a central feature of Dionysus' cult in every Greek city-state, but at Athens Dionysus, as Dionysus Eleuthereus (The One Who Sets Free), was also patron of dramatic and certain choral productions.

Figure IV.14 A bearded Dionysus, with a cantharus drinking cup in his right hand and branch of ivy in his left, has the central position on this Athenian black-figure amphora of about 535 B.C.E. Small satyrs climb in the vine around him, harvesting the bunches of grapes into baskets. Courtesy Museum of Fine Arts, Boston, inv. no. 63.952. Photograph © Museum of Fine Arts, Boston.

Figure IV.15   The Theater of Dionysus, with the Odeon (roofed theater) of Pericles in the background. Watercolor by Peter Connolly. Photograph: AKG London.

At his major festivals there, and only at his festivals, tragedies, comedies, and *dithyrambs* (choral songs and dances celebrating the god's birth and adventures) were produced annually in his sanctuaries.

The common thread linking Dionysus to both drama and wine is that the god created in his worshipers a state of *ecstasy*, which is, literally, a state of "standing (*stasy*) outside (*ec*) of oneself." In a state of Dionysiac ecstasy one becomes, as it were, "different," "free" from one's usual self. That wine can create such an effect requires no argument, but dance and song can also produce it. It is especially apparent in the theater where as an actor in a tragedy an ordinary Athenian male might become for a few hours King Agamemnon or even Princess Antigone. The audience, too, as they watched the tragedies, were transported from their usual daily concerns to the distant age of great kings and queens. The comedies of Aristophanes and others kept the spectators in their contemporary world but reshaped that world in bawdy, humorous, and often fantastic ways. These are all experiences of the Dionysiac just as much as are the drunken revels concluding many Dionysiac festivals. What is missing, however, from

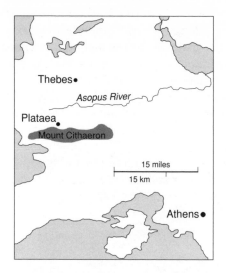

Map IV.2　Map illustrating sites of cult of Dionysus of Thebes.

the Athenian cults of Dionysus are the *maenads* and many other elements that we traditionally associate with Dionysus in cult, myth, and art, and for those we must turn to his cult in Thebes.

Thebes was the dominant city in the region of Boeotia north of Attica. There, according to Greek myth, Dionysus was born, the son of Zeus and Semele, the mortal daughter of King Cadmus. Semele, when pregnant, asked to see Zeus in all his splendor, and when he granted her request, she was incinerated by a thunderbolt. Zeus snatched up the yet unborn Dionysus, sewed him up in his own thigh until he came to term, and, when he "delivered" him, sent him abroad to Nysa in Asia Minor to escape detection by his jealous wife Hera. Years later Dionysus, with a following of young women, returned to Thebes to claim his status as a god in his homeland. Euripides in his *Bacchae* dramatized this myth of Dionysus' return, and that wonderful play should be read as a primary source for the nature of Dionysus and his role in Thebes. It is, much like the *Hymn to Demeter*, a panhellenized foundation myth of Dionysus' cult, but it is also integrally related to cult sites and rituals at Thebes. In the *Bacchae* Pentheus is now king of Thebes in place of the aged Cadmus. Semele's sisters and the Thebans in general have rejected Semele's claims to have conceived a god from Zeus, and Dionysus returns to establish his own authority and to restore the reputation of his mother. Dionysus has enmaddened the doubting women of Thebes, and they have left their homes to live in the wilds of the nearby mountain Cithaeron. They are the mythical, prototypical *maenads* (mad women), dressed in fawnskins and carrying the *thyrsos*, a long stick with a bundle of ivy or a pine cone affixed to the top. Pentheus, disturbed by the flight of the Theban women, is perplexed by the appearance of a mysterious, androgynous stranger with a retinue of Asian women. In a series of encounters Pentheus, despite the warnings of Cadmus and the seer Teiresias, mocks and tries to interrogate and imprison the stranger and his followers. Pentheus is, however, always bested, sometimes by miraculous phantoms and once by an earthquake. The stranger, who is of course Dionysus, finally maddens Pentheus and entices him, dressed as a maenad, to spy on the Theban women on the mountainside. Pentheus is spotted by them, and they tear him limb from limb. Eventually Agave, his mother, returns to Thebes carrying his head,

Figure IV.16   Roman copy of a late fifth-century B.C.E. relief sculpture of a *maenad* holding in her right hand a *thyrsus*. Courtesy of the Metropolitan Museum of Art, Fletcher Fund, 1945, inv. no. 35.11.3.

thinking it is the head of a lion. Dionysus then lifts the madness of Agave, and she recognizes what she has done. Dionysus has demonstrated his power as a god, in maddening both the women of Thebes and Pentheus and in using a whole series of miracles to crush human opposition. His status as a god in Thebes is established, and the reputation of his mother Semele is restored.

In the *Bacchae* Dionysus causes immense suffering for those who reject him, but countering this are the praises of Dionysus sung by his Asian devotees:

> Blessed is the person who, happy, knows
> the rites of the gods, who is pure in his life
> and joins the Dionysiac dance groups,
> the one who celebrates the Bacchic rites in the mountains.
>
> (lines 72–6)

> The god, the child of Zeus,
> delights in banquets and
> loves the goddess Peace, the giver of prosperity,
> the nurse of the young.
> He has an equal gift for the rich and the poor –
> the painfree pleasure of wine.
> But he hates the person not interested in living
> the good life night and day.
>
> (lines 417–25)

The Dionysus of Euripides' *Bacchae* is, as the god himself declares, "most terrible, and yet most gentle, to mankind" (line 861).

The pattern of this myth is like the foundation myth we have seen of Demeter at Eleusis. A god initially angered is eventually appeased by humans, with the result that a cult is established and that deity becomes a benefactor to his or her worshipers. The god's anger and appeasement belong to the mythical history of the cult, but the worshipers of historical times enjoy, through the cult, the benefits that the deity can bestow. From the foundation myth, however, the thought always lingers that this is a powerful deity who must be treated carefully and who must be honored and worshiped properly.

Semele, her union with Zeus and her death, Cadmus the king, Teiresias the seer, the maenads roaming the mountainside dressed in fawnskins and carrying the *thyrsos*, the dismemberment of a living being, and Dionysus' gift of wine were themes known and represented in art and literature throughout the Greek world, but the actual cult based on these combined elements was centered in Thebes, the city in which the myth placed them.

Dionysus had two major sanctuaries at Thebes, both associated with his mother Semele. In one his epithet was Cadmeios, which indicated location because the sanctuary was on the Cadmeia, the large hill on which the city of Thebes was situated. The Cadmeia itself took its name from Cadmus who was both founder of Thebes and the maternal grandfather of Dionysus. Cadmus undoubtedly had a hero sanctuary in the city, but no evidence of that survives. Although neither of Dionysus' sanctuaries has been discovered, ancient reports indicate that on the Cadmeia there was an altar and two statues, one a bronze image and another, much more ancient, a log adorned with bronze. It was claimed that this log fell from the sky when Zeus incinerated Semele with his thunderbolt and was itself called Dionysus Cadmeios. This image of Dionysus, like the similarly ancient statue of Athena Polias in the Athenian Erechtheum, would have been a focal point of the cult, an object of special veneration. As we have seen, Euripides' *Bacchae* makes it a mission of Dionysus to restore his mother's reputation, and in his sanctuary on the Cadmeia were the remnants of Semele's bedchamber, probably a *heroön*. Like many places struck by Zeus' lightning in Greece, the spot took on special significance. It was deemed to be an *abaton*, that is, a place that "could not be entered" by humans. There is no mention of a temple of Dionysus Cadmeios although there probably was one, to shelter the "log" statue of the god.

At his other sanctuary in Thebes, near one of the gates, Dionysus' epithet was Lysios (The One Who Sets One "Loose"). According to the ancient sources, Dionysus received this epithet for rescuing some Theban prisoners of war, but the epithet also recalls his epithet in Athens, Eleuthereus. Both could refer to Dionysus' role of inducing the state of *ecstasy* in his worshipers. In this sanctuary were a temple, a theater, and a statue of Semele. Nearby, or perhaps even in the sanctuary, was the tomb of Semele. The theater was perhaps a later addition, to accommodate dramatic competitions that were held in the late fourth century and later as part of Dionysus' festival there. And, finally, even the soothsayer Teiresias had monuments. The place where he observed omens was still being shown to visitors in the second century c.e., and neighboring Boeotian towns had sanctuaries and a tomb for him, probably as a hero. And so major characters of the Dionysus myth as told by Euripides had a role in the practiced cult of the Thebans.

We know little of the Agrionia (Of the Wilds), the festival of Dionysus Cadmeios at Thebes in the fifth century, but that little suggests that Euripides' dramatized account of Dionysiac activity in Thebes is, on the whole, accurate. The festival gave its name to the Boeotian month Agrionios, which fell in March/April, about the time of the major Dionysiac drama festival in Athens. The foundation myth for the festival is that Dionysus

Figure IV.17 An Athenian red-figure *crater* from about mid-fifth century
B.C.E. depicting Dionysus in the center holding a cantharus and a *thyrsus*.
The woman on the left holds an oenochoe (wine-pouring vessel) and a snake.
The other woman wields a *thyrsus* and a dismembered fawn. The whole scene
is typical of the Theban maenadic cult of Dionysus. Courtesy of the Shefton
Museum of Greek Art and Archaeology, University of Newcastle-upon-Tyne,
inv. no. 629.

arrived in Thebes but was not welcomed by the royalty. He then drove three
princesses mad, and they killed the king who was resisting Dionysus.
Thereafter the god was accepted. In all probability this foundation myth
was reenacted every other year at the Agrionia. Here the women of Thebes,
or a contingent of them, were organized into three dance groups (*thiasoi*),
and rushed off to Mount Cithaeron with ritual cries of "to the mountain."
As "mad women" (maenads) and devotees of the god (*Bacchai*), they

pursued and killed – perhaps by dismemberment (*sparagmos*) – the king. The king quite possibly was represented by a goat, an animal sacred to Dionysus, and the maenads may have eaten the meat of the goat raw (*omophagia*) or sacrificed it to Dionysus. The maenads' defeat of Dionysus' antagonist would lead to a reconciliation with the god, and eventually the women were freed from their madness and returned to Thebes and their usual lives. But for the time of the festival they would have had an intense Dionysiac, ecstatic experience. The Agrionia was celebrated in several Greek cities, especially in Boeotia. Although each Boeotian city had its own distinct foundation myth for it, the patterns are much the same: the arrival of Dionysus, resistance to him, flight of the women to a mountain, killing of Dionysus' persecutor, and eventual reconciliation with the god.

Thebes' coins bore the image of Dionysus on one side and on the other a large wine-drinking cup, the *cantharos*. In the third century B.C.E., when an Asia Minor city wanted to create a maenadic cult of Dionysus, the Delphic Oracle bid them to send to Thebes for both instruction and three professional maenads. Thebes was, in fact, as Euripides represents her to be, the center of maenadic Dionysiac cult, and here we can see, as we did with the cult of Demeter at Eleusis, how the cult elements of divine epithets, sanctuaries, statues, monuments, and festivals of a specific place can help us understand the cult realities ultimately underlying the poetic reshaping of local foundation myths such as Euripides' *Bacchae*, and how, in turn, the poetic versions of the myth can then bring to life the cultic elements.

Figure IV.18 Head of Dionysus, with an ivy wreath, on a silver *stater* (two-drachma coin, about $200) from Thebes, about 395–387 B.C.E. Courtesy of the Trustees of the British Museum, inv. no. BMC Thebes 104.

> Go to the holy plain of Thebe so that you may get
> maenads who are from the family of Ino, daughter of Cadmus.
> They will give to you both the rites and good practices,
> and they will establish dance groups (thiasoi) of Bacchus in your city.
>
> Delphic oracle to Magnesians of Ionia, a Roman copy of a third
> century B.C.E. inscription, *IMagn.* 215(a), lines 9–12

Apollo Pythios of Delphi

North of the Gulf of Corinth, nestled on a ledge on the steep slopes of
Mount Parnassus, is the sanctuary of Apollo Pythios of Delphi. It offers

Figure IV.19   An Attic red-figure *crater* (wine-mixing bowl) of about
460–450 B.C.E., attributed to the Villa Giulia Painter. It depicts Apollo in the
center, his mother Leto to the left, and his sister Artemis to the right. Apollo
wears a crown of laurel and holds both a lyre and an offering bowl. The name
of each deity is written to its right. The vase is 37 cm. high. Courtesy of the
Metropolitan Museum of Art, Fletcher Fund, 1924, inv. no. 24.97.96.

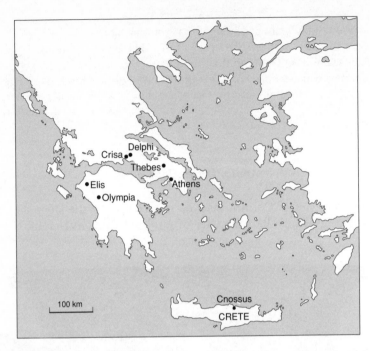

Map IV.3   Map of Greece and Crete, featuring sites discussed in Chapter IV.

an awe-inspiring view, with the cliffs of Parnassus rising behind, with
the gorge of the Pleistus river below and the mountains of the northern
Peloponnesus standing out clearly across the Gulf of Corinth.

This was the site of the Oracle of Apollo, and, as the *Homeric Hymn to
Apollo* tells us, the god himself chose this very site. This *Hymn*, like that
of Demeter, is rich in language and detail and should be read in its
entirety, but here we offer extracts and a summary of essential elements.

> Apollo traveled the Greek world, searching for a place for his oracle. He even-
> tually settled on a site near the city Crisa:
>
>> From there you went rushing to a mountain ridge,
>> and you reached Krisa beneath snowy Parnassos,
>> a foothill looking westwards, with a rock
>> hanging above it and a hollow and rough glen
>> running below it. There the lord Phoibos Apollon
>> resolved to make a lovely temple and spoke these words:
>> "Here I intend to build a beautiful temple
>> to be an oracle for men who shall always
>> bring to this place unblemished hecatombs;

as many as dwell on fertile Peloponnesos
and on Europe and throughout the sea-girt islands
will consult it. It is my wish to give them unerring
advice, making prophecies inside the opulent temple."
With these words Phoibos Apollo laid out the foundations,
broad and very long from beginning to end; and on them
the sons of Erginos, Trophonios and Agamedes,
dear to the immortal gods, placed a threshold of stone.
And the numberless races of men built the temple all around
with hewn stones, to be a theme of song forever.[12] (281–99)

Apollo had first, however, to slay the Python, a savage dragon that was causing much suffering for the local residents and their flocks. This he did, leaving the corpse "to rot" (*pythein* in Greek), and from that the place was named Pytho and Apollo received his local epithet, Pythios. Apollo next needed a priesthood to serve his Oracle, and for that he waylaid off the southern Peloponnesus a ship of Cretan men from Cnossus. He approached them in the shape of a dolphin and hurled himself on the deck of their ship. The ship then miraculously set its own course, along the west coast of the Peloponnesus, into the Gulf of Corinth, and to Crisa. Apollo then revealed himself to the Cretan men, and told them of his purpose:

"Strangers, up to now you dwelt about Knossos
with its many trees; now you shall no longer be
on the homeward journey, bound for your lovely city,
your beautiful homes and dear wives, but you shall keep
my opulent temple which is honored by many men.
I am the son of Zeus and proudly I declare that I am Apollon.
I brought you here over the vast and deep sea,
entertaining no evil thoughts, but here you shall have
my opulent temple, which is greatly honored by all men,
and you shall know the will of the immortals, by whose wish
you shall be honored forever to the end of your days." (475–85)

"Since I, at first on the misty sea
in the form of a dolphin, leaped onto the swift ship,
so pray to me as Delphinios." (493–5)

The Cretans accepted Apollo's words and commission, and

They walked up the hill unwearied and soon reached
Parnassos and the lovely place where he was destined
to dwell honored by many men; he led them there
and showed them the sacred sanctuary and opulent temple. (520–3)

Just as Demeter established her sanctuary and had her first temple built at Eleusis, so Apollo, according to this *Hymn*, chose Delphi and built his first temple. Just as Demeter established the Eleusinian royalty as the priesthood for her Mysteries, so Apollo handpicked men from Crete to serve as the priests of his Oracle. The *Hymn* further explains the two names given to the site in antiquity – Pytho, from the "rotting" corpse of the dragon Python, and Delphi, from the "dolphin" whose shape Apollo assumed in leading his priests to his new Oracle. Also reflected in the *Hymn* is the immense popularity and resulting wealth which Apollo's cult at Delphi enjoyed from Homer's day well down into Roman times. But perhaps most important in religious terms is the idea clearly stated in the *Hymn* that Apollo's act of establishing an Oracle is one of pure benevolence: he wanted men to be able to know "the will of the immortals." As we shall see, for centuries thousands of Greeks, Romans, and even Persians and other non-Greeks came to Delphi to partake of this benefit, either for their personal needs or on behalf of their countries.

Demeter's cult at Eleusis was probably initially intended only for the inhabitants of Attica and only gradually developed an international clientele of initiates. As the *Hymn to Apollo* indicates, Apollo's sanctuary at Delphi was from its beginnings panhellenic, with the Oracle speaking to all Greeks and even foreigners. In the fifth century, although it was autonomous internally, Delphi was protected by a consortium (*amphictiony*) of twelve peoples which included neighboring states and also Sparta and Athens. Unlike most cults in Greece, it was a full-time religious center, and with its stream of consultants and visitors it offered a full-time occupation for the priests and other religious personnel. It was also filled with dedications and treasuries from cities throughout the Greek and non-Greek world.

By the fifth century Apollo's original temple had long since disappeared, and the temple a fifth-century visitor saw had been built just after 548 B.C.E. Its great altar stood immediately to the east, a dedication of the residents of the island of Chios for having been spared by the Persians in their invasions of Greece. Unlike many temples, the Temple of Apollo, like Demeter's Telesterion at Eleusis, played a major role in the cult. A special room in its *cella* was Apollo's "innermost shrine," the *adyton*, the "place that could not be entered." It was from there that Apollo's prophetess, the Pythia, spoke to enquirers the words of Apollo himself. Apollo's *temenos* was roughly rectangular, 128 × 183 meters, rising steeply in terraces from its gate in the south-east corner. As one climbed the winding Sacred Way from the gate to the Altar of the Chians and finally to the Temple, one saw on both sides of the Sacred Way treasury buildings and dozens of dedications. Many of these had been made by either satisfied or hopeful

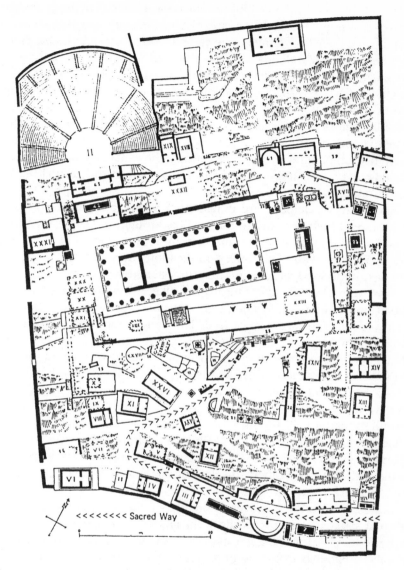

Figure IV.20 A plan of the sanctuary of Apollo Pythios at Delphi. The Temple of Apollo, in the center, housed the Oracle. To its right is the Altar of the Chians. The theater in the upper left was the venue for some events of the Pythian Games. The entrance, at the lower right, leads to the Sacred Way which passed, on its way to the Altar and Temple, numerous treasuries and dedications.

clients of the Oracle, but Delphi was also a place which many prominent Greeks and non-Greeks visited, and many states and kingdoms erected monuments there to commemorate and publicize their victories over other countries. An outstanding example of the latter from the fifth century was the magnificent gold tripod on a stand of three intertwined bronze snakes, which stood probably seven or eight meters high near the Altar of the Chians. The Greeks had inscribed this monument with the names of the thirty-one allied states and erected it as a thank-offering and memorial of their united victory over the Persians in 479 B.C.E. Delphi was already "rich" in Homer's time, and by the fifth century the sanctuary was filled with silver, gold, bronze, and marble dedications made by the most gifted and famous artisans of the time.

The priests of Delphi were drawn from aristocratic families who no doubt traced their ancestry to the Cretans brought to Delphi by Apollo. Why Apollo should have chosen Cretans is uncertain, but Crete was known for men who could offer "purification" from religious pollution, and Delphi became, at least in literature, a center of such purification. In Aeschylus' *Oresteia*, after Orestes has killed his mother Clytemnestra, Apollo sends him first to Delphi to be "purified" of the murder and only then to Athens to face a legal trial. The Oracle, too, offered means of expiation for religious crimes. Two priests were appointed for life to serve Apollo. Two were probably required by the volume of religious activity there.[13] They were assisted by five *Hosioi*, "Holy Men," who helped the priests in the performance of the rites and other duties. In addition there would have been a staff, who, like Ion portrayed in Euripides' *Ion*, kept the sanctuary clean and tidy. We should also imagine, outside the *temenos*, a large establishment of Delphians to transport, house, and feed the many visitors to Delphi. There, too, would have been the workshops of the artisans who crafted the dedications and built the buildings of the sanctuary.

Of greatest interest, however, is the Pythia, the prophetess who in the oracular session spoke the words of the god in response to the questions of the enquirers. Unlike the priests and Hosioi, she was a local woman with no special family background or training. Once appointed she served for life, lived in a special house in the *temenos*, and had to remain chaste. She is generally portrayed in art as a young woman, but one account says that in later times she was in fact a woman over fifty years of age who dressed in the clothing of a young woman.[14] Her role was of immense importance in the functioning of the Oracle because she served as the medium for the god. In the oracular session she spoke, but the words she spoke were Apollo's words. When in giving an oracle she said, "*I* say it is better for you to do x and y," that "*I* " is Apollo himself.

In the fifth century formal oracular sessions were apparently held on the seventh day, Apollo's sacred day, of each month, excluding the three months of winter. The Pythia began her oracular day with a "bath" in the waters of the nearby spring Castalia. Just as an ordinary worshiper would "purify" himself with a sprinkling of water at the *perirrhanterion* at a sanctuary's gate, so the Pythia, who would be having a very close encounter with a deity, "purified" herself with water. As the Pythia entered the Temple she would have seen all about many precious dedications to Apollo. On her right, on the front porch, was a massive silver *crater* (mixing bowl) dedicated in 546 B.C.E. by Croesus, king of the Lydians. It held 21,730 liters and was used for mixing wine at one of the festivals of Pythian Apollo. Its mate, a gold *crater* also dedicated by Croesus, weighed 225 kilograms and was now stored in one of the treasury buildings. In the *cella* of the Temple she would have encountered statues of two Moirae (Fates) and of Zeus and Apollo, both with the epithet Moiragetes (Leader of the Moirae). There, too, was an altar on which burned an eternal flame, fed by pine wood. This was "pure fire," and, if ever extinguished, it had to be rekindled with mirrors from the sun's rays. The Pythia would also have passed by the "sacred weapons" of Apollo and an iron chair on which, reportedly, the lyric poet Pindar had sat when he wrote his songs for Delphic Apollo. The Pythia then entered the *adyton* of the Temple, and she would have seen there a large tripod, a small altar of Apollo, statues of Apollo and Dionysus, and the *omphalos*.[15] The *omphalos* was a large stone, shaped like a protruding navel and wrapped in fillets of wool. Delphic lore held that the site of the Oracle was in fact the "navel," that is, the "center," of the earth. It was here that two eagles met when they were released from the opposite ends of the earth by Zeus. Dionysus earned his place of prominence in the *adyton* because he tended the sanctuary during Apollo's winter holiday.

On an oracular day the Pythia burned laurel leaves and barley meal on the altar. Laurel was the plant sacred to Apollo, and the Pythia also wore a crown of it in her hair and held a branch of it in her hand. She then sat on the tripod, a covered bowl suspended by three legs (*tripod* = "three-footed"), and perhaps drank some water piped into the *adyton* from the spring Cassotis. The Pythia is thus seated, surrounded by the most familiar symbols of the Pythian Apollo: his statues, the *omphalos*, the tripod, and the laurel. She is now inspired by the god and ready to give Apollo's answers to questions directed to her. But by what was she inspired? Many and contradictory answers have been given by ancient sources and modern scholars. Some claim that the fumigation of laurel leaves affected her, some that she even ate laurel leaves and was intoxicated by the small bit of prussic acid in them, and some that she worked herself into a

Figure IV.21   On this Athenian red-figure *crater* of the fifth century B.C.E. are represented, inside the Temple of Apollo, from right to left, Apollo Pythios, seated, with crown and branches of laurel; the tripod and *omphalos*; an attendant with a staff, probably one of the Hosioi; the elaborately dressed Pythia; and an attendant. Courtesy of the Museo Archeologico Nazionale di Ferrara.

hypnotic trance. Recent geological and archaeological work has, however, remarkably confirmed the claims of our best ancient source for Delphi, the biographer and scholar Plutarch, himself a priest of Pythian Apollo at Delphi. He wrote that vapors arose from a chasm in the rock beneath the *adyton* and that the Pythia was "inspired" by these vapors. He attributed the decline of the Oracle in his time, in the second century C.E., to the disappearance of these vapors (*On the Failure of Oracles*). The recent studies have shown that intoxicating vapors, including in particular ethylene, do emerge from fault lines in the rock formations of the Delphi area and, most importantly, that there was one such fault *directly* beneath the *adyton* of Apollo's temple.[16] Plutarch's claims, long dismissed by modern scholars, are proving to be the most likely physical explanation of the Pythia's "inspiration."

We now have the Pythia in the *adyton*, attended by priests and Hosioi, seated on the tripod, inspired, and awaiting the first question. Let us now look at the oracular session from the point of view of the enquirer, the one who has brought his question for Apollo to answer. We should imagine a long line of enquirers, stretching well down the Sacred Way from the Altar of the Chians. All the enquirers would be male. If a woman had a question for Apollo, she had to entrust it to a male representative. First in line would be the Delphians. Next would be those to whom the Delphians gave priority in return for services rendered in the past. Behind them would be the others, some with questions concerning their private lives, others as ambassadors with questions that their country was directing to the god. The place of these enquirers in line was determined by the drawing of lots. Each enquirer had to pay a fee, which we know was for one Asia Minor city-state in the early fourth century four obols ($66) for a private inquiry, seven drachmas and two obols ($733) for a state inquiry.[17] The fees are not insignificant, but Delphi's great wealth came not from them but from the precious gifts of satisfied customers. Each enquirer had with him also a goat which he would present as he approached the Altar of the Chians. A religious official would sprinkle the goat with cold water. If the goat shook the water off – as it normally would –, that was a sign that the god was willing to address the enquirer, and the goat would be sacrificed. If the goat did not shake, the god rejected the enquirer, and the enquirer and his goat would not be permitted to continue. Since the god had to give truthful – if not always clear – answers to each question, the "goat test" afforded him the opportunity to avoid those questions and enquirers he chose not to deal with.

If the enquirer passed the "goat test," he would proceed into the temple accompanied by his Delphic sponsor. Although there is much dispute about this, the enquirer as he entered the *cella* probably saw the Pythia face to face. He would already have given his question to one of the priests, and the priest, not the enquirer, would address the Pythia. The Pythia then responded, and, although there is also much dispute about the nature of her response, the best evidence is that she simply spoke Apollo's words to the enquirer in intelligible Greek.[18] Some Delphic oracles come down to us in prose, others in metrical form, the latter usually in the dactylic hexameter of epic language and style. Some modern scholars think that the Pythia spoke only prose and that the verse oracles were later reworkings of the original oracle, perhaps by poets employed by Delphi. But the Greeks of the time believed that both the prose and verse oracles were the words of the Apollo himself. The oracular consultation was then ended, and the enquirer was not allowed a follow-up question. Enquirers then went home, most of them simply remembering the god's response. Ambassadors and others could, on request, have a written copy made of the responses they received.

There have come down to us from antiquity over 600 oracles that were credited, by someone in antiquity, to Apollo Pythios of Delphi.[19] They range in date from the oracle in Homer's *Odyssey* that Agamemnon would capture Troy only after the best of the Greeks quarreled among themselves

(8.75–81), to what was reputedly the last response from Delphi, the sad reply to the emperor Julian who, in the middle of the fourth century c.e., wanted to revive the Oracle: "Tell the Emperor that the well-wrought house has fallen to the ground. Apollo no longer has even a hut, nor the prophetic laurel, nor the talking spring. Even the talking water has been quenched" (Fontenrose, Q263). Many Delphic oracles derive from poetic literature, especially Greek tragedy. A good example of those is the oracle to Oedipus, that he was fated to kill his father and marry his mother (Fontenrose, L18). Some come from the historians. Herodotus (7.139–144) reports that when the Persian invasion of their land was imminent, the Athenians inquired at Delphi and were told to abandon their land and seek the protection of the "wooden wall." The oracle concluded with the lines,

> Divine Salamis, you will destroy the children of women,
> either when Demeter is sown, or when she is gathered.

After much debate the Athenians decided that the "wooden wall" was their navy of wooden ships and that the closing reference to Salamis promised victory and not defeat. That interpretation led them to contrive a naval battle against the Persians at Salamis, and so the Athenians and Greeks won their great victory there in 480 b.c.e. Many other oracles are to be found in the official records of individual states, inscribed on stones which survive to this day. We have seen an example of this in the text that records that, on the basis of their "ancestral practices" and a Delphic oracle, the Athenian farmers dedicated to Eleusinian Demeter 1/600 of the barley and 1/1200 of the wheat they harvested.

We would like to know which of these many oracles were in fact given by Apollo at Delphi and which have been created by poets and other writers to enrich their stories. We can put most trust in those oracles which appear in inscriptions and other writings close to the time at which the oracle was given.[20] In 402, for example, the Athenian Xenophon was invited to join the expedition of Cyrus the Younger against the King of Persia. Xenophon went to Delphi and asked Apollo "to which god he should sacrifice and pray to make his intended journey successfully, to fare well, and to return in safety." The Oracle told him what gods to sacrifice to, including Zeus Basileus (King), and Xenophon made the sacrifices and went on the expedition (*Anabasis* 3.1.5–8). Here a trustworthy historical source describes an oracular consultation that he himself participated in, and we can take the oracle he received to be genuine. There are 75 such oracles in the collection of Delphic oracles, and 56 of these concern religious matters, including the foundations of new cults, sacrifices and offerings that should be made, and the establishment or violation of religious laws

Private inquiries to Oracle of Zeus Naios at Dodona, recorded on lead tablets found at the sanctuary:

Gods. May I have good fortune.
Evandros and his wife consult Zeus Naios and Dione. To whom of the gods or heroes or divinities should they pray and sacrifice so that they themselves and their household may fare better both now and for all time? (#1)

God. Gerioton asks Zeus about a wife. Is it better for him to take one? (#6)

Heraclides asks Zeus and Dione for good fortune. He asks the god about a family. Will he have one from his current wife Aigle? (#7)

Lysanias asks Zeus Naios and Dione whether or not the baby with whom Annula is pregnant is from him. (#11)

Nicocrateia asks to which god she should sacrifice in order to fare better and to stop her disease. (#15)

Although private enquiries such as these were no doubt made at all Greek oracles, extensive records of them survive only from the Oracle of Zeus at Dodona.

From H.W. Parke, *The Oracles of Zeus* (Cambridge, MA, 1967), pp. 263–73

The greatest, finest, and first matters of legislation are not our business but that of Apollo at Delphi: the establishment of sanctuaries, sacrifices, and the other services of the gods and heroes. Also the tombs of the dead and what services it is necessary to provide to the dead so that they are appeased. We do not understand these things, and as we found a city we will trust no one else, if we are wise, nor will we use any other expert than our ancestral one. Apollo, seated at the navel of the earth, as the ancestral expert gives guidance about such things to all men.

Socrates, in Plato's *Republic* 4.427b–c

and practices. Six deal with relations between states in international affairs, two with the foundation of new cities, three with secular laws, and four with war. A common formula for these inquiries was, "Is it better to do X?" Many times the god was asked to choose between alternatives the enquirer proposed. It would appear from this that the "real" Delphic Oracle dealt primarily with religious questions – for example, whether to found a new cult of Athena and Ares in Attica (Fontenrose, H27), or whether to rent out some sacred land in Eleusis (H21), or what offerings to make to Demeter of Eleusis (H9). For many Greeks Delphi was the authority to consult on religious questions of cult foundation, sacred laws, and sacrileges that could not be settled locally. The Oracle was not, in any clear sense, predicting the future. It was telling the enquirers unambiguously that it was "better," or perhaps "not better" to do what they were planning to do in religious matters. A positive response would indicate that their plans were acceptable to the gods, and this would be reassuring to a society which lacked, locally, any divinely inspired religious authority.

In addition to these clearly "historical" oracles there are 268 oracles which are recorded by historians or inscriptions many years, sometimes centuries, after they were purportedly given at Delphi. The "wooden wall" oracle is an excellent example. Herodotus gives the first account of it, fifty years after he says the Athenians received it. These are termed "quasi-historical" oracles, and, unlike the "historical" oracles, the plurality (39.4%) concern plagues, famines, and wars. They also treat subjects found in historical oracles, including the founding of cities and colonies, omens, and religious matters. The Greeks believed many of these "quasi-historical" oracles to be genuine, such as that of the "wooden wall," but each one must be individually studied to determine the likelihood that it was genuine. The remaining Delphic oracles fall either into the "legendary class" – occurring in stories of the remote past – or into the "fictional" class – clearly invented by poets and other writers to develop their stories. It is unlikely that many of the "legendary" or "fictional" oracles are genuine, that is actually issued by Delphi, but they offer much of interest. We have seen two such "legendary" oracles in the cult myths of Icarius and Artemis Brauronia (Chapter III, Myths #4 and 5), and they were most likely believed "genuine" by the worshipers in those cults. Many of the "fictional" oracles, like that given to Oedipus, occur in the great works of Greek literature and capture our imagination. If we wish, however, to understand the role of the Delphic Oracle in the life of fifth-century Greeks, we do best to concentrate on the "historical oracles" and then, with more caution, to look to the "quasi-historical" ones. There we find that the Oracle assisted primarily with difficult religious questions in the founding of cults of gods and heroes, in the establishment of religious laws, in the expiation of religious crimes, and, to a lesser extent, in the sending out of colonies and in the undertaking of war. In most of these the Oracle did not simply *tell* the enquirers what to do, but told them if "it was better to do or not to do" what they were already planning to do. The historical Oracle offered more guidance than instruction, and a positive response from Delphi significantly increased the confidence of the enquirers in the undertaking they were proposing. It is easy for some today to dismiss the Delphic Oracle as a contrivance of charlatans to deceive the naive, but, in terms of the religion of its time, we must remember that virtually all Greeks and many non-Greeks put their trust in the Oracle. Even Plato, much of whose work was devoted to exposing falsehoods and charlatans, entrusted to Delphi many of the religious decisions to be made for the states he created in the *Republic* and the *Laws*.

Zeus Olympios of Olympia

At Delphi every four years in August a major panhellenic festival, the Pythian Games, was held for Apollo. Delphic myth told that the Games were celebrated to commemorate the death of Python, the dragon that Apollo slew to gain control over Delphi. According to local tradition, there was originally just one contest, the singing of a hymn which probably related how Apollo killed the Python. By the fifth century many other contests had been added, including athletic events in the stadium, equestrian events in the hippodrome, and more musical contests. The prizes for the

Figure IV.22 The head of Zeus Olympios on a silver *stater* (two-drachma coin, about $200), about 421–370 B.C.E., from Elis, the city-state that controlled Olympia. The head is probably modeled on that of Phidias' statue of Zeus at Olympia. Courtesy of the British Museum, inv. no. BMC Elis 54.

winners were crowns of laurel leaves, Apollo's favored plant. Most Greek city-states would have had local games in honor of some of their deities, but the Pythian Games were one of four sets of games termed by the Greeks *stephanitic*, that is, internationally recognized games awarding "crowns" (*stephanoi* in Greek). At the sanctuary of Poseidon of Isthmia, whom we came to know in Chapter II, stephanitic games were also held, biennially in April or May, and there chariot and horse races were featured. The prizes were crowns of dry celery leaves. The Nemean Games were held also biennially, in August, in the sanctuary of Zeus Nemeios of Nemea in the central Peloponnesus, and the prizes there were crowns of fresh celery leaves. Although these games were held in the sanctuaries of Apollo, Poseidon, and Zeus, the foundation myth of each associates it closely with the death of a figure important in the Olympian's cult: at Delphi, with the death of the Python; at Isthmia with the death of Palaemon, a local hero; and at Nemea with the death of the heroized boy Opheltes. These games appear in their foundation myths to have originally been funeral games that were then repeated, quadrennially or biennially, in the decedents' honor. Achilles' funeral games for his slain companion Patroclus in Book 23 of the *Iliad* would serve, on the human level, as a parallel to such games. As time passed, the stephanitic games became more identified with the god, with Apollo at Delphi, Poseidon at Isthmia, and Zeus at Nemea, and the ties with the local hero survived

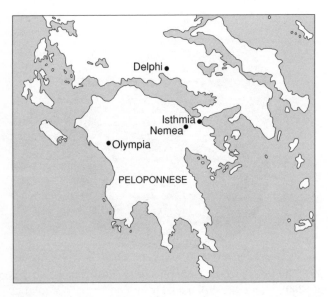

Map IV.4   Map of the four sites of the international stephanitic games of the Classical Period.

only in myth or in some rituals directed to the hero during the celebrations of the games.

The Games of Zeus of Olympia, the Olympic Games, were the most famous and prestigious of the four stephanitic "game" festivals. According to the ancient tradition (that is just now being questioned from archaeological finds), they were founded in 776 B.C.E. That was the first year of the first Olympiad, the most widely known fixed date in Greek history. This was the date from which Greeks, when writing for an international audience, dated subsequent events. The Olympic Games were, however, just one feature of Zeus' cult at Olympia, and we will return to them after we have surveyed the sanctuary and cult context in which they were held.

Olympia lay in a lush and wooded valley between the Alpheius and Cladeius rivers on the western coast of the Peloponnesus. Like Delphi it was not a city-state but a religious sanctuary. The city-state Elis claimed ownership of the sanctuary and closely controlled it, providing all the priests and officials. In the middle of the site was the *temenos* of Zeus Olympios, called the Altis (Grove), a rough square approximately 220 meters on a side. The Altis was flanked on the north by treasury buildings and on the east by the famous Stadium, running roughly perpendicular to the Altis for 192 meters. By the second century B.C.E. the Altis was bounded on the

Figure IV.23 Photograph of British Museum model of Olympia as it would have appeared about 100 B.C.E. The fifth-century Temple of Zeus stands out in the upper right and, in the upper center, the Temple of Hera. In front of the Temple of Hera are athletic training facilities. Courtesy of the Trustees of the British Museum.

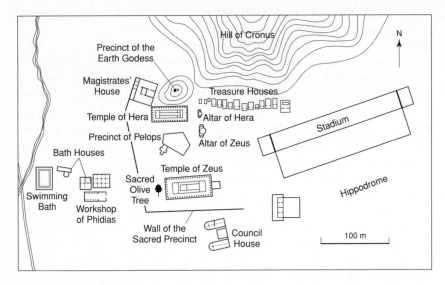

Figure IV.24   Plan of fifth-century B.C.E. sanctuary of Zeus at Olympia.

west by training facilities – a palaestra for wrestling and a gymnasium for other athletic events. Overlooking it all, from the north, was the Hill and sanctuary of Cronus, Zeus' father. Of the many, many buildings and monuments at Olympia, we begin with the monumental Altar, Temple, and Statue of Zeus Olympios.

As our guide here and for all of Olympia we have Pausanias, a second-century C.E. visitor to Olympia, who in Books 5.7–6.21 of his *Description of Greece* gave a remarkably full and vivid description of the sanctuary from what he saw, read, and heard from guides.[21] Here he describes the great Altar of Zeus:

> The Altar of Zeus Olympios is about equally distant from the Pelopion and the sanctuary of Hera, and it is in front of both. It has been made from the ash of the thighs of the victims sacrificed to Zeus. The first level of the Altar has a circumference of 38.1 meters; the circumference of the second level is 9.7 meters. The total height of the Altar reaches 6.7 meters. They sacrifice the victims on the lower level, but they carry the thigh pieces up to the highest part and burn them there. The steps that lead up to the first level from each side are made of stone, but those leading from there to the second level are made, like the Altar itself, of ashes. Women and girls, when they are not excluded from Olympia, may ascend to the first level, but only men may climb to the second level. Even when the festival is not being celebrated, sacrifice is offered to Zeus by private individuals and also daily by the Eleans. Every year the soothsayers, keeping carefully to the nineteenth

Figure IV.25 One possible reconstruction of the Altar of Zeus at Olympia. As described by Pausanias, it was 6.7 m. high, 38.1 m. in circumference at its base, and 9.7 m. in circumference at its second level. The upper level was made from the ash of burnt sacrifices to Zeus. With permission, from J. Swaddling, *The Ancient Olympic Games*, 1999, p. 16.

day of the month Elaphius, bring ash from the Town Hall. They then apply this as a paste to the Altar. The paste may be made only with the water of the Alpheius River, and for this reason the Alpheius is thought to be the dearest of the rivers to Zeus Olympios.

(Pausanias 5.13.8–11, abbreviated and paraphrased)

Matching the monumentality of the Altar was Zeus' Temple and the Statue it housed. The great Doric Temple of Zeus, one of the largest of its time in Greece, was completed before 456 B.C.E. The marble sculpture of the east pediment, the front of the Temple, represented preparations for the chariot race between Pelops and Oenomaus, with Zeus standing in the center between the two contestants. Later we will consider the significance of this in terms of the relationship of Zeus and Pelops at Olympia and the founding of the Olympic Games. The west pediment portrayed a battle of the Lapiths and Centaurs at the wedding of the Thessalian prince Pirithous, a son of Zeus. It was a battle scene of the type we saw on the Temple of Poseidon Soter at Sunium in Chapter I, and it represents the victory of order and good (the Lapiths) over disorder and evil (the Centaurs). On metopes in the interior of the Temple were represented twelve labors of Heracles, each a victory of Zeus' son.

Figure IV.26 Photograph of the Temple of Zeus in the British Museum model of Olympia. The temple was completed in 456 B.C.E. and housed Phidias' gold and ivory statue of Zeus Olympios. Note the dedications of statues in the area. Courtesy of the Trustees of the British Museum.

In the *cella* of the Temple, facing east, was the Statue of Zeus Olympios, which came to be known as one of the seven wonders of the ancient world. He was seated on an ivory and ebony throne richly adorned with gold and gems. Zeus Olympios was sculpted by Phidias, the sculptor of the Athena Parthenos in Athens, and like her he was made of gold and ivory, with the ivory for exposed flesh and gold for the robes. He wore a gold crown of olive leaves, and held, as did Athena Parthenos, a gold and ivory statue of a Nike (Victory) in his right hand. In his other hand, however, he held not a spear as Athena did but a scepter topped by an eagle – the scepter a symbol of his rule as king of the gods, the eagle the bird sacred to him. The whole composition, including the pedestal, the throne, and Zeus himself, rose probably 12 meters high, and it was said in antiquity that if Zeus had risen from his throne, he would have knocked the roof off from his Temple.

The stately, seated Zeus, the scepter, and the monumentality of the Statue, Temple, and Altar all strongly suggest *power*, and those expressions of power were appropriate to the king of the gods. We will want, however,

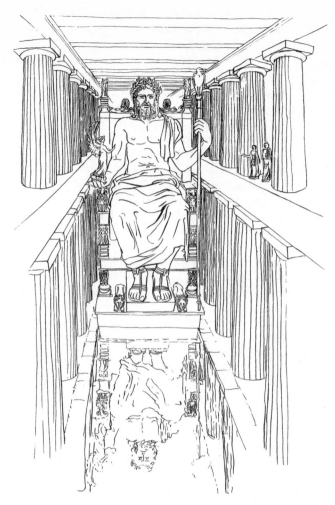

Figure IV.27   Drawing of Phidias' gold and ivory statue of Zeus Olympios in his temple. The pedestal and statue together were probably about 12 m. high. In front of the statue was a reflecting pool. Zeus holds in his left hand a scepter surmounted by an eagle, in his right hand a winged Nike (Victory). His crown is of gold olive leaves. With permission, from J. Swaddling, *The Ancient Olympic Games*, 1999, p. 18.

to define more clearly which Zeus this Zeus Olympios was. That is, what did Zeus with the epithet Olympios provide for his worshipers? Zeus was, like all Olympians, worshiped under many different aspects in the Greek world and even at Olympia itself. We can most fully appreciate this and in addition see the divine community associated with Zeus Olympios from Pausanias' description of the altars in the Altis:

> Let us now treat all the altars in Olympia, and I will describe them in the order in which Eleans customarily sacrifice on them. They sacrifice to Hestia (Hearth) first and second to Zeus Olympios on the altar inside the Temple. Third they sacrifice, on a shared altar, to Zeus Laoitas (Of the People?) and Poseidon Laoitas. Fourth they sacrifice to Artemis, fifth to Athena Leitis (Gatherer of Booty), and sixth to Athena Ergane (Of Crafts). The descendants of Phidias, called the "cleansers," have received from the Eleans the privilege of cleaning off the dirt that settles on the Statue of Zeus, and they sacrifice to Athena Ergane before they begin to polish the Statue. Near the Temple there is another altar of Athena and next to it a square altar of Artemis. Then there is one altar on which they sacrifice to Alpheius and Artemis together. Not far from that is another altar of Alpheius and next to it one of Zeus Areios (Of War). The Eleans say that Oenomaus used to sacrifice to Zeus Areios on this altar whenever he was about to begin a chariot race with one of the suitors of Hippodamia. After this there is an altar of Heracles Parastates (Attendant),[22] and there are also altars of the brothers of Heracles. Two altars stand at the place where are the foundations of the house of Oenomaus: one is of Zeus Herkeios (Of the Courtyard), which Oenomaus appears to have built himself, and the other of Zeus Keraunios (Of the Thunderbolt) which I believe was built later, after the thunderbolt had struck the house of Oenomaus.[23] The Great Altar I have already described. It belongs to Zeus Olympios. Near it is an altar of the Unknown Gods, and after this an altar of Zeus Katharsios (Purifier), and one of Nike (Victory), and another of Zeus Chthonios. There are also altars of all the gods there as well as one of Hera Olympia. It, like the Great Altar, is made of ash. After this there is a shared altar of Apollo and Hermes because the Greeks have a story that Hermes invented the lyre and Apollo invented the lute. Next there are altars of Homonoia (Concord), Athena, and the Mother of the Gods. Close to the entrance of the Stadium there are two altars, one of Hermes Agonios (Of Competitions) and one of Kairos (Opportunity). In a hymn, Ion of Chios makes Kairos the youngest child of Zeus. Near the treasury of the Sicyonians there is an altar of Heracles. At the sanctuary of Ge (Earth) there is an altar of her, and it, too, is made of ashes. At a place called the Stomion (Mouth) an altar for Themis (Right) has been built. Also near the Great Altar is an altar of Zeus Katabaites (Descender) surrounded by a fence. By the *temenos* of Pelops is a shared altar of Dionysus and the Charites (Graces), and between it and the Pelopion are altars of the Muses and the Nymphs.
>
> (Pausanias 5.14.4–10, abbreviated and paraphrased)

Pausanias adds to this list an altar of all the gods in Phidias' workshop and various other altars of Aphrodite, the Horae (Seasons), the Nymphs, Artemis

Agoraia (Of the Market Place), Despoinae (Mistresses), Zeus Agoraios, Apollo Pythios, Dionysus, the Moirae (Fates), Hermes, Zeus Hypsistos (Highest), of the Cladeius River, Artemis Coccoca (meaning of epithet is unknown), Apollo Thermios (Of Law), and Pan. Associated with the Hippodrome for chariot races were altars of Poseidon Hippios (Of Horses), Hera Hippia, Ares Hippios, Athena Hippia, the Dioscuri, Agathe Tyche (Good Luck), Pan, Aphrodite, the Nymphs, and Zeus Moiragetes (Leader of the Fates). Before the doors of The Town Hall of the Eleans, which was in the Altis, was an altar of Artemis Agrotera (Of the Wilds), and inside it was one of Pan. There, too, was a perpetual fire, the ashes of which were applied once a year to the Great Altar. On all of these altars the Eleans each month burned incense with wheat kneaded with honey, added a sprig of olive, and poured a wine libation. They also, Pausanias says, poured libations to all their heroes and the heroes' wives. As an interesting footnote, Pausanias reports that the Eleans also sacrificed to Zeus Apomyios (Averter of Flies). According to myth, when Heracles was sacrificing at Olympia he was much bothered by flies, and so he sacrificed to Zeus Apomyios, and the flies then were turned away to the other side of the Alpheius River.

Thanks to Pausanias we have the fullest description of the altars and deities worshiped at any single Greek panhellenic sanctuary.[24] We have moved to the opposite extreme from the simple model sanctuary with one altar for one deity that we introduced in Chapter I. The deities who shared the Altis of Zeus Olympios included, foremost, members of his "family": his wife Hera; his brother Poseidon; his daughters and sons, Athena, Artemis, Apollo, Dionysus, and Heracles. For many of these gods Pausanias gives the epithet, distinguishing, for example, between Athena Ergane, Athena Leitis, and Athena Hippia. For a few he gives their founding myth or specific function known to the local people, and we should assume that each deity Pausanias lists had such a myth or role but that Pausanias chose to pass over most. The local river Alpheius, "sacred to Zeus," had two altars, one associated with Artemis who, as we saw with Artemis Brauronia of Athens, preferred rural locations near sources of water. Most of these deities were also represented on the pedestal or the throne of the great Statue of Zeus in the Temple.

The Temple and Great Altar belonged to Zeus Olympios, but around him were clustered a host of Zeuses, each with a distinct epithet and most with distinct functions. Zeus Keraunios and Katabaites alike were the Zeus of thunder and lightning, and any spot struck by lightning, like Oenomaus' house in the Altis or Semele's bedchamber in Thebes, was sacred to him. Zeus Agoraios tended the *agora* (marketplace) in many cities. Zeus Areios, like Athena Areia in rural Attica, was concerned with war. Zeus

Moiragetes at Olympia was associated with the Hippodrome, probably affecting the fortunes of the competitors. Zeus Herkeios was a protector of homes, watching over the wall (*herkos* in Greek) that surrounded the house and its courtyard. Here in the Altis he is associated with the house of Oenomaus. Zeus Katharsios refers to his role of purification, which, like Apollo, he could on occasion assume. Zeus Chthonios is the under-world aspect of Zeus, often identified with Hades himself. Last we have the wonderful Zeus Apomyios who, when duly honored with sacrifices, kept the annoying flies away from the Altis.

All these Zeuses shared the name Zeus, but, as we saw in Chapter II, each was also a distinct deity with his own epithet, function, and altar. All but Zeus Apomyios were also worshiped in many places elsewhere in Greece. We should not imagine that Zeus Olympios of Olympia – he of the monumental Temple and Great Altar – was simply identical to these other Zeuses of his sanctuary or a composite of them. Pausanias and the Eleans clearly marked Zeus Olympios out as a separate deity with his own epithet, statue, and altar. To understand better him and what he provided mankind, we must turn to the dedications made to him.

Pausanias took a special interest in the statues of Zeus at Olympia, and he claims to have described them all (5.21.1–25.1). In addition to the great Statue of Zeus in the Temple, he found forty-three others. They ranged in size from a "small" one on a pedestal to the eight-meter tall one dedicated by the Eleans themselves to celebrate their victory over the Arcadians in the 360s. Most, perhaps all, were made of bronze. A bearded and helmeted Zeus stood, appropriately, beside the seated statue of Hera in her temple. One was a statue of Zeus as a boy, two represented him without a beard, but the others were bearded, sometimes with a crown of flowers. When Pausanias tells us what Zeus held in his hands, it was sometimes a scepter, sometimes an eagle, but most commonly a thunderbolt, sometimes in both hands, sometimes with the scepter or eagle in the other hand. Eighteen of these Zeuses were imposed as fines on those who violated the rules of the games, usually by bribing their opponents to "throw" a match, and the earliest set of these was erected in 388 B.C.E. Most of the other Zeuses were erected from the spoils of victory in war. Most famous was the four and one-half meter tall bronze statue of Zeus erected by all the Greeks after their victory over the Persians. This, like its counterpart, the golden tripod dedicated at Delphi, had inscribed on it a list of the Greek states that had contributed to the Greek victory. The Spartans, too, erected a statue of Zeus, near the Temple, three and one-half meters tall, after their victory over the Messenians who had revolted from Sparta about 490 B.C.E. Even the Roman general Mummius dedicated two Zeuses from the spoils of his victories over the Greeks in 146 B.C.E.

In addition to these and other dedications from war were two Zeuses standing beside the chariots of winners in the games. To Pausanias the most "terrifying" Zeus was that erected by the Eleans in their Council Hall:

> The Zeus in the Council Hall most of all the statues of Zeus has been created to bring terror to unjust men. His epithet is Horkios (Of Oaths), and he holds a thunderbolt in each hand. It is the custom that the athletes and their fathers, brothers, and trainers stand beside this statue and swear on cut up offerings of boar's meat that they will commit no wrong against the games of the Olympia. The athletes also swear that continuously for ten months they have followed exactly the regimen for training. Those who select the boys (for the boys' competitions) or the foals from the horses swear an oath that they made their decisions justly and without bribes, and that they will keep secret all matters relating to those who were selected or rejected. . . . Before the feet of Zeus Horkios is a bronze plaque, and on it elegiac verses are inscribed, verses which are intended to frighten those committing perjury.
>
> (Pausanias 5.24.9–11)

Another major group of dedications also concerned victory in wars. The Eleans, in fact, built the great Temple and Statue of Zeus from the spoils they took in their victory over their neighboring city-state Pisa in about 470 B.C.E. If we limit ourselves to just a few dedications from the early years of the fifth century, we have the Zeus that the Greeks dedicated from the Persian Wars and a helmet taken from the enemy in those wars. Miltiades, the Athenian commander at Marathon in 490 B.C.E., dedicated another helmet, perhaps the one he wore at the battle. There was also a bronze helmet commemorating the victory of Hieron, tyrant of Syracuse, over the Etruscans in Italy in 474 B.C.E. Such dedications of bronze and iron weapons and armor, usually taken as spoils in battle, are the most common fifth-century dedications found in the excavations at Olympia. The third large group of dedications was statues of kings, tyrants, and rulers from throughout the Greek and later Roman world. Such "dynastic" statues became common only in the fourth century and later, but even in the fifth century there were statues of Hieron, tyrant of Syracuse, a multiple victor and patron of Olympia. Pausanias saw statues and monuments of Alexander the Great, his father Philip II, and his successors Ptolemy I, Antigonus I and his son Demetrius, and Seleucus, and of the Roman emperors Augustus, Trajan, and Hadrian, and a host of rulers of lesser renown.

All these dedications reflect the two aspects of Zeus Olympios we saw in his great Statue in the Temple: victory and the power of kingship. The magisterial Zeus held the scepter of royal power, and human non-democratic "rulers" obviously turned to him. In Athens, too, the "kingly" side of Zeus Olympios comes to the fore. The tyrant Pisistratus began construction on Zeus' monumental temple, the Olympieion, in the middle of the sixth century. When the democracy was restored in 508/7, the project was abandoned, and centuries passed before the non-Athenian monarch Antiochus IV of Syria (174 B.C.E.) took it up and the Roman Emperor Hadrian (132 C.E.) finished it. It was a monument of tyrants, kings, and emperors, and democratic Athenians wanted nothing to do with it.

Victory in athletic competitions and in war both brought dedications to Zeus, and Zeus Olympios himself was surrounded by symbols of "victory." He held in his right hand a statue of Nike, four statuettes of Nikae stood at the feet of his throne, and two more were at the base of the pedestal supporting his throne. The east pediment of his Temple represented a chariot competition, and at its apex stood a gilded Nike. Beneath that Nike was affixed a gold shield which the Spartans dedicated from their victory over the Argives, Athenians, and Ionians in the battle of Tanagra

Figure IV.28   A bronze votive statuette, 22.6 cm. high, of Zeus hurling the thunderbolt. It was found at Olympia and now is in the Olympia Museum. Courtesy of the Deutsches Archäologisches Institut, Athens, neg. no. Ol 5615.

in 457 B.C.E. Many of the Zeuses described by Pausanias and many of the bronze statuettes of Zeus found in the archaeological excavations wield the thunderbolt, sometimes in both hands. Zeus' thunderbolt is often taken to be an indication of his original function, that of the sky and weather god, but at Olympia, I think, it has become more, in association with his scepter, a symbol of power – the most awe-inspiring display of raw power known to the Greeks. Zeus elsewhere was certainly worshiped as the sky/weather god, especially on mountain tops, but at Olympia that was not foremost. There Zeus Olympios wielded power, supported powerful kings, tyrants, and monarchs, and gave victory in both war and his own Games.

According to Pausanias (5.4.5–6 and 5.7.6–8.6), some experts at Elis traced the first games at Olympia back to the times of Zeus' father Cronus and saw them as a celebration of Zeus' overthrow of his father. In these first games the gods Apollo, Hermes, and Ares were the competitors. The games were then refounded fifty years after the great flood in the time of Deucalion and were held by a succession of kings, among them Pelops and Heracles. They were again renewed, in 776 B.C.E., by Iphitus, king of Elis. At the time all Greece was suffering from war and plague, and Iphitus went to Delphi to ask how these evils might be brought to an end. Apollo bid him and the Eleans to refound the Olympic Games, to declare a sacred truce for the Games, and to sacrifice to Heracles. This, in the Elean tradition, was the beginning of the succession of Olympic Games that was to last until they were abolished by the Christian emperor Theodosius in 393 C.E. The poet Pindar, however, offers an alternative version to the complicated Elean tradition (*Olympian Ode* 10.24–77). He has Heracles himself consecrate the Altis to his father Zeus and found the Games at the "ancient" tomb of Pelops. In another poem (*Olympian Ode* 1.67–88) Pindar seems to offer a foundation myth for the chariot races at the Games, when he describes Pelops' victory in the chariot race over Oenomaus to win Oenomaus' daughter Hippodamia and kingdom. This is, of course, the chariot race featured on the east pediment of Zeus' Temple, and it brings together a number of Olympian themes, including the chariot race, Pelops, the succession of Elean kingship at Olympia, and Zeus' oversight of the whole event. By his victory over Oenomaus Pelops succeeded to the kingship of Elis. He married Hippodamia, and their sons eventually ruled throughout the peninsula, which, appropriately, came to be named "the Island of Pelops," that is, the Peloponnesus. The Eleans could thus view their Pelops as not just a local hero but as a hero significant for all Greeks in the Peloponnesus.

Pelops' role in the games, whether as one who once held them, or as one who initiated the chariot races, or as one at whose tomb they were originally held, is reflected in cult. Nearly in the center of the Altis,

Figure IV.29 Photograph of British Museum model of Olympia, showing, in right center, the Temple of Hera. To the left of it is the irregularly shaped *heroön* of Pelops. Below the Temple of Hera is the smaller Temple of Rhea, Zeus' mother. Note the treasuries lined up in the lower right. Courtesy of the Trustees of the British Museum.

halfway between Zeus' and Hera's temples, he had a large *heroön*, the Pelopion. The Stadium, before the sanctuary was reorganized and expanded, began near his *heroön*. Each year the Eleans sacrificed a black ram to him as a holocaust, and he presumably received an offering at each celebration of the Olympic Games. He, as a hero, stood to Zeus in much the way that Erechtheus stood to Athena in Athens, or Palaemon to Poseidon at Isthmia, or Opheltes to Zeus at Nemea. In each case it is possible that the games were originally in the hero's honor, probably as funeral games, but as the years passed the glory of the games fell more to the Olympian deity.

According to Olympian tradition as described by Pausanias (5.8.6–9.3), the Games of 776 B.C.E. had just one event, a footrace the 192 meter length of the Stadium. The contestants ran barefoot and naked, and throughout the history of the Games this remained the most prestigious event. In 724 was added the double race, out and back in the Stadium, and in 720 the "long" race, twenty lengths (3.77 kilometers) of the Stadium. The pentathlon

Figure IV.30　An early fifth-century B.C.E. bronze votive statuette (10.2 cm. high) of a runner at the starting line of an Olympic race. On his right thigh is inscribed, "I belong to Zeus." Found at Olympia and now in the Olympia Museum. Courtesy of the Deutsches Archäologisches Institut, Athens, neg. no. Emil, Olympia 811.

(running, long jump, the javelin and discus throws, and wrestling) and wrestling were introduced in 708, boxing in 688. The first four-horse chariot race was held in 680, and the *pancration* (a brutal combination of boxing and wrestling) and a horserace in 648. In 632 the first events for boys were added, running and wrestling. Boxing for boys was first held in 616, a race in armor for men in 520, and a two-horse chariot race in 408. Some events were also introduced but quickly dropped in these times and, later, in the Hellenistic and Roman periods, various other events were added. In the Classical period at Olympia, as contrasted to Delphi and Athens, there were only athletic and equestrian contests, none of music and poetry. Heralds and trumpeters were regular features of the games, however, and in 396 a competition was introduced for them.

Figure IV.31   A depiction of a *pancration* contest on a black-figure vase of the sixth century B.C.E. The *pancratist* on top holds his opponent by the throat, and the opponent is reaching to tap the other man's shoulder and thereby concede defeat. The judge's whip appears from the right. Courtesy of the Metropolitan Museum of Art, Rogers Fund, 1906, inv. no. 06.021.49.

We can imagine a typical fifth-century celebration of the Games. It was August in Olympia, hot and sometimes humid in the low-lying valley. The flies, at least, had been driven off by Zeus Apomyios. Thousands of spectators, among them many celebrities of the Greek world, camped in tents in a meadow adjoining the sanctuary. Unmarried girls might have been there too, but not married women. With the exception of a few priestesses, they were excluded from watching the competitions. The spectators and competitors had arrived in Olympia under the sacred truce proclaimed throughout Greece that forbade war with the host country and guaranteed competitors and visitors safe passage to and from Olympia. All about, too, were the Olympic officials, athletes, trainers, horses, chariots, and their sponsors. The Elean *agonothetai* (Producers of the Games) were lay officials presiding over the games. There were only two in the fifth century, but in the fourth century they were increased to nine or ten and then called the

Hellanodikai, the "Judges of the Greeks." The *agonothetai*, the judges, and all the competitors had sworn the oath before the fearsome, thunderbolt-wielding Zeus Horkios in the Council House. In 472 B.C.E. the program of the festival was remodeled to its final form, and the Games began with the pentathlon and horse races. Then came the day of sacrifice, with the priest of Zeus Olympios and his attendants sacrificing 100 bulls in the morning at the Great Altar. There may have been some events in the afternoon, and in the evening a great feast was held. The following three days were devoted to the remaining events. The festival was closed with sacrifices and a celebratory banquet for all the Olympic victors and officials. Amidst the competitions, which were keenly watched, there were many diversions, among them hawkers selling their wares and professional orators giving demonstration speeches. We are told that the historian Herodotus read a portion of his *Histories* on the back porch of the Temple of Zeus during the festival. One listener in the audience, reputedly, was Thucydides.

Competitors had to be legitimate sons of free Greek parents, without a criminal record, and official citizens of their cities. Herodotus in his *Histories* (8.144.2) has the Athenians define "being Greek" as having the same blood and language, common sanctuaries of the gods and sacrifices, and similar customs. Olympia and the festival of Olympian Zeus are the prime example of a common sanctuary and sacrifice that contributed to making Greeks Greek, and this rule of participation kept the festival Greek. The designation of being a Greek was much prized in the Classical period, and Alexander I, king of Macedon, sought and received this from Olympic officials in 476. His descendants Philip II and Alexander (III) the Great sponsored chariot teams and erected elaborate dedications at Olympia. Already in the fifth century many of the competitors in the athletic events were professionals, devoting their lives to training for the stephanitic games. Kings, tyrants, and aristocrats sponsored chariot teams, and if their team won, they, not their charioteers, were declared the victors. The Games, like war, were about winning, and only the winners received prizes. The most prestigious prize was, of course, the traditional crown of olive leaves, taken from a sacred olive tree in the Altis. Beginning in 544 B.C.E. it became the regular practice for victors, their families, or their city-states to commemorate victories in the games with a statue of the victor himself, his race horses, or his chariot. Pausanias (6.1–18) selects only what he considered the more famous athletes and more noteworthy statues that he saw in the Altis. He describes 194 such statues, and often gives the event won, the father and city-state of the victor, victories the victor had won at other stephanitic games, and other miscellaneous information that he had read on the inscriptions on the statues. A victor might also commission a poet to write an *epinician* (victory) ode celebrating his victory and family, and we have from Pindar a series of such odes for victors at the Olympic, Pythian, Isthmian, and Nemean games. By his victory the victor also brought glory to his city, and some cities gave their victors large cash rewards. According to one report, the lawgiver Solon in 594 established at Athens that victors in the Olympic games receive fifty drachmas ($5,000), but only ten drachmas ($1,000) for a victory in the Isthmian Games. Athens and some other city-states also gave their Olympic victors free dining privileges in the state dining room for life. In the eyes of many Greeks, despite occasional criticisms from philosophers, a victory at the Olympic Games was the pinnacle of human accomplishment.

A few deserters from Arcadia came to the Persians, in need of food and wanting to be part of the action. The Persians took them to the king and asked what the Greeks were now doing. . . . The Arcadians said the Greeks were holding the Olympic festival and were watching athletic and equestrian contests. The Persian then asked what prize they were competing for. And the Arcadians said the prize given was a wreath of olive. At this point Tritantaechmes, the son of Artabanus (and a Persian general), expressed a very noble opinion but one for which he incurred a charge of cowardice from the king. For when he heard that the prize was a wreath and not money, he could not keep silent and said for all to hear, "Alas, Mardonius, against what kind of men did you lead us to fight, men who compete not for money but for virtue?"

> Conversation among Persians, before battle of Thermopylae
> in 480 B.C.E. (Herodotus, *Histories* 8.26)

My songs, lords of the lyre,
which of the gods, what hero, what mortal shall we celebrate?
Zeus has Pisa; but Herakles founded the Olympiad
out of spoils of his warfare;
but Theron, for his victory with chariot-four, is the man
we must sing now, him of the kind regard to strangers,
the tower Akragantine,
choice bud of a high line guarding the city.

> Opening lines of Pindar, *Olympian Ode* 2, praising Olympic victory
> of Theron of Acragas in Sicily in 476 B.C.E. (Lattimore translation)

The quadrennial Olympic festival, with its sacred truce, games, and honoring of Zeus Olympios, was the premier expression of panhellenism among the always independent-minded and often contentious Greek city-states. This feature of the Olympic festival is well summarized by the orator Isocrates in a speech he wrote for the Games of 380 B.C.E.:

> "We rightly praise those who first established the panhellenic meetings at which we Greeks make a truce with each other, dissolve our existing enmities, and come together, and sharing in prayers and sacrifices remember the ties of kinship that unite us and come to be better disposed towards one another for the future, renewing old friendships and making new ones."
>
> (Panegyricus 43)

NOTES

1. The evidence is difficult to interpret, but some modern scholars claim that the *heroön* of Erechtheus was a separate building close to the Erechtheum. If this is so, then that should properly be called the Erechtheum, and the building we call the Erechtheum should be called the Temple of Athena. For a concise statement of the problems and various theories and a defense of the position I have taken, see Hurwit, *The Athenian Acropolis*, pp. 200–2.
2. At the Greater Panathenaea each fifth year Athena may have been presented with a second, much larger *peplos*. This would also have been decorated with scenes of the battle of the gods and Giants and may have served as a tapestry for the temple's interior walls.
3. Some would put the *pannychis* in the night following the sacrifices, not in the night preceding them.
4. There is no explicit evidence for competitions at the annual Panathenaea, and some scholars would have such competitions only at the quadrennial Greater Panathenaea. Several days were, however, kept open on the Athenian calendar before and after Hekatombaion 28 *every* year, not just in the years of the Greater Panathenaea, and I presume these were kept open for "local" competitions.
5. This and the following translations of the *Hymn to Demeter* are from A.N. Athanassakis, *The Homeric Hymns* (Baltimore, 1976).
6. On the women's festival of the Thesmophoria, see Chapter V, pp. 144–5.
7. Myth #4 in Chapter III.
8. Lesser Mysteries were held at the sanctuary of the Mother in Agrae, about one kilometer southwest of Athens, in the month Anthesterion, seven months before the Mysteries at Eleusis. Initiation into these Lesser Mysteries was required before initiation at Eleusis. The identity of the Mother is uncertain. It may have been Mother Earth, or Rhea, mother of the gods, or perhaps even Demeter, as mother of Kore.
9. For other events of the Mysteries and for differing views on which days various events occurred, see Mikalson, *The Sacred and Civil Calendar of the Athenian Year* (Princeton, 1976), pp. 54–60, 65 and, under Further Reading, Mylonas (1961) and Clinton (1988 and 1992).

10. For an attempt to reconstruct all of the events and secret rituals of the Mysteries at Eleusis, see Clinton, 1992, 84–95, under **Further Reading**.

11. The "child" was probably not Demophon, despite his prominence in the *Hymn*. Demophon was probably a local Eleusinian hero whose cult featured annual mock war games by boys as described in the *Hymn*, lines 263–7.

12. This and the following translations from the *Hymn to Apollo* are from Athanassakis, 1976.

13. In addition to the priests (*hiereis*) there is also a record at Delphi of a *prophetes* (prophet). It is uncertain whether the term indicates a separate official with special duties or is simply another name for the priests.

14. Diodorus Siculus 16.26.6.

15. Late reports also indicate that in the *adyton* was a "tomb" of Dionysus.

16. J.Z. de Boer and J.H. Hale, "Was She Really Stoned?" *Archaeological Odyssey*, vol. 5, no. 6 (2002), 47–53 and J.Z. de Boer, J.R. Hale, and J. Chanton, "New Evidence for the Geological Origins of the Ancient Delphic Oracle," *Geology* 29 (2001), 707–10.

17. G. Rougemont, *Corpus des Inscriptions de Delphes*, vol. 1, #8.

18. There is also some evidence, though disputed, that the Pythia responded to some inquiries by the drawing of lots, perhaps from the tripod. Such a method would be effective and efficient when the question was posed in the form of alternative actions.

19. For the collection of these, see Parke and Wormell, 1956. For a catalogue of them, classed by type, subject, and genuineness, see Fontenrose, 1978.

20. In what follows I use the categories of oracles and statistics concerning them of Fontenrose, 1978.

21. On the high quality and accuracy of Pausanias' descriptions, and especially those of Olympia, see Habicht (1998), esp. 32 and 149–51.

22. For his importance at Olympia, see Pausanias 5.8.1.

23. On the house of Oenomaus, see Pausanias 5.20.6–7.

24. Pausanias visited Olympia in the second century C.E., but most of the altars he saw there were probably standing already in the fifth century B.C.E.

FURTHER READING

Athena Polias of Athens

Hurwit, J.M., *The Athenian Acropolis* (Cambridge, UK, 1998)

Goddess and Polis, ed. J. Neils (Princeton, 1992), especially essays by Neils, "The Panathenaea: An Introduction," 13–28 and "Panathenaic Amphoras: Their Meaning, Makers, and Markets," 29–52; H.A. Shapiro, "Mousikoi Agones: Music and Poetry at the Panathenaea," 53–76; D.G. Kyle, "The Panathenaic Games: Sacred and Civic Athletics," 77–102; E.J.W. Barber, "The Peplos of Athena," 103–18; and B.S. Ridgway, "Images of Athena on the Akropolis," 119–42.

Worshipping Athena: Panathenaea & Parthenon, ed. J. Neils (Madison, 1996), especially essays by A.L. Boegehold, "Group and Single Competitions at the Panathenaia," 95–105; D.G. Kyle, "Gifts and Glory: Panathenaic and Other Greek Athletic Prizes," 106–36; Neils, "Pride, Pomp, and Circumstance: The Iconography of Procession," 177–97; E.B. Harrison, "The Web of History: A Conservative Reading of the Parthenon Frieze," 198–214; and H.A. Shapiro, "Democracy and Imperialism: The Panathenaea in the Age of Perikles," 215–25.

Tracy, S.V., "The Panathenaic Festival and Games: An Epigraphical Inquiry," *Nikephoros* 4 (1991), 133–53.

Demeter Eleusinia and the Eleusinian Mysteries

Burkert, *GR*, 285–90

Price, *RAG*, 80–1, 102–7

Zaidman and Pantel (1989), 132–40

Burkert, *Ancient Mystery Cults* (Cambridge, MA, 1987)

Camp, J.M., *The Archaeology of Athens* (New Haven, 2001), 283–9

Clinton, K.A., *Myth and Art* (Stockholm, 1992) and "Sacrifice at the Eleusinian Mysteries," pp. 69–80 in *Early Greek Cult Practice*, edd. R. Hägg, N. Marinatos, and G.C. Nordquist (Stockholm, 1988)

Mylonas, G.E., *Eleusis and the Eleusinian Mysteries* (Princeton, 1962)

Richardson, N.J., *The Homeric Hymn to Demeter* (Oxford, 1974)

Zaidman, L.B., *Le commerce des dieux*, 73–84

Dionysus Cadmeios of Thebes

Burkert, *GR*, 161–7, 237–42, 290–5

Zaidman and Pantel (1989), 198–207

Burkert, *Homo Necans* (Berkeley, 1983), 173–9 (on Agrionia)

Carpenter, T., *Dionysian Imagery in Fifth-Century Athens* (Oxford, 1997)

Henrichs, A., "Changing Dionysiac Identities," 137–60, 213–36 in *Jewish and Christian Self-Definition*, vol. 3, edd. B.F. Meyer and E.P. Sanders (London, 1982) and "Greek Maenadism from Olympias to Messalina," *Harvard Studies in Classical Philology* 82 (1978), 121–60

Schachter, A., *Cults of Boiotia, Bulletin of the Institute of Classical Studies*, Supplement 38, (London, 1981–1994)

Apollo Pythios of Delphi

On oracles and divination in general:

Parker, R., "Greek States and Greeks Oracles," pp. 298–326 in *Crux, Essays Presented to G.E.M. de Ste. Croix*, edd. P. Cartledge and F.D. Harvey (London, 1985)

Zaidman, L.B., *Le commerce des dieux*, 57–71

On Apollo and Delphi:

Fontenrose, J., *The Delphic Oracle* (Berkeley, 1978)
Parke, H.W. and D.E.W. Wormell, *The Delphic Oracle*, 2 volumes (Oxford, 1956)
Price, S., "Delphi and Divination," pp. 128–54 in *Greek Religion and Society*, edd. P.E. Easterling and J.V. Muir (Cambridge, UK, 1985)
Roux, G., *Delphes: son oracle et ses dieux* (Paris, 1976)

Zeus Olympios of Olympia

Burkert, *GR*, 125–31
Zaidman and Pantel (1989), 113–21
Habicht, C., *Pausanias' Guide to Ancient Greece* (Berkeley, 1998)
Finley, M.I. and H.W. Pleket, *The Olympic Games: The First Thousand Years* (London, 1976)
Sinn, U., *Olympia: Cult, Sport, and Ancient Festival* (Princeton, 2000)
Swaddling, J., *The Ancient Olympic Games*, second edition (Austin, 1999)
The Archaeology of the Olympics, W.J. Raschke, ed. (Madison, 1988), especially, A.E. Raubitschek, "The Panhellenic Idea and the Olympic Games," pp. 35–7; W.J. Raschke, "Images of Victory," pp. 38–54; A. Mallwitz, "Cult and Competition Locations at Olympia," pp. 79–109; H.M. Lee, "The 'First' Olympic Games of 776 B.C.," pp. 110–18; and J. Fontenrose, "The Cult of Apollo and the Games at Delphi," pp. 121–40

V

Religion in the Greek Family and Village

୮ฆ୮ฆ୮ฆ୮ฆ

In our survey of the cults of Apollo Pythios of Delphi and Zeus Olympios of Olympia we have seen the most panhellenic of Greek religious institutions. We now shift our focus to religion as it was practiced in family and village life by individuals and small groups. Panhellenic cults and festivals were open to all Greeks, but probably very few had the money or the opportunity to travel to Delphi and Olympia to participate directly in them. All Greeks, however, were engaged in the religious activities of their families and villages, and these were probably their most common and most immediate religious experiences. The settings for this aspect of Greek religion are the house, the family cemetery plot, and the village, and we will describe each as we come to it. Let us now look at the religious activities of the various members of the Greek family.

The Father

Greeks usually lived together as extended, not nuclear families, and the male line was dominant. Daughters-in-law joined the household of their husbands. The household would consist of the father, mother, their sons and their sons' wives and children, any unmarried daughters, and slaves. The father was the religious authority and priest of the family in that he made the offerings and performed the rituals that concerned the household. He as the eldest son would have inherited this role or been ceded it by his own father. Probably every day and in a special way on certain days each year he made offerings to the three deities of his home: Zeus Ktesios, Zeus Herkeios, and Apollo Agyieus.

The characteristic Greek house was one or two stories high, along three sides of an open, sometimes colonnaded rectangular courtyard. The fourth

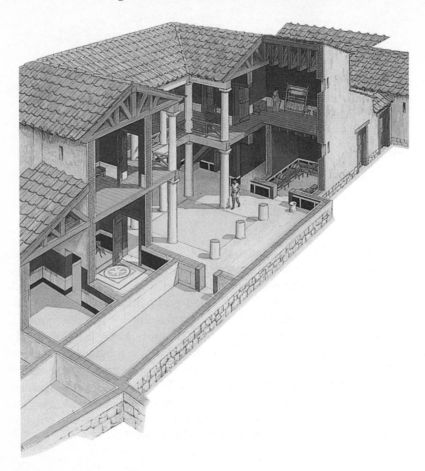

Figure V.1   A cutaway view of a two-story house near the Agora in Athens.
Watercolor by Peter Connolly. Photograph: AKG London.

side of the courtyard would be a high wall separating the house from the
street. One of the inner rooms of the house would serve as the storeroom,
and there Zeus Ktesios (Of Property) had his station. He was represented
by a two-handled jar draped in a white woolen fillet and filled with a
variety of seeds, water, and olive oil. Zeus would also have a small altar
there, and we have the following charming description by a grandson of
his grandfather's offerings at this altar in his home:

> When Ciron sacrificed to Zeus Ktesios, a sacrifice about which he was
> especially serious, he did not admit either slaves or non-family members.
> He did everything himself, but we shared in this sacrifice and joined with

him in handling and placing the sacrificial victims and in doing the other things. He prayed that the god give us health and good "property," and this was only natural because he was our grandfather.

(Isaeus 8.16)

Another more sociable Athenian invited to his honoring of Zeus Ktesios his slave mistress and a male friend, and the sacrifice was followed by libations, the burning of incense on the altar, and, finally, a dinner party, at which, unfortunately, the host and his friend were accidentally poisoned and killed by the mistress (Antiphon 1.15–18). From these and other ancient accounts Zeus Ktesios appears more the "Giver of Wealth" (*Ploutodotos*) than the "Protector of Wealth," and, to judge by his "jar" and his location in the storeroom, that "wealth" was still, in an old-fashioned way, conceived of primarily as agricultural produce.

Zeus Herkeios (Of the Fence), by contrast, was the protector of the "enclosure" of the house. His altar stood in the courtyard and he, from the inside of the house, protected it against intruders. Odysseus had such an altar in his palace on Ithaca (Homer, *Odyssey* 22.333–6), and Oenomaus, as we saw at Olympia, had this deity in his home also. Zeus Herkeios was so identified with the home that, if an Athenian wanted to know where another Athenian's home was, he could ask him, "Where is your Zeus Herkeios?"

The door of the house was protected, from the outside, by a statuette or perhaps merely a small pillar called Apollo Agyieus (Of the Street). Either he or a similar representation of Heracles stood on the street, just by the house door, and both were thought of as "Averters of Evil" (*Apotropaioi*). We do not know why Apollo was thought to assume this domestic role, but the mighty Heracles is a natural choice as a divinity to ward off any evil that might threaten the house.

We should imagine that the father of the family each day, perhaps with just a word, perhaps with a small offering, acknowledged the contribution of each of these household deities. And each deity would have one day each year for special attention. The wealth and security of the family and possessions depended upon them, and, in the Greek tradition, they must be shown proper respect.

The father would also be concerned with the religious aspects of the home's hearth.[1] From earliest times the Greeks gave special veneration to the hearth, and from it evolved a goddess, Hestia (Hearth). Hestia lacks the developed mythology of most Greek gods, but her importance to religious life was significant. When a large number of deities received offerings, she was almost always included, often, as for the Eleans at Olympia, first in line (Pausanias 5.14.4, above in Chapter IV). Zeus Herkeios seems to symbolize the family to outsiders, but Hestia does that for the family members themselves. Children, brides, and slaves were formally accepted into the family by being led to or around the hearth, often in a shower of dried fruits and nuts, a ceremony no doubt performed by the father with all the other family members present.

A Greek father's primary religious obligations were to maintain his household cults *and* to tend the tombs of his ancestors. Greek cemeteries in the fifth century characteristically did not adjoin houses nor were they set apart as special precincts as in modern times. The graves were strung alongside the roads leading out from the villages, and Greek families would commonly have their own plots along these roads. In the plot the individual graves would be marked by simple tombstones. Inscribed on the tombstone would be the name of the deceased, and, if a man, his father's name, if a woman, her husband's name. Those relatively few tombstones with more information we will discuss in connection with Greek conceptions of death and the afterlife in Chapter VII. The father no doubt had ultimate authority over the proper performance of funerals, but many of the funerary rituals were performed by the women of the family and we will treat them in our account of the Greek mother. Our concern now is rather the all important "tendance" of the family tombs, and that involved two aspects. The first is the physical care of the tombs and tombstones themselves. In the Greek tradition a person's inscribed stone tombstone was his "memorial," the most tangible and lasting remnant of his memory. That is a major reason why the Greeks made extraordinary efforts to recover and bury at home the bodies of soldiers killed in battle and sailors lost at sea. But the concerns would be much the same if a person's tombstone should be neglected, overgrown with weeds, and perhaps even lost. The memory of that person would be erased, and that was one of the great horrors for Greeks. Greek fathers were responsible for these tombs, and one of their greatest concerns was to leave behind a male heir to carry on the tradition. If no male heir were born or survived, married couples would adopt a son to maintain the household cults and tombs. The second aspect in the tendance of the family grave plot is the offerings made, one day each year, at the tombs of the family's deceased. We know little of the nature of these offerings, but they probably included adorning the tombs with garlands, making libations of milk and honey and such things, and, perhaps, a meal at the grave plot. In a sense a visit by the family to their family graves would reunite the living and dead members of the family and provide the opportunity for the living to show their respect and honor for the family's deceased members. A speaker in a courtroom oration of Isaeus (2.46, paraphrased) summarizes nicely what the lack of an heir meant to a Greek in this regard: "He lies dead and childless and nameless, so that no one gives the honor

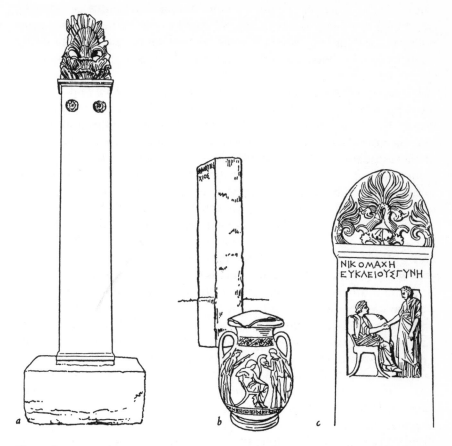

Figure V.2 (a) Athenian late fifth-century grave stele adorned with two rosettes and acanthus leaves.
(b) Athenian mid-fifth-century plain grave stele with name of deceased. It was placed over the red-figure vase used as a cremation urn.
(c) Athenian late fifth-century grave stele adorned with acanthus leaves. Relief represents common scene of a handshake in departing. The inscription reads, "Nicomache, wife of Eukleies." Courtesy of John Boardman.

of the ancestral sacrifices for him and no one performs the rites of the dead for him each year, but his honors are all taken from him."

Several prominent Athenian families traced their ancestry to distant relatives in Athens' legendary past. Those individual families who traced their origins to the same legendary ancestor were termed a *genos* (Clan), and the *genos* was named after their ancestor. The families that claimed descent from the Eumolpus we met in the Eleusinian Mysteries were called the Eumolpidae. The original ancestor, like Eumolpus, was usually worshiped as a hero. If our family belonged to one of these noble *gene*, the father and his sons would join fellow *gennetai* once a year in making offerings and perhaps having a banquet at the *heroön* of their common eponymous ancestor.

The father of our family would also have a religious role to play in the life of his village, probably a prominent role if he were a member of a noble *genos*. By villages we mean not the great cities like Athens and Thebes but the towns, some very small, scattered about the countryside. Most of the 139 demes (townships) of Athens we encountered in Chapter II were centered on such small, preexisting villages. Not all Greek cities had formed "townships," but villages existed throughout Greece and we should imagine many of the same religious activities there. As the place for our family to reside we choose the Athenian deme Erchia, a mid-size deme in the midlands of Attica with a population of about 500 male adult citizens and with perhaps 2,000–3,000 residents in all. As we saw in Chapter II, the Erchian annual calendar of religious events survives on an inscription from the fourth century B.C.E., and from it we find that the Erchians as a group had 25 days of sacrifice each year. They sacrificed in a year 59 animals, including 31 sheep, 11 goats, and 10 pigs. No cows, however. Cows were very expensive (from $4,000 to $9,000), were rarely sacrificed in deme festivals, and normally could be afforded only for the larger state festivals such as the Panathenaea. For their sacrifices the Erchians spent 547 drachmas ($54,700) each year, and the costs were probably assigned annually to five of the wealthier demesmen. The Erchian deities, as always in practiced religion, are distinguished by epithet and locale, even within Erchia. There are, for example, six Apollos: Apotropaios (Averter of Evil), Delphinios (Of Delphi), Lykeios (Of Wolves), Nymphegetes (Leader of the Nymphs), Paion (Healer), and Pythios. The father of our family may well have served as priest of one of these Apollos or perhaps of one of the seven Zeuses. Or he may have served one of the local heroes, three of whom (Epops, Leucaspis, and Menedeius) are unknown anywhere else in Greece. As the priest of a deme cult he would have sacrificed and prayed on behalf of all his fellow demesmen. He would also have attended many of the sacrifices and mini-festivals of the other deities of this small community, and he may have been one of the delegation of Erchians who in late summer, on Metageitnion 12, walked the 32 kilometers to Athens and sacrificed there, on behalf of the Erchians, to Apollo Lykeios and, on the Acropolis, to Zeus Polieus and Athena Polias and, in her sanctuary in Athens, to Demeter Eleusinia. Finally, if our family were one of the wealthier ones in Erchia, the father may have been chosen to contribute $10,940 to support the year's sacrificial program of the Erchians.

The economy of a rural deme like Erchia was based largely on grape-cultivation and farming, and both are reflected in the deme's religious activities. The men of Erchia, perhaps together with men of neighboring demes, would each fall celebrate a local *Proerosia*, a "Pre-Plowing" festival which probably involved, amidst offerings and vows, the plowing of a small tract of land sacred to Demeter. The plowing of the land was the first step in the new agricultural cycle, and it was an appropriate time for the demesmen to honor Demeter, the goddess who would watch over their new crop. After the harvest in the spring they would, as we have seen, dedicate and send to Demeter of Eleusis 1/600 of the barley and 1/1200 of the wheat they produced. Dionysus was, of course, the patron of the grape vines, and in the spring, on Anthesterion 2, when the grape vines were blossoming, the Erchians sacrificed to him at his sanctuary in Erchia a kid, at a cost of five drachmas ($500). The Erchians as a community also would participate, each year, in their own or a neighboring celebration of a Rural Dionysia. These festivals were held for Dionysus in the country-side in the winter month of Posideon. Most consisted of a procession which featured a large and prominently displayed phallus, lots of wine drinking, and a sacrifice of a billy goat to Dionysus.[2] Some Rural Dionysia in the demes were quite elaborate, with productions of tragedies and comedies like those of the great state festival of the City Dionysia. The Rural Dionysia would have been a highlight of the religious year of the villages, and even city folk came to the countryside to participate in them. We should imagine that our father would have taken his sons and perhaps even his wife and daughters to join in these Dionysiac festivities.

> When you first begin plowing,
> pray to Zeus Chthonios and holy Demeter,
> that the holy grain of Demeter be heavy when ripe.
> Hesiod, *Works and Days* 465–7

The father of a Greek family thus had a range of religious activities and obligations. They included serving as the priest for the deities who offered prosperity and security to his house and family, the tendance of the family cemetery plot and the annual offerings to kin buried there, and participation in and financial support of the cults of the many deities that saw to the interests of his village and its residents. This father would also, as a citizen of Athens, participate in several of the cults of the state, mostly centered in Athens, and these we will describe when we treat, in Chapter VI, state religion.

The Mother

The Greek woman lacked many political and legal rights taken for granted in modern western societies. In Athens she was not a "citizen" and could not vote or hold political office. In social and legal terms she was always dependent on a male "protector," either her father or her husband or, if widowed, her son. We have seen how, at marriage, she passed from the household of her father to the household of her husband. The bride would be in her middle teens, the groom in his early or middle thirties, and this age disparity would put her at a disadvantage in the relationship. Her "property" – in the form of a dowry or an inheritance – was held in trust for her by her husband or, after his death, by another male family member. The wives and daughters of middle- and upper-class Athenian citizens led a cloistered life in the home, with the responsibility for tending the stores of the house and keeping it clean, working the wool and weaving the clothes for the family, preparing the meals, and tending the children and ill of the family. In a poor family the women would perform these tasks alone and might well have field work to do in addition. In the more prosperous families the women would have slaves to share the domestic work and do the shopping but then had the additional responsibility of assigning and overseeing the work of the domestic slaves.

Given this familiar picture of the limited political rights, subordinate social position, and home-centered environment of a woman's life, one might expect the woman's role in religion to be limited to her family and home.

A woman with whom an adulterer is caught is not permitted to enter any of the public sanctuaries. The laws granted permission even to foreign women and slave women to enter the sanctuaries in order to see them and make supplications. But the laws forbid the entering of public sanctuaries to a woman with whom an adulterer is caught, and if they do enter and transgress the law, the law allows them to suffer without redress any punishment, except death, at the hands of anyone who wishes to inflict it, and the law has granted to any passerby the right to exact the punishment for these matters. The law provides that she may in no way get redress when she has been maltreated in all other ways except death so that pollutions and impieties may not be in the sanctuaries. The law creates for women fear sufficient to motivate temperate behavior, the avoidance of wrongdoing, and a law-abiding desire to stay at home, because it teaches them that if a woman commits any such wrong she will at the same time be thrown out from her husband's home and from the sanctuaries of the city.

[Demosthenes], *Against Neaera* 86

But quite the contrary is true, as we shall see here in her activities in family and village life. In Chapter VI we will look to the woman's role in state cult, but, as a telling example of that, we should note that in Athens women held about forty state priesthoods and that a woman served as the priestess of Athena Polias, the patroness and protectress of the whole state.

In the home Zeus Ktesios, Zeus Herkeios, and Apollo Agyieus were all tended by the father, the male head of the household. We know of no similar religious activities of women *inside* the house. The mother is often represented on votive sculptured panels with her husband and children participating in sacrifices at sanctuaries outside of the home. In some of these the deity is male and the father is presenting the offering, and the mother and children are in the background as part of his entourage. But it is important for understanding her and the family's role that she and the whole family are there. Despite restrictions in some cults, the female members of the family were apparently often present at sacrifices to male deities.

Figure V.3 A fourth-century B.C.E. sculpted relief, 58 cm. high, depicting a sacrifice to Artemis Brauronia. Artemis stands majestically to the right before the altar, with a bow in her left hand and an offering plate in her right, and with a deer standing behind her. Attending the sacrifice are four couples, each with a child, and, probably, slaves holding the cow and carrying the basket. An inscription along the top reads, "Aristonice, the wife of Antiphates of the deme Thorae, dedicated this to Artemis after making a vow." The relief was found at Brauron and is now in the Brauron Museum, inv. no. 1151. Courtesy of the Greek Archaeological Society.

The mother of the family independently furthered the interests of her family through several cults *outside* of the home, and these activities concerned especially the deities Artemis, Asclepius, Athena, and Demeter. Her religious duties thus took her outside of the home to the village and, occasionally, to the city. We know of these activities primarily through surviving dedications made by mothers, and they most often concern the birth and welfare of their children.

Athenian women turned in particular to Artemis and, after 420 B.C.E., to Asclepius for assistance in childbirth. Dedications of articles of clothing and images of breasts and other female reproductive organs to Artemis are usually taken as expressions of gratitude for successful childbirths. Some reliefs dedicated to Artemis even represent pregnant women. The statuettes of male infants found in Artemis' sanctuary at Brauron may indicate the successful or hoped-for birth of a male heir. For problems with childbearing many women turned to Asclepius. Images of breasts and other male and female reproductive organs were common dedications at Asclepieia, and in Asclepius' sanctuary at Epidaurus a long series of miraculous "cures" was recorded, including the following:

> Andromache of Epirus: for the sake of offspring. She slept in the Temple and saw a dream. It seemed to her that a handsome boy uncovered her, after the god touched her with his hand, whereupon a son was born to Andromache from Arybbas.[3] (*IG* IV² 1.121–2, #31)

> —— of Troezen: for offspring. She slept in the Temple and saw a dream. The god seemed to say to her she would have offspring and to ask whether she wanted a male or a female, and that she answered she wanted a male. Whereupon within a year a son was born to her. (#34)

> Nicasibula of Messene: for offspring. She slept in the Temple and saw a dream. It seemed to her that the god approached her with a snake which was creeping behind him; and with that snake she had intercourse. Within a year she had two sons. (#42)

Among the more remarkable of these records of miracle cures is the following:

> Cleo was with child for five years. After she had been pregnant for five years she came as a suppliant to the god and slept in the *Abaton*. As soon as she left it and got outside the temple precincts, she bore a son who, immediately after his birth, washed himself at the fountain and walked about with his mother. In return for this favor she inscribed on her offering: "Admirable is not the greatness of this tablet but the god, in that Cleo carried the burden in her womb for five years, until she slept in the Temple and he made her sound." (#1)

In the Erchian calendar Artemis is paired with Kourotrophos (Nurse of the Young), and from throughout the Greek world we have many dedications by mothers to Artemis for the welfare of their children. In the two following, Telestodice erected two statues for Artemis, one together with her husband, the second on her own:

> Democydes and Telestodice together vowed
> and erected me, this statue, for the maiden Artemis,
> the daughter of aegis-bearing Zeus, on her sacred land.
> Increase their family and livelihood, free from suffering.
> > (*IG* XII 5.1, no. 215) (Hansen #414)

> Telestodice erected this statue for you, Artemis.
> She is the mother of Asphalius, and daughter of Therseles.
> > (*IG* XII 5.1, no. 216) (Hansen, #413)

After the introduction of his cult in Athens in 420/19 B.C.E., Asclepius became a favored recipient of dedications on behalf of children. A father and mother might together make a dedication:

> Meidias and Danaïs
> Erected this after having made a vow to Asclepius
> On behalf of their children Hediste, Sosicles, and
> Olympiodorus.
> > (*IG* II² 4403)

The mother might also on her own, perhaps when widowed, make such a dedication, as this one to Athena,

> Micythe dedicated me, this statue, to Athena.
> She vowed it as a tithe
> on behalf of her children and herself.
> > (*IG* I³ 857) (Hansen, #273)

or even to Heracles,

> Lysistrate dedicated this
> to Heracles
> on behalf of her children.
> > (*IG* II² 4613)

With the women of her deme the Erchian mother would have participated in local sacrifices, conducted by priestesses, to Artemis and Kourotrophos, to Hera Thelchinia, to Ge (Earth), to Dionysus' mother Semele, to the Athena of Erchia, to Hera Teleia (Of Marriage) at her sanctuary shared with Zeus, to Apollo's mother Leto, to Athena Polias, Aglaurus, and Pandrosus. She would also have attended sacrifices to the heroines, including, in addition to Semele and Aglaurus and Pandrosus, the Heroinae and Basile (Queen). If the woman's husband belonged to a prominent *genos*, she may well have served as a priestess of one of these goddesses or heroines. If she served Semele, the Erchians specified that all the meat of the sacrifice to Semele and to Dionysus was to be given only to the women and that the skins of the two goats sacrificed were to go to the priestess. These provisions reflect the prominence of women in the cult of Dionysus as we saw also in Chapter IV.

A major festival celebrated exclusively by women in Athens and throughout most of the Greek world was the Thesmophoria for Demeter Thesmophoros. In Athens it was a three-day festival held in September both in the city and at a number of sanctuaries of Demeter throughout Attica. During this festival the mother and the other married women of her household, in a rare excursion from the home, "camped out" at a nearby sanctuary of Demeter. The women of the deme selected two of their fellow demeswomen to lead them, perform rites, and assist the priestess of Demeter. In one deme these two "leaders" of the Thesmophoria were required, at their husbands' expense, to provide four liters each of barley, wheat, barley meal, wheat meal, and dried figs, three liters of wine, $1^1/2$ liters of olive oil, $1/2$ liter of honey, one liter each of white sesame and poppy, cheese weighing not less than one pound, two pounds of onions, a torch, and four drachmas ($400) in cash.[4] The first day of the festival consisted of the procession "up" to the local Thesmophorion and, no doubt, of setting up camp. For the second day the women fasted, and on the third day they celebrated the Kalligeneia (Beautiful Birth). The rituals of the festival, as at Eleusis, were secret, and we know little, but the central rite appears to have been fetching up from a deep pit (*megaron*) the rotted remains of pigs which had been sacrificed and deposited there at a previous festival. These remains were placed on the altar of Demeter and mixed with some of the grain seeds that were, just at this time of the year, to be planted by the farmers. The Thesmophoria and Demeter Thesmophoros may have owed their names to these "deposits" ("*thesmo-*" in Greek) that were "brought forth" ("*phor-*"). The festival was also sexually charged, with symbols of phalluses and obscene jokes, and the rituals obviously concerned both agricultural and human fertility. The day of sadness (the fast) was followed by a day of celebration (the Kalligeneia), and during that celebration the women no doubt feasted on the vegetarian foods and wine their leaders had provided. They may, as at the Mysteries at Eleusis, have been joyfully welcoming a new beginning of the agricultural cycle, particularly of grain crops. The day of sadness followed by the day of celebration is reminiscent of the sequence of the Eleusinian Mysteries (Chapter IV), and the myth of the separation and reunion of Demeter and Kore served as the foundation story for this festival as well. In the Thesmophoria, as in most Greek fertility and agricultural festivals, women played the major or even sole role. Aristophanes sets his *Thesmophoriazusae* on the fast day of the Thesmophoria and in his comic way provides glimpses into the festival, though never violating its secrecy, as he has the women of the Thesmophoria detect and pursue a male intruder. Modern scholars have been fascinated by the secrecy and sexual symbolism of this festival, by the women setting up their own temporary "city-state" during it, by their hostility to men, by the ribald humor, and by the apparent reversal of social conventions restricting the behavior of women. Discussions of these and other features of the Thesmophoria may be found in items in Further Reading.

> "I say that for every man everywhere it is best to be wealthy, healthy, honored by the Greeks, to reach old age, to bury well his own parents when they have died, and then himself to be buried well and grandly by this own descendants."
>
> Hippias in Plato's *Hippias Major* 291d9–e2

The married women of the family through their religious activities held primary responsibility for the birth and health of family members, and these activities were complemented by their major roles in the family's funerals. The Greek funeral consisted of 1) preparing the body, 2) the *prothesis* ("display") when the body was placed on a bier in the courtyard of the house for a day, 3) the *ekphora* ("carrying out"), when the body, in a procession, was transported to the tomb, and 4) the burial or cremation of the body at the tomb. Only women over the age of sixty or a very close relation could do the washing, anointing, dressing, and adorning of the body. During the *prothesis* the women of the family or hired professional keeners sang ritualized laments and dirges, tearing their hair and striking their heads and breasts. To limit public display and the exposure of the women to the public, the Athenians required the *ekphora* to be held in early morning before sunrise and allowed only women over sixty years of age or within the degree of second cousin to participate. Festivals and funerals were the prime occasions when Athenian women would be seen in the streets of Athens, and the occasional ancient Greek love story begins with a young man's glimpse of a beautiful girl in these settings. In the

Figure V.4   A red-figure Athenian *loutrophoros* (bathwater vessel) from the mid-fifth century B.C.E., attributed to the Bologna Painter. The scene represents the *prothesis* of a funeral, with the older woman on the right holding the head of the deceased and the younger woman on left tearing her hair in mourning. Courtesy of the Acropolis Museum, Athens, inv. no. 1170.

procession the body was carried by pall-bearers or taken on a cart, and the men led the way and the women and children followed. A flautist would play somber music suited to the occasion. The cremation or inhumation of the body and the offerings at the tomb were men's work, but the women, probably superintended by the mother of the household, had performed all the necessary preparations before the burial. They too no doubt prepared for the mourners the dinner held back at the house after the burial. In Athens the family remained in mourning for one month, and, as we saw in Chapter I, the women and men who participated in the funeral would be considered "polluted" for a designated time and could not enter sanctuaries of the gods. We have also seen that the father was responsible

Figure V.5   An Athenian white-ground Athenian *lekythos* (funeral vessel for oil), 36.5 cm. high, of 475–450 B.C.E. A weeping woman stands beside a tombstone decorated with a fillet. She carries in her hand another fillet with which to decorate the tomb. Courtesy of National Museum, Athens, inv. no.1958.

for tending the family tombs and making the annual offerings there, but a large series of vases show women too visiting and decorating the tombs of their family members.

Despite the considerable restrictions on their social, political, and personal lives, within the family and village Greek mothers contributed, through their religious activities, significantly to the welfare of their society, especially in terms of the fertility of crops and humans, of health, and, finally, in the last rites for the dead. We shall now look to the Greek daughter, both as she was trained to take on the roles she would have as a mother herself and as she participated in certain festivals and ritual roles intended only for her.

The Daughter

Girls in ancient Greece married early, at about the age of fifteen, and the bride joined the family of her groom. She was ritually accepted into their house, lived there with her husband, and participated in the religious rituals and the funerals and tomb cult of her new family. A daughter was, therefore, only a temporary member of her birth family – from birth to about the age of fifteen. In Athens as a baby she was named and formally accepted into the family by a ritual around the family's hearth, but she was not, as a son would be, formally registered, amidst religious ceremony, on the citizen roll of her father's deme. However much she may have been loved by her parents – and tombstones of girls often reflect parents' love –, she was a financial burden to the family because a substantial dowry had to be provided for her. The fact that she was expected to reside with her birth family only those few years is critical to understanding her religious life. As a result of this she was given no role in the religious activities of her birth family except to attend family sacrifices and some of the deme and state festivals. Not surprisingly, though, such festivals were a highlight of these girls' lives, and the early teenaged heroines of Greek tragedy such as Antigone and Electra, when faced with imminent death, count among their losses marriage, children, and the pleasures of festivals.

The daughters of Greek families thus were excluded from major roles in family and deme cult, but, interestingly, some were given significant responsibilities in state cult. In a moment of unusual seriousness in Aristophanes' *Lysistrata*, the chorus of elderly Athenian women makes a claim to its right to contribute to the discussion of public policy. They begin by listing the religious services they had performed as girls:

> "When I was seven, I immediately served as an *arrephoros*
> Then, at ten, I was a *aletris* for Athena Archegetis.
> Then, wearing the saffron dress, I was a bear at the Brauronia.
> And once I, a beautiful child, was a basket-carrier, wearing a necklace
>   of dried figs."
>
> (Lines 641–7)

Three of these roles concerned the cult of Athena Polias on the Acropolis. Four *arrephoroi*, as we saw in Chapter IV, served for a year and participated in the weaving of Athena's *peplos* for the Panathenaea. They also, once a year in May, performed a secret ritual, the *Arrephoria*. Pausanias (1.27.3) offers the fullest description of this ritual:

Two maidens have a dwelling not far from the temple of Athena Polias, and the Athenians call them *arrephoroi*.[5] For a period of time they have their life with the goddess, and when the festival (of the Arrephoria) occurs they do the following at night. They place on their heads what the priestess of Athena gives them to carry. Neither the priestess nor the girls know what this is that they carry. In the city, not far away, there is a *temenos* of Aphrodite In The Gardens, and there is a natural underground passage through it. The maidens descend by this passageway. Down there they leave the things they are carrying, and they take and bring back something else that is hidden from view. After this festival they dismiss these girls and bring other maidens to the Acropolis in their place.

The foundation myth for this ritual was that in very early times Athena herself entrusted Aglaurus, Herse, and Pandrosus, the daughters of King Cecrops, with a basket and forbade them to open it. That night Aglaurus and Herse opened it nonetheless, and they saw in the basket the baby Erechtheus. When a snake leapt out of the basket, the two girls in a panic jumped to their death from the heights of the Acropolis. Aglaurus' *heroön* has been identified off the sheer east end of the Acropolis, and Pandrosus, the one guiltless daughter, had her sanctuary with the sacred olive tree adjoining the Erechtheum. Although much of the Arrephoria remains unknown and many interpretations of the rituals and myth are possible,[6] it seems that the young *arrephoroi* in the fifth century and for centuries to come reenacted, in some form, this myth which brought together central figures of Athenian state cult: Athena Polias, Erechtheus, the daughters of Cecrops, and the snake.

We know little of the *aletrides* (grinders) except that they were daughters of noble families who, each year, ground the meal for the cakes which on various occasions would be offered to Athena on her altar. Like animal offerings, cakes given to the goddess had to be carefully and specially prepared, and that was the task of these ten-year-old girls. "Carrying the baskets" was the last in this series of activities for girls, done probably when they were nearing marriageable age. They carried these baskets, which probably contained implements for the sacrifice, in the Panathenaic procession, and in the fourth century the state provided gold jewelry for 100 such "basket-carriers." Aristophanes' basket-carriers have necklaces of dried figs which, if not an Aristophanic joke, may be symbols of fertility. We should assume that Athenian girls were specially selected for these roles, probably based on family connections. In the Hellenistic period proud parents dedicated to Athena on the Acropolis statues of their daughters who had served as *arrephoroi* or basket-carriers.

As *arrephoroi*, *aletrides*, and basket-carriers the select Athenian girls were appropriately, as both females and virgins, serving the virgin goddess

Figure V.6   A fourth-century marble statue of a girl, found at Brauron and now in the Archaeological Museum at Brauron. She may be an *arktos*, one of the many Athenian girls who "played the bear" in the rituals of Artemis Brauronia. Courtesy of the Greek Archaeological Society.

who protected the state at large. They were also doing "women's work" – weaving, preparing food, and tending a baby. It was, as the chorus of old women in the *Lysistrata* presents it, a service to the state. The same may true of their "being bears," the ritual of the *Arkteia* (*arktos* = "bear" in Greek) at the Brauronia, the quadrennial festival of Artemis Brauronia, but the Arkteia concentrated more directly on the girls' own concerns and roles in society. Apparently, *every* Athenian girl had to "play the bear" before she could marry. The chorus in the *Lysistrata* place their service at Brauron after the "grinding" of the ten-year-olds and before the "basket-carrying," and we would imagine the girls to be 10–14 years old.[7] These girls had assembled in the sanctuary of Artemis at Brauron, a village 32 kilometers southwest of Athens. Other girls may have performed their Arkteia at other Artemis sanctuaries in Attica. The girls would dress in special saffron robes, sacrifice to Artemis, and, in some type of initiatory ceremony, "play the bear" for Artemis. Included in the festival were processions, dancing, and even footraces for the girls. Modern theories about the meaning of the ritual abound,[8] but the simplest explanation may be that through the rituals of the Arkteia these girls, as they approached puberty and marriage, were being formally initiated into the cult of the goddess who would be of major importance to their lives as women in the future. Artemis is the goddess most invoked by women in casual conversation ("By Artemis, . . ."), and as Lochia (Of the Child-Bearing Bed) she assisted women in childbirth – a critical new role facing these girls. Women apparently dedicated garments to Artemis at Brauron after childbirth. We have also seen mothers offer dedications to Artemis on behalf of their children. Through the Arkteia the girls were, essentially, initiated into the cult of the goddess to whom they as women would turn for help in childbirth and for the care of their own children, the goddess to whom they as women would pray and sacrifice for the rest of their lives. This would be one religious affiliation that the girl, as a bride, would take with her from her birth family to the family of her husband. It bridged the world of her childhood in her birth family and that of her motherhood in her new family. The foundation myth of the Brauronia, as we saw it in Myth #5 of Chapter III, has, however, a different emphasis. According to it, the girls were "playing the bear" in a ritual reenactment of the original appeasement of the angry goddess. Making and keeping Artemis "happy" is certainly an important service to the state, and that may be why the chorus of the *Lysistrata* include it in their list. But in their rituals of "playing the bear" the girls were also developing a close association with the goddess who would play a major role in their personal lives as women and mothers.

For daughters of married parents marriage meant the end of girlhood. The purpose of this union between a fifteen-year-old girl and her thirty-something groom was quite explicit. At the betrothal, with the settlement of the dowry, the bride's father promised her to the groom "for the plowing of legitimate children." The bride was soon to be a mother, giving the family male heirs. If she did not accomplish this, she might soon be replaced by another. There was a marriage ceremony with established, formal elements: the betrothal arranged between the groom and bride's father; special baths for bride and groom on the wedding day, the water for which in Athens was fetched in a procession in a special vase, the *loutrophoros* (bath-water carrier), from a special fountain house; a large, festive banquet and "unveiling" of the bride to the groom at her father's home; a torch-lit, joyful procession that evening, when the bride, riding on a cart and accompanied by the groom, was delivered by her mother to her mother-in-law in her new home amidst wedding songs with their distinctive refrain "Hymen oh Hymenaios"; and then more wedding songs outside the new couple's bridal chamber. It may be overly schematic to attempt to separate

Figure V.7 An Athenian red-figure cup, 11 cm. high, attributed to the Amymone Painter, after 460 B.C.E. The bride's mother, to the far right, escorts the bridal couple with torches. The groom's mother, at the house to the left, receives the couple, also with torches. Note the wreaths worn by the groom and the musician. Courtesy of the Antikensammlung, Staatliche Museen zu Berlin, Preussischer Kulturbesitz, inv. no. F 2530.

out "religious" elements from secular ones in this ceremony, but certain aspects of it do involve familiar deities even though an ancient Greek marriage was not, apparently, a union pledged before god. When the bride arrived at her new home, she would be showered with coins, dates, dried fruits, figs, and nuts at the hearth as would any new person, free or slave, who was being joined to the household. Before the wedding the bride made an offering, often of childhood toys and such, to Artemis, an offering to the virgin goddess symbolizing the end of her own virginity.

> Before her marriage Timareta dedicated, as was
>   fitting for a maiden to a maiden, to Artemis Limnatis
> her drums, her lovely ball, the net that protected her hair,
>   and her dolls and the doll's clothing.
> Daughter of Leto, hold your hand over Timaretus' child
>   and protect the pious girl in a pious way.
> A dedication from one of the several cults devoted to Artemis
>   Limnatis (Of the Lake), *Palatine Anthology* 6.280

The bride also deposited one drachma ($100) as an offering in a special collection box in, appropriately, the sanctuary of Aphrodite, and Aphrodite figures prominently in the many wedding scenes depicted on vases. We do not know if they were invoked in the wedding ceremony itself, but in Athens and in many other places in Greece Hera Teleia and Zeus Teleios oversaw the institution of marriage. In the deme Erchia both receive offerings on the same day in Gamelion, the month "of marriages," on the day of the festival Theogamia (The Marriage of the Gods). The festival celebrated the marriage of Hera and Zeus, and, interestingly, the sanctuary belonged to Hera, not Zeus, and was served by a priestess. Zeus, as we have seen, had many roles to play in Greek religion, but this cultic arrangement at Erchia reflects Hera's primary role in the divine pantheon as protectress of marriage.

The girl has thus become a married woman and is expected soon to be a mother. As a married woman she can now turn to Hera Teleia and Aphrodite for her needs as a wife, and, as we have seen, to Artemis, Demeter, and Asclepius for her other needs as a woman and a mother.

The Son

The son of an Athenian family would, like his sister, receive his name and be formally introduced into the family at the hearth within ten days of his birth, but after that the son proceeded through very different stages of life, each with religious elements. First, as a proof of his legitimacy, he was presented to the *phratry* ("brotherhood") of his father. When he was sixteen years old, he was again formally presented to the phratry, and the successful completion of that rite meant that at the age of eighteen he could be entered onto the citizen rolls of the deme and state. He then entered one or two years of public service, the *ephebeia* (*ephebos* = "young man" in Greek). On the completion of that he was a full citizen, with the obligation for military service and with voting membership in the Athenian *Ekklesia*, the general Assembly of all Athenian male, adult citizens. In some ways, however, his "youth" came to an end only when he reached thirty years of age. Then he could serve in the Athenian *Boule*, the Council of 500 representatives from the demes, on the law courts, and in administrative positions in the government. And then, as we have seen, his and his family's thoughts would turn to his marriage. He might well soon become a father himself, but he would become the head of the extended family only when his own father died or ceded authority to him. And, lastly, he was obliged to tend his parents and to see to a proper burial for them.

The 139 demes and 10 new tribes that Cleisthenes established in Athens in 508/7 B.C.E. as foundations of the new democracy were superimposed on an earlier social organization based on the phratries ("brotherhoods") and four tribes. The original four tribes largely disappeared, but the phratries persisted. After Cleisthenes each Athenian family belonged to a phratry. Membership was inherited in the male line, and the phratry decided on the legitimacy and hence citizenship of male children. There were at least thirty phratries and perhaps nearly as many as the demes themselves, and they seem, like the demes, to be regionally based. Each had its own cult center, and the patron deities of the phratries were Zeus Phratrios and Athena Phratria. In Athens and in other Ionian cities claiming descent from Athens the phratries individually held an annual three-day festival, the *Apatouria* (Of the Same Father), in early October. The procedures varied some from phratry to phratry, but the general scheme was that the first evening was devoted to a feast well provided with wine, the second day to sacrifices to Zeus Phratrios and Athena Phratria, and, on the third day, the members introduced their sons into the phratry. The father would first present his son at a celebration of the Apatouria within a year after the son's birth and would sacrifice a sheep to Zeus and Athena. He would also swear an oath that this boy was his legitimate child, and thereafter the son would probably regularly attend the annual Apatouria of his father's phratry. At about the age of sixteen the boy was again presented by his father to the members of the phratry at the Apatouria. On this occasion the boy made an offering of hair which for boys typically symbolized the transition from childhood to adolescence. The father again swore an oath to the legitimacy of his son and presented a sacrificial victim for Zeus and Athena. Any member of the phratry could challenge the father's claim by leading the victim away from the altar. This, of course, would be a shocking event, and the dispute would eventually be settled by a vote of the members of the phratry. If the offering was accepted by the members, the animal was sacrificed, the meat was distributed to the members of the phratry, and the boy became a full member of the phratry. This, in turn, was a necessary step to his being accepted, at age eighteen, by his deme and the state as a citizen.

After becoming a citizen, the Athenian young man joined a group of his peers for military training and community service, the *ephebeia*. We know little of the structure of this program in the fifth century, but in the late fourth century it was a two-year program, highly regulated, with adult officials training the youth in military and civic matters. For some of the time the young men garrisoned outposts on the Athenian borders. They also attended, as a group, meetings of the Ekklesia. They were being prepared as soldiers and citizens for the civic life of an Athenian adult, and part of that civic life was, of course, religious. The corps of *ephebes*

toured the sanctuaries of Attica, provided escorts for religious processions, participated in games at festivals, and themselves made offerings
at sanctuaries with strong patriotic connections, as at the tomb of the
heroic dead of the Battle of Marathon. At the beginning of their ephebic
service the young men swore the following oath which embodies many
Athenian ideals:

> I will not bring shame upon these sacred weapons nor will I abandon my
> comrade-in-arms wherever I stand in the ranks. I will defend both the holy
> and profane things. I will not hand on the fatherland smaller than I received
> it, but larger and better, so far as it lies in my power with the assistance
> of all the other citizens. I will obey the officials who govern wisely and the
> laws, both those which are already established and those which are wisely
> established in the future. If anyone attempts to destroy them, I will not allow
> it, so far as it lies in my power with the assistance of all the other citizens. I
> will hold in honor the ancestral sanctuaries. The following gods are witnesses:
> Aglaurus, Hestia, Enyo, Enyalius, Ares and Athena Areia, Zeus, Thallo, Auxo,
> Hegemone, Heracles, the territory of the fatherland, the wheat, barley,
> vines, olive-trees, and fig-trees.
>
> (M.N. Tod, *Greek Historical Inscriptions*, vol. 2, no. 204)

Here the ephebes by an oath with gods (and others) as their witnesses
put their civic responsibilities under divine sanction. In Athens "to not
obey the officials" would not have been a religious crime in itself, but by
this oath the young men subjected themselves to the anger of the divine
witnesses if they violated any promise made in the oath. Aglaurus, as
we have seen, was a daughter of Cecrops, and in one version of her myth
she willingly sacrificed herself to save her country in the midst of a war.
It may have been for that reason that the ephebes, who were expected
to do the same, swore their oath in her sanctuary and saw themselves
under her supervision. Hestia is the hearth of city-state, maintained with
a perpetual fire in the *Prytaneion*, the state's official dining building.
Enyo, Enyalius, and Ares and Athena Areia are military deities and, by their
prominent position in the oath, reflect the primarily military orientation
of the *ephebeia*. Zeus may be present as the protector of oaths (Horkios).
Thallo (Flourishing) and Auxo (Growth) are personifications, and the nature
of Hegemone (Leaderess) is uncertain. Heracles is relevant both as one
who wards off evil and because these young men had, at their Apatouria,
each made an offering of wine to him before the cutting of their hair.
Finally the land and its agricultural products are invoked, not as gods, but,
in this context, as revered objects these young men are obliged to defend
and protect. This oath was essentially the citizens' oath of Athens, and these
new citizens could expect to hear it invoked in speeches in the Ekklesia,
in the law courts, and on the battlefield for the rest of their lives.

Our young male citizen would now continue for ten years many of the religious activities he had begun in boyhood. He would attend many of the deme sacrifices and festivals with the rest of his family. He no doubt would regularly attend the major festivals in the city. He might well compete in the senior division of many of the same athletic contests of the Panathenaea that he had entered before as a junior. There were, as well, in the Classical period at least four other major annual festivals in Athens that featured some form of athletic competition for young men, and more were added in the Hellenistic period. The young man might also compete as an adult member of his tribe's fifty-man chorus in performing a *dithyramb* in Dionysus' honor at the City Dionysia festival, much as he had done as a member of the junior chorus of his tribe. Throughout these years he would be, essentially, serving a long, informal apprenticeship, begun in the *ephebeia*, in military, political, civic, and religious affairs, preparing himself for roles as military commander, government official, and, quite possibly, if he was of the right family, as a priest of a local or state cult.

The Slave

All but the poorest Greek families probably owned slaves. These slaves might be other Greeks or non-Greeks taken as prisoners of war. They would have formerly been free, but many also had been born to slaves of the family and had known nothing but slavery. Some worked in the home doing household chores, weaving, and tending the children; others worked in the fields or factories; and others were hired out for excruciatingly hard and dangerous work in the mills and the mines. Slaves were members of the "family," but primarily as property, like the land and the farm animals. Slaves' status was above that of animals, however, because they were formally accepted into the family, like newborn children and new wives, by ceremonies at the family's hearth. Also, they could not be killed without incurring pollution. Some may, at the discretion of their master, have had limited participation in the religious activities of the family. We saw earlier that Ciron did not allow slaves even at his family celebration of Zeus Ktesios, but another Athenian had his slave mistress – a special case, to be sure – share in the same occasion (Isaeus 8.16 and Antiphon 1.15–18, above). Slaves are occasionally shown on scenes of a family sacrifice, attending one of the participants, carrying baskets, or leading the sacrificial victim. They no doubt did much of the tending of sacrificial animals and of the cooking for the feasts that accompanied many religious events. But, of course, their "membership" in the family was very limited. Household slaves involved in the rearing of the children might be given a modest tombstone, but even they were usually not buried in the family cemetery plot.

In tragedy and comedy slaves are portrayed as invoking the gods, praying, and swearing by the gods much as their masters do, but not sacrificing or performing other religious rituals. In Athens slaves were permitted to enter state sanctuaries "to see and to make supplications," but there is no evidence that they could or did sacrifice or perform other religious rituals there. They were explicitly banned from some festivals such as the Thesmophoria, but in a few others they had specific roles. In Athens at the Cronia, the festival honoring Cronus, the father of Zeus, masters and slaves dined together with no distinction of status, and masters may even have served slaves. Such festivals reversing the usual social order were not uncommon elsewhere in Greece. Freed slaves marched carrying oak boughs in the procession of the Panathenaea. The slaves who worked at Demeter's sanctuary in Eleusis were initiated into the Mysteries, probably because they otherwise could not have had access to parts of the sanctuary. But the evidence suggests very little slave participation in public cults, and even this little bit would be subject to the will of the master.

Slaves have left no evidence of a religious life of their own, apart from the communities of citizens. No deities and no cults were directed to them, and for the Classical period there is no evidence that Greek or non-Greek slaves worshiped the gods of their homelands either individually or in groups. Asylum, as we described it in Chapter I, offered one of the few protections for slaves. A slave might lay hold of the altar, perhaps of Zeus Herkeios, in the home if he feared the wrath of his master. If he entered a sanctuary, he would, like any other person, have "sanctuary" there and could not be removed against his will. In Athens the *heroön* of Theseus and the altar of the Semnae (Revered Goddesses), both near the Acropolis, were recognized specially as sites of asylum for slaves.[9] There a slave would be safe until his complaints were adjudicated, probably by a state official. The decision might be that his master must sell him to another master, or, as in Sicily, that the master was required to swear an oath that in the future he would treat the slave humanely (Diodorus Siculus 11.89.6–8).

NOTES

1. Greek palaces in the Mycenaean period had large permanent hearths, but in the Classical period the Greeks apparently used braziers or temporary hearths. This seems not, however, to have diminished their devotion to the hearth.
2. One can get a sense of such Rural Dionysia from the one held by Dicaeopolis in Aristophanes' *Acharnians*, lines 237–79.

3. The translations of this and the following Epidaurian epigraphical texts are from E. and L. Edelstein, *Asclepius* (Baltimore, 1945).
4. Isaeus 8.19–20 and *IG* II² 1184 (for the full text, see Price, *RAG*, 173–4).
5. The number of *arrephoroi* is disputed. In the Classical period there were probably four, not two as is sometimes claimed.
6. For some of these interpretations, see under Arrephoria in Further Reading.
7. One ancient source, however, says the "bears" were five to ten years old, and several scholars accept this. On this, and for a reinterpretation of the whole passage, see C. Sourvinou-Inwood, "Aristophanes, *Lysistrata* 641–47," *Classical Quarterly* NS 21 (1971), 339–42.
8. See under Brauronia in Further Reading.
9. It is probably not coincidental that slaves were not permitted to participate in the annual procession to the sanctuary of the Semnae.

FURTHER READING

Family and village life in general:

Price, *RAG*, 89–107
Lacey, W.K., *The Family in Classical Greece* (Ithaca, 1968)
Osborne, R., *Demos: The Discovery of Classica Attica* (Cambridge, UK, 1985), esp. 154–82
Whitehead, D., *The Demes of Attica* (Princeton, 1986), esp. 176–222
Lambert, S.D., *The Phratries of Attica* (Ann Arbor, 1993), esp. 143–90 and 205–36

On children's and women's role in religion:

Dillon, M., *Girls and Women in Classical Greek Religion* (London, 2002)
Kron, U., "Priesthoods, dedications, and euergetism: what part did religion play in the political and social status of Greek women?" pp. 139–82 in *Religion and Power in the Ancient Greek World*, edd. P. Hellström and B. Alroth (Uppsala, 1996)
Demand, N., *Birth, Death, and Motherhood in Classical Greece* (Baltimore, 1994), esp. 87–101, 107–21
Golden, M., *Children and Childhood in Classical Athens* (Baltimore and London, 1990), esp. 23–32, 41–50, 65–72, and 76–9

On the Thesmophoria:

Burkert, *GR*, 242–6
Clinton, K., "The Thesmophorion in Central Athens and the Celebration of the Thesmophoria in Attica," pp. 111–25 in R. Hägg, *The Role of Religion in the Early Greek Polis* (Stockholm, 1996)
Demand, 1994, esp. 114–21
Dillon, 2002, 110–20

On funerals:

Dillon, 2002, 268–92
Kurtz, D.C. and J. Boardman, *Greek Burial Customs* (Ithaca, 1971), esp. 91–161
Garland, R., *The Greek Way of Death* (Ithaca, 1985), esp. 21–47

On Arrephoria:

Dillon, 2002, especially 57–60
Burkert, *Homo Necans* (Berkeley, 1983), 150–4
Robertson, N., "The Riddle of the Arrephoria at Athens," *Harvard Studies in Classical Philology* 87 (1983), 241–88

On Arkteia and Brauronia:

Dillon, 2002, especially 19–23, 220–1
Camp, J.M., *The Archaeology of Athens* (New Haven, 2001), 277–81
Cole, S.G., "The Social Function of Rituals of Maturation: The Koureion and the Arkteia," *Zeitschrift für Papyrologie und Epigraphie* 55 (1984), 233–44
Demand, 1994, 88–91, 107–14
Kahil, L., "Mythological Repertoire of Brauron," 231–44 in *Ancient Greek Art and Iconography*, ed. W.G. Moon (Madison, 1983)
Osborne, 1985, 154–74

On marriage:

Zaidman and Pantel, *RAGC*, 68–72, 186–8
Dillon, 2002, especially 215–28
Demand, 1994, 11–18, 25–6
Oakley, J.H. and R.H. Sinos, *The Wedding in Ancient Athens* (Madison, 1993)

On Apatouria:

Cole, 1984, 233–44
Lambert, 1993, 143–90 and 205–36

On slave's role in religion:

Klees, H., *Sklavenleben im Klassischen Griechenland* (Stuttgart, 1998), esp. 208–10, 262–73, 379–88

VI

Religion of the Greek City-State

⌐⌐⌐⌐

The deities, cults, and religious activities of a Greek city-state as a political unity were enmeshed with those of its constituent elements, the families and the villages. We may first distinguish state cults and religious activities from those of a family and village in that they were directed to the welfare of the city-state as a whole, were financed by state revenues, and were open, barring any specific cultic regulations, to all citizens of the city-state and their families. The state at its expense provided through elected, allotted, or appointed officials the sacrificial animals, administered and provided prizes for games, built the temples and other major buildings, and had general oversight over the performance of ritual activities. In Athens the priesthoods of most state cults remained with individual families in the fifth century, but the state had lay commissioners to superintend the property, expenses, and even the timely and appropriate performance of the rituals.

In these ways state cults were distinct elements of a Greek's religious life, but in a variety of other ways they either drew from or contributed to religious activities at the family and village levels. Each family, for example, worshiped Hestia (Hearth) in its own home. The Athenian state, which was in essence a large extended family into which its citizens were born, had a state cult of Hestia in the Prytaneion, the state dining room. Just as a single Athenian family entertained guests at its hearth, so the Athenian state entertained and fed foreign ambassadors, official visitors, and Olympic victors at its hearth in the Prytaneion. The state Hestia of the Prytaneion is the Hestia of all the individual Athenian families writ large. With Hestia we probably have a familial deity for whom the state, reputedly under Theseus (Thucydides, 2.15.2) established a centralized, national cult to develop the sense of the state as itself a family. Zeus Herkeios, another major deity of the individual family, was probably given a similar unifying role when an altar was dedicated to him by the state on the Acropolis beneath the sacred olive tree in the sanctuary of Pandrosus. In both cases the state was, at the least, recognizing nationally the importance of these family deities. Some scholars would further claim that by establishing such cults it was establishing or claiming authority over such domestic cults.

We see Athens also bringing into its orbit cults of the Attic countryside. On the Acropolis itself the state had a sanctuary of Artemis Brauronia whose cult center, as we have seen, was in the village of Brauron thirty-two kilometers southwest of the city. Likewise the Athenians dedicated to Demeter an Eleusinion below the northern slopes of the Acropolis, a sanctuary which linked Eleusis and the Eleusinian Mysteries more closely to the city and the political center. One may also see the City Dionysia with its annual presentation of dithyrambs, tragedies, and comedies as the state's unified celebration of the Dionysus worshiped in the demes in the many Rural Dionysia, some also with tragedies and dithyrambs. The movement of religious cult might be away from the city-state center as well as towards it. The cult of Cecrops' daughter Aglaurus was, as we have seen, firmly rooted on the Acropolis, but one day each year the demesmen of Erchia sacrificed to Aglaurus on their own Acropolis in Erchia. In their sacrifices to her and at other times to Athena Polias they were clearly, at the village level, rendering honor to the state deity. In this case the religious impulse emanated from the state center to the outlying areas.

State cult is not distinct but is part of a continuum of religious life of Greek individuals. An Erchian might one day attend sacrifices to Athena Polias at her sanctuary in his village; another day he might go with a few fellow demesmen to sacrifice to her on the Acropolis in Athens on behalf of the Erchians; and on still another day he and his family might join all the residents of Attica in the procession of the Panathenaea, watch the sacrifices on the Great Altar on the Acropolis, and then enjoy the contests and feasting that followed. And, of course, if he thought he personally received some favor from Athena, he could privately erect a dedication for her either in Erchia or on the Acropolis in Athens.

Many deities, as we have seen, were worshiped only at the village level, some only at one village. Cult at the state level was the widest scope that most Greek deities attained. The Athena Polias of the Acropolis was, for example, worshiped only by Athenians. The few exceptions are the panhellenic deities we encountered in Chapter IV, but they too fit into the continuum within the state. Apollo Pythios of Delphi was worshiped, at Delphi, by all Greeks. But the Athenians had for him in Athens a state sanctuary, the Pythion, with a temple and altar southeast of the Acropolis, and on special occasions they sent a chorus and state offerings to him at Delphi. And, finally, the Erchians sacrificed to him on two days each year at Erchia, once to him as Pythios and once as Delphinios. Apollo Pythios and, in many city-states, Zeus Olympios were among the very few gods who could extend their reach from the local villages beyond the city-state to all Greeks.

The needs for which the citizens of a state as a group turned to the gods were much the same as those of individual families and villages: 1) fertility of crops, animals, and human beings; 2) good health; 3) economic prosperity; and 4) safety in the dangers of war and seafaring. In addition, we need to consider, at the state level, national identity and some specifically national needs. We can perhaps best understand the range and nature of state cult by seeing how it responded to these needs. The deities and cults answering to these needs would have varied, often significantly, from one city-state to another, but, again, we will take Athens as our model because we have for her the best evidence.

Fertility of Crops, Animals, and Human Beings

The major crops of Athens were grapes, olives, and grain, and in previous chapters we have seen Olympian gods involved with each. Dionysus was the patron of the vine and wine, and through the myth of Icarius (Chapter III, Myth #4) the Athenians explained how Dionysus, not without difficulties, introduced both to Athens. The tasting of the new wine was featured in a Dionysiac festival in the spring, and, of course, wine played a role in the other major state as well as deme festivals of Dionysus. In Athens Athena was the patroness of the olive. It was her gift to the city, in fact the gift that won her the city (Chapter III, Myth #1), and the prizes for many of the contests of her Great Panathenaea were amphoras of olive oil. Grain, as we have seen (Chapter IV), was Demeter's gift to the Eleusinians. Eleusis was, or was soon to be, part of Athens, and so all Athenians were the direct beneficiaries of this gift. Athenian farmers, before they planted their grain crops, performed a plowing ritual for Demeter, their wives celebrated the rites of the Thesmophoria to bring Demeter's blessing to the grain seeds, and, at harvest, the farmers dedicated a portion of their yield to Demeter of Eleusis. Each of these deities, understandably, had sanctuaries and was worshiped in the countryside where the farmers actually lived and worked, but the state also had, in the fifth century, a centralized cult center for each: the sanctuary of Dionysus with its theater and temple on the south slope of the Acropolis, the Acropolis sanctuary of Athena, and the Eleusinion of Demeter beneath the north slopes of the Acropolis.

Among her various roles Artemis was both huntress and protectress of wild animals, as the foundation myth of her cult at Brauron and the girls' "playing the bear" there suggest (Chapter III, Myth #5 and Chapter V, pp. 150–1). Cattle, goats, sheep, and pigs were raised in Attica and tended by herdsmen. Although certain domesticated animals are associated with specific gods as favored sacrificial victims, the goat, for example, for Dionysus or the piglet for Demeter, divine attention seems focused on the herdsman and not the animal. Commonly Hermes was a patron of the herdsman. He cleverly steals a herd of cattle in the delightful *Homeric Hymn to Hermes*, and the swineherd Eumaeus in the *Odyssey* (14.435) makes an offering to him. Pan too assumed this role in some countries. We hear little of them in these roles in highly agricultural and mercantile Athens, but they are prominent in the more mountainous areas of Greece such as Arcadia, Hermes' and Pan's homeland in the Peloponnesus. The rural and nomadic nature of herding and herdsmen may partially explain why the Athenians established no centralized, state cult to acknowledge this function of those deities. The fertility and welfare of animals raised in the home and farm probably were included in the prayers and offerings by the family to Zeus Ktesios, the promoter of the family's prosperity in material terms.

Fertility of human beings began with Aphrodite, the goddess of sex. She had a sanctuary near the Athenian marketplace, and, as we have seen, brides gave her a gift of one drachma ($100) before their marriages. Athenian married women in their annual celebration of the Thesmophoria for Demeter performed various rituals aimed at promoting sexuality and fertility. Artemis, as we have seen, was a goddess for women, and at Brauron numerous dedications resulted from or looked to the birth and welfare of children, particularly male children. There apparently was no special state Thesmophorion, and the Athenian government left it to women to promote this aspect of fertility in the sanctuaries of their villages. But the state did provide, in Athens, sanctuaries of Aphrodite and Artemis Brauronia.

Good Health

Infertility might, of course, result from medical problems, and miniature reproductions of genitalia were dedicated especially at sanctuaries of Artemis and Asclepius. For much of the fifth century b.c.e. the Athenians turned to local deities and various Physician Heroes in the demes for heal- ing. Athena as Athena Hygieia (Of Health) had an altar on the Acropolis, but she probably looked to the health of Athenians in general terms, only rarely dealing with individual patients. But in the years 431 to 423 the Athenians, at the beginning of the Peloponnesian War, suffered a devastat- ing plague, perhaps of measles, typhus, or smallpox, which may well have killed nearly a third of the citizens, including the leading statesman Pericles and much of his family. Part of the despair resulting from the plague was, as Thucydides reports in his *History of the Peloponnesian War* (2.47.4), that "all the supplications at the sanctuaries and all inquiries at the oracles and such things were of no help." Soon after, in 420/19 B.C.E., the Athenians imported from Epidaurus the cult of the healing god Asclepius whom we encountered in Chapter V. Two major sanctuaries were established, one in Piraeus and one on the south slope of the Acropolis. These sanctuaries would have been medical clinics as well as cult sites, and the Athenians flocked to them. We do not have for Athens the elaborate records of cures that we saw from Epidaurus in Chapter V, but hundreds of dedications do survive from the sanctuary on the south slope of the Acropolis, and many represent miniature models of body parts such as legs, arms, torsos, eyes, and ears. There were also more elaborate dedications of altars, chests, and small reliefs, statues, and statuettes portraying the god. These, unlike the dedications of craftsmen to Athena, were not tithes but usually payments of vows taken by fathers, mothers, and children on behalf of family members. Typical, and typically simple, is this inscription on a marble pillar:

> Meidias and Danais dedicated this
> To Asclepius after they made a vow
> On behalf of their children Hediste,
> Sosikles, and Olympiodorus.
>
> (*IG* II² 4403)

These many dedications give testimony to the Athenians' belief that Asclepius had healed their diseases or had warded off diseases from their loved ones. Here we may recall Socrates' last words, to his old friend Crito: "Crito, we owe a cock to Asclepius. Give it to him and do not neglect it" (Plato, *Phaedo* 118a7–8). Socrates, a man of humble means, may well have vowed to sacrifice a cock to Asclepius if he lived a healthy life. Here he, on his death bed, bids Crito to fulfill that vow for him.

Economic Prosperity

For farmers and vintners economic prosperity derived from their crops. In addition to the fertility of their crops discussed above, they also needed rain in sufficient quantities and at the right times. For this they turned to Zeus who was, throughout Greece, the sole giver of rain. This Zeus was worshiped in Attica in at least eleven mountain and hilltop sanctuaries, as close to the sky as possible. Sometimes he was named after the mountain

Figure VI.1 The Hephaisteion, the temple of Hephaestus and Athena Hephaistia, overlooking the Athenian Agora from the west. Construction was probably begun about 460–450 B.C.E. and completed about 420. Author's photograph.

(Zeus Hymettios – of Mt. Hymettus), and sometimes he had the epithet Ombrios (Of Rain). He probably received annual offerings but also would be appealed to with sacrifices and prayers in times of special need.

Artisans who used fire in their crafts, especially smiths and potters, had their patron in Hephaestus. The Athena of the Acropolis, with the epithet Ergane ("Workeress"), looked to all the crafts, and she and Hephaestus, linked also in myth (Chapter III, Myth #2), shared a temple, the Hephaisteion, on the hill west of the Agora in the Ceramicus, the "Potters' Quarter" of the city. They shared an annual festival, the Chalkeia (Of Bronze), which was celebrated especially by the smiths. The inscriptions of dedications to Athena by at least four potters (*IG* I³ 620, 628, 633, and 824) and probably of twenty-four others survive from the fifth century, many probably works of the potters themselves. One potter dedicated seven marble *perirrhanteria* (926–32). Athena also received dedications from a carpenter (606), a shipbuilder (589), a tanner (646), fullers (616 and 905), a scribe (841), a perhaps foreign bakeress (546), a washerwoman (794), and a woman who supported her family with her weaving (*IG* II² 4334). Each of these craftsmen probably gave their statues and other dedications to Athena as a tithe of their profits, and dozens of other such tithe dedications to Athena, though without designation of the dedicators' occupations, also survive. These dedications, by women and men, indicate the contribution of the state's Athena to the financial prosperity of individuals, and sometimes, as in the following dedication, this is made explicit:

> Lady Athena, Menandrus of Aigilia, the son of Demetrius, dedicated this to you as a first-fruits offering, fulfilling a vow, returning favor (*charis*) to you. Protect his prosperity, daughter of Zeus, having favor (*charis*) for this.
>
> (*IG* I³ 872)

One tithe dedication to Athena, perhaps by a woman, captures well the sentiment of these craftsmen:

> It is good for wise men to develop their skill in a craft,
> because whoever has a craft has a better livelihood.
>
> (*IG* I³ 766)

The surviving dedications suggest that such Athenian craftsmen turned almost exclusively to Athena in the pursuit of their careers. Very rarely is such a dedication given to another god, and then always for obvious reasons, as, for example, to Hermes, the herald of the gods, by a herald (776). In Athens of the fifth century Athena dominated the interest of the craftsmen who were able to afford these expensive dedications.

The Agora of Athens was a major political, religious, social, and commercial center. In the Classical period the large central square was kept open as a "commons" where each day retail merchants and bankers would set up tables and do business. Overseeing this activity at Athens and some other Greek cities was Zeus Agoraios. We would like to know what Zeus' oversight here entailed: assisting the merchants, protecting the customers, or, more generally, guaranteeing fairness of dealings? In several cities he was concerned with the administration of justice in the Agora, and among the Greeks many financial and commercial dealings were sealed with an oath. Zeus Agoraios may have been regularly invoked as a witness of such dealings in the Agora.

Much of the economy of Athens depended on trade by sea, and merchantmen and sailors invoked Poseidon before, during, and after their voyages throughout the Aegean and Mediterranean. Merchant ships putting in at the Sunium harbor had to pay a small tax for the support of the sanctuary (*IG* I³ 8). A tithe of the profits from a trade venture could be given to Poseidon or another state deity. Merchants from Samos, after huge financial success from a trading voyage into the Atlantic, gave six talents ($3,600,000), one tenth of their profits, to Hera, the major deity of

Samos, and from this a magnificent, monumental bronze crater was made (Herodotus 4.152.4). Several Greek cities involved in sea trade established cult centers of their own major deities in large international ports. At Naucratis of Egypt, for example, Aegina, Samos, and Miletus each had a sanctuary of their major state deity, and a number of Greek cities in Asia Minor founded there, as a consortium, a joint sanctuary, the Hellenion. These Greek sanctuaries in Egypt would have been used by the Greeks of the respective states during their stays in this foreign port (Herodotus, 2.178). In a similar way, apparently, the Athenians allowed a few cults of foreign peoples in their harbor at Piraeus.

The silver mines of southern Attica brought great wealth to both Athens and individuals, and one might expect that of all human activities mining might especially be subject to the chthonic deities, but that does not seem to be the case. Several of the mines were named after Olympian gods, for example, Artemisiakon, Aphrodisiakon, Apolloniakon, and Athenaikon. It is not known whether these mines were, in a sense, dedicated to these deities or whether, as is more likely, they simply took their names from local sanctuaries which would serve as landmarks for identifying them.

We see, then, that major elements of the state economy, including farming, crafts of all types, international trade, and mining were subject, to some degree, to divine oversight. Some of these were local by nature, and then the state tended to create a national, centralized cult of the deities involved, without, however, encroaching on the local cults. For activities more national by nature, such as trade and commerce, the state developed national cults, as, for example, those of Poseidon and Zeus Agoraios.

Safety in Seafaring and Warfare

Where men hold in reverence the gods, train in military matters, and practice obedience, how is it not reasonable that here all things are full of good hopes?

Xenophon, *Agesilaus* 1.27

Warfare was a national concern, and that is reflected in cultic religion. In Athens, as we have seen, Athena Polias as the national patroness was a war goddess, represented with helmet, shield, and spear. In her sanctuary and temples on the Acropolis victory in a variety of wars was celebrated by elaborate and expensive dedications. In a sanctuary in northern Attica with a major temple she was explicitly associated with Ares, as Athena Areia.

The Athenians' conceptions of the role of their Athena and other gods in war may perhaps best be seen in events of the Persian Wars when the Persians twice invaded Greece. In the first invasion of 490 ordered by King Darius the Persians were repulsed at Marathon by the Athenian army, and in the much larger invasion of 480 led by Xerxes they were defeated by the combined force of several Greek states at Salamis, Plataea, and, finally, at Mycale in Asia Minor. We learn, from Herodotus and others, not so much what Athena and the other gods actually did in these wars but rather how the Athenians expressed their gratitude to them. From the spoils of their victory at Marathon, for example, the Athenians had Phidias sculpt the towering Athena Promachos on the Acropolis. The goddess was also depicted as fighting in the battle in a famous painting of the battle in the Stoa Poicile in the Agora. It may also be that the early Parthenon, the temple under construction when destroyed by Xerxes in 480, was intended as a commemoration of the battle of Marathon. During the second invasion a Delphic oracle told the Athenians that Athena had unsuccessfully tried to convince her father Zeus to prevent the occupation and devastation of her city. In the face of the Persian occupation of Attica in 480 Athena herself joined the evacuation: the large snake that lived in her temple stopped eating the offerings put out for it, and Athenians concluded that the goddess had left the city and that they should do the same. But soon after the Persians occupied the city Athena's sacred olive tree miraculously gave Xerxes an indication of the future: on the second day after the burning of the Acropolis it sent up a one and one-half foot sprout. It was an unmistakable sign that, whatever the current situation, Athena would see to the revival of her city. And, on the eve of the battle of Salamis, an old oracle was brought forward, assuring the Athenians that Zeus and (Athena) Nike would bring on Greece's day of freedom. Because of the devastation after the occupation the Athenians were unable, for a generation, to reward their war goddess properly. But under Pericles the Athenians built the new Parthenon, the Erechtheum, and the temple of Athena Nike with its representation of Greeks defeating Persians. The rebuilding of the Acropolis sacred buildings in the form we know them today may well have been in good part a tribute to Athena's contribution to the victory over the Persians.

Athena was not the only Athenian deity to contribute to the war effort. As the great Persian fleet was making its way south to Athens along the east coast of Greece in 480, the Athenians were bid by Delphi to summon the aid of their "son-in-law." They took this to mean that they should sacrifice and pray to Boreas, the north wind, and his Athenian wife Oreithyia. This they did, and a great storm came up and destroyed almost a third of the Persian ships. In gratitude the Athenians founded a sanctuary of Boreas in Attica alongside the Ilissus River. In the storms and sea battles of the second Invasion Poseidon also played his part. After the victory at Salamis the Greeks as a group gave, as dedications, captured Phoenician ships to Poseidon's sanctuary at Isthmia and, as we saw in chapter I, at Sunium. The unwarlike Athenian Artemis had her role too in these difficult times. The battle of Marathon probably occurred just days before the festival of Artemis Agrotera at Agrae very near Athens, and the Athenians before the battle vowed that they would sacrifice to her at her festival each year a female goat for each enemy they killed. The Athenians killed more Persians than they had expected (6,400), however, and compromised with sacrificing 500 female goats to Artemis, a sacrifice which they continued each year well into the Roman period. In the battle of Salamis the Persians drew up their ships initially near the sanctuary of Artemis Mounichia, and for centuries afterwards the Athenians held a regatta celebrating their victory at her annual festival. Even Demeter of Eleusis, like Artemis not naturally a war goddess, joined the action. Xerxes in his occupation of Attica burned the Telesterion at Eleusis, and Demeter in anger at this sacrilege sent before the battle of Salamis an omen favorable to the Greek forces and later denied the Persians refuge in her sanctuary near the battleground of Plataea. Even the heroes of Attica joined the fray. Theseus assisted the Athenians at Marathon, and Ajax, whose home was on Salamis, with members of his family helped the Greeks in the battle there. Ajax received for his sanctuary on Salamis the third of the Phoenician ships the Greeks dedicated after their victory, and for centuries thereafter the Athenians honored him for his contributions in this war.

> I say to the city-protecting gods of this land,
> both those dwelling in the plains and those watching over the market,
> and to the streams of Dirce and to the waters of Ismenus,
> if we succeed and if our city is saved,
> we will bloody the altars of the gods with sheep
> and, in the temples, we will set up as trophies
> the spoils taken by spear from the enemy.
>
> Eteocles, facing the attack of the Argives on his native Thebes,
> Aeschylus, *Seven Against Thebes*, 271–8

Such were the deities who came to Athens' aid in her darkest hours of these wars. After victory the Athenians expressed, in dedications or sacrifices, their gratitude, but it is worthwhile to consider also the motives of the gods themselves in these wars as the Greeks described them. Several (Athena, Demeter, Artemis, and Ajax) seem, in the Greek accounts, to be acting primarily to protect their own sanctuaries or to be avenging sacrilegious destruction of them. Some (Demeter, Artemis, and Ajax in particular) were drawn into the conflict because their sanctuaries happened to be in the field of battle. Only Athena and Poseidon, by nature gods of warfare, seem to show concern for the welfare of the Athenians themselves. In a sense we have represented here two sides of cultic religion: on the one, supportive deities, prayer, sacrifice, granting of the prayer, and expressions of gratitude for that; on the other, the anger of the gods when their property and sanctuaries are impiously violated. In the first case the Athenian gods and heroes helped the Athenians who prayed, sacrificed, and made dedications to them; in the second they took vengeance on the Persians. Both contributed to the Greek and Athenian victories in these wars.

The Athenians and other Greeks recognized the help they received from their gods and heroes in war, but in war, as in the areas of agriculture, economic prosperity, and health, they did not give credit solely to the gods for their accomplishments.

> If men plan reasonable things, they generally occur. But if men plan unreasonable things, not even the god is willing to support their plans.
> Themistocles, in Herodotus, *Histories* 8.60.g

They took considerable pride in their own contributions to their successes. In the Persian Wars they prayed to the gods not to give them "victory," but to make it a "fair fight." After the gods evened the odds by destroying many of the Persian ships in a storm, these veteran Greek soldiers and sailors thought they could handle the rest.

The thousands of dedications in the hundreds of Greek sanctuaries are certainly expressions of gratitude to the deities, but they are equally monuments of human achievement, and usually the human achievement is given considerably more emphasis than the deity's contribution. After their great victory over the Persians at Plataea the Greeks inscribed their grand dedication of a golden tripod to Apollo at Delphi as follows:

> The saviors of Greece with its broad dance floors dedicated this,
> after they saved their cities from hateful slavery.
> (Diodorus Siculus 11.33.2)

There is not a word of Apollo's help, not even his name. The Athenians, after a victory over the Boeotians and Chalcidians in 506, erected as a dedication to Athena on the Acropolis a bronze four-horse chariot, with this inscription:

In deeds of war the children of the Athenians defeated
the peoples of the Boeotians and Chalcidians.
They quenched their hybris with painful iron chains,
and they dedicated, as a tithe, these mares to Pallas Athena.

(Herodotus 5.77.4 and *IG* I³ 501)

Again, the monument and its text reflect as much human accomplishment as divine help, and this is characteristic of virtually all Greek dedications. Just as many dedications result from a tithe, a tenth-part, of the success of the individual or state, so often nine-tenths of the text inscribed on these dedications describe the humans who made the dedication and their accomplishments. The Greeks looked to their deities for assistance and protection in war, agriculture, economic activities, and health, but in no sense passively expected their deities to do it all for them. The Greek attitude is nicely captured in a line from Aeschylus' *Persae* (742): "Whenever someone himself shows eagerness, the god also lends a hand." It is this view of divine help which contributed much to the dynamism of Greek culture in the Archaic and Classical periods.

I think I have come to learn that the gods made it impermissible for men to succeed without knowing what must be done and without taking care that these things be done. To some who are wise and diligent they give prosperity, but not to others. Therefore I begin by serving the gods, but I also try, as is right for me when I pray to the gods, to act in a way to find health and strength of body, honor in the city, goodwill among friends, honorable safety in war, and wealth which is honorably increased.

Ischomachus, in Xenophon, *Oeconomicus* 11.8

National Identity and National Needs

The Zeus Herkeios and Ktesios, Apollo Agyieus, and Hestia of a family were worshiped by and would be concerned with only that family. So too only the demesmen of Erchia would sacrifice to and receive the benefits from the deities in their sanctuaries. The Athenians as a group were, like a family or a deme, one very extended birth group, all descended from the earth-born Erechtheus, and the cults and deities of their state were expected to serve the interests of, and in turn be served by, only the members of that extended birth group. A Spartan visiting Athens for a few days on a diplomatic mission would have no rights or interest in sacrificing to an Athenian deity, even if that deity might have the same name as a deity he worshiped at home. Those many wealthy and talented non-Athenians resident and working in Athens in the fifth and fourth centuries, themselves citizens of other Greek states, would be largely excluded from Athenian religious cults and cult practices. They could, as we have seen, be initiated into the Eleusinian Mysteries, and the resident aliens were given a specially demarcated role in the procession of the Panathenaea and in a few other festivals, and they might make occasional dedications of gratitude to Athenian deities. But, beyond that, they were at best spectators at the many Athenian festivals and sacrifices. They, like slaves, were not part of the Athenian "family" and had no significant role to play in Athenian cult. Athenian state cult was for Athenians alone.

In the Classical period each Greek city-state, like Athens, practiced this same exclusivity of its religious life, and each had, in varying degrees, its own pantheon of deities, its own myths, and its own program of sacrifices and festivals. Even festivals with the same name such as the Thesmophoria might vary considerably in ritual from city to city. A city-state's collection of deities, myths, sacrifices, and festivals thus contributed to its distinctiveness, to its national identity viewed in comparison to that of other city-states. But, interestingly, it is a characteristic of Greek religion that no city-state claimed that its religious system or deities were superior to or more effective than those of any other city-state or even of non-Greek countries. The Athenians worshiped their own gods, but to show disrespect for any god – in Greece or elsewhere – or to rob or desecrate their sanctuaries was dangerous and might well bring forth the vengeance of that god. The Athenians actively worshiped their own gods, but respectfully accepted the worship of other gods elsewhere in the world by other Greek and non-Greek peoples.

Internally a city-state's religious system also contributed significantly to that state's image of itself and its customs and political institutions. As we saw in Chapter III, Myth #2, the Athenians took great pride in being *autochthonous*, that is, in being born from the earth of Attica itself. The land itself was, they claimed, literally their mother, and they, unlike most Greeks, had lived in that same land since the conception of their ancestor Erechtheus. The myth also made all Athenians one birth family, the Erechtheidae, descended ultimately from Erechtheus and, if not sons of Athena, at least sons of her favorite foster child. Some individual families might be more socially, economically, and politically prominent, but still all Athenians were of the same larger family and, in that sense, equal, and this, the Athenians thought, inclined them to democratic government.

But within this "democratic family" the only true citizens of Athens, the only full members of the family, were the descendants of Erechtheus in the male line. A boy born of an Athenian father and a foreign mother would become an Athenian citizen. A son of an Athenian mother and a foreign father would not. Only after Pericles' legislation in 451/0 did citizenship depend on having both an Athenian mother and father, but even then women were never termed "citizens," rather "Athenian women." Males alone still had the political rights to serve in the legislative and administrative positions, the legal rights to own property and participate personally in the court system, and the social right to move about freely in their own country.

The divisions between male and female were reflected and, in a sense, validated and reinforced by Athenian religious institutions. In addition to being a family, Athens was even in the fifth century a warrior society, with all males expected to serve, as needed, from ages 18 to 60 in the army, navy, or cavalry of the state. We have seen this reflected in the Ephebic Oath in Chapter V and, of course, in the warlike nature of Athena Polias, the patroness of the city, and in her Panathenaea. Most of the specifically Athenian contests in that festival featured military skills, dances in armor, cavalry exercises, and such, and Athenian youth in the junior divisions were being trained in these and the young men in the senior divisions were showing their skills. Similar activities, like the regatta for Poseidon of Sunium or the competitions at Theseus' festival, promoted and show-cased military expertise. The Acropolis, Athena's sanctuary, was filled with dedications celebrating Athenian victories over Greek and foreign foes. In other settings too, the value of the military side of Athenian life was highlighted. The ephebes visited and made offerings to the war dead and heroes of great Athenian military victories, and even in Dionysus' City Dionysia with its comedies and tragedies the Athenians staged a procession, in armor, of the male youth who, as orphans of fallen soldiers, were being raised at state expense.

Women's activities centered on childbearing and rearing, and, as we have seen, the festivals of Artemis and Demeter featured these roles, usually with the exclusion of men. It was also the women who tended Aphrodite and Hera Teleia (Of Marriage). Greek women contributed to the family economy by weaving, and so in Athens the four *arrephoroi* wove the *peplos* for the city's patroness. In the Parthenon frieze representing the Panathenaic procession, the young men ride horses and carry spears, the young women carry baskets with the implements for the sacrifice. The one hundred young women carrying baskets, with their fine clothes and jewelry, added beauty to the procession; the young men provided the military heft. These and other divisions of labor between men and women were inculcated in the youth by the whole program of Athenian religious activities.

Religion also offered support to the political fabric of Athens. An Athenian who, as an adult, wished to hold an archonship, was asked, in front of the

Boule, the following questions: "Who is your father, and from which of the demes is he? Who is your grandfather? Who is your mother? Who is her father, and from which of the demes is he? Do you have an Apollo Patroös and a Zeus Herkeios, and where are their sanctuaries? Do you have family tombs, and where are they? Do you treat your parents well? Do you pay your taxes? Have you participated in military campaigns?" Each question but the last two had a religious component. Legitimate birth from an Athenian citizen was asserted and validated, as we saw in Chapter V, in the festival of the Apatouria at the altar of Zeus Phratrios and Athena Phratria. The possession of a sanctuary of Zeus Herkeios assured a permanent home in Athens. Tombs were evidence of proper care and tendance of the dead. And the treatment of parents, as we will see in Chapter VII, had a religious sanction.

The Apollo Patroös (Ancestral) of this inquisition introduces a new aspect of the Athenian self-image. He was not among the early patrons of Athens such as Athena, Poseidon, and Hephaestus, but he was eventually given an important place in the genealogy of the Athenians and of all the people, the Ionians, who were descended from them and established colonies on the coast of Asia Minor. The myth that makes him Patroös to the Athenians is dramatized in Euripides' *Ion*, a play which should be read in its entirety both for its exciting plot and what it reveals about early Athenian myth. In very short form, Apollo of Delphi, as Euripides describes it, raped Creusa, a daughter of Erechtheus. She conceived a child, abandoned it in a cave of the Acropolis, and Apollo had it brought to Delphi and raised as a temple servant. The boy, Ion, is eventually discovered by his mother and returned to Athens where he will become king. Ion becomes the eponymous hero for all the *Ion*ians, including the Athenians, and his four sons become the eponymous heroes of the four tribes characteristic of Ionian peoples. Apollo is thus claimed as the original source, through Ion and his sons, of the pre-Cleisthenic four-tribe structure of Athenian male citizenry, and in the sixth century an Athenian would be an Erechtheid by descent from Erechtheus but, say, a member of the tribe of Geleon from descent from that child of Ion. In that sense Apollo Pythios of Delphi was Patroös, Ancestral, to the Athenians, and also, through their Ion, the Athenians could claim some at least mythical authority over the Ionian colonies in Asia Minor. Thus each Athenian citizen should be able to demonstrate his worship of Apollo Patroös. The state, just as it had a national cult of Hestia, had a state sanctuary for Apollo Patroös in the Agora.

In Athens the four Ionian tribes were largely outmoded by Cleisthenes' introduction, for political organization, of the ten tribes. In a system of regional and proportional representation, each deme was assigned to one

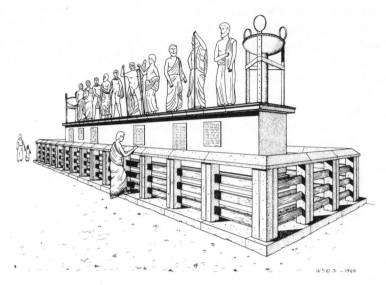

Figure VI.2 Drawing of the state monument of the ten eponymous heroes after whom the Athenian tribes were named. It stood in the Agora and on its base were posted, under the appropriate hero, public notices concerning his tribe's affairs. Courtesy of the American School of Classical Studies at Athens: Agora Excavations.

of these new tribes. The tribes became the basic political and military units of Athens, with each sending fifty members to serve in the Boule and with the army arranged into tribal units. Many of the contests at the festivals, as that of dithyrambs at the City Dionysia, of the regatta at Sunium, and of several at the Panathenaea, were competitions between these tribes. Important in religious terms is that each tribe was assigned, by the oracle at Delphi, a preexisting Attic hero as its eponymous hero, and so, for example, one tribe was named after Theseus' father Aegeus, another after the Salaminian hero Ajax. After the Cleisthenic reforms of 508/7, an Athenian would identify himself as an Erechtheid as a descendant of Erechtheus; as, for example, an Erchian by deme; and lastly as a member of Aegeus' tribe to which Erchia belonged. Each of these ten eponymous heroes had his own sanctuary where his tribe's members would assemble each year for a sacrifice and feast and where, if victorious in state competitions, they might erect dedications. The state, again, had in the Agora one unifying sanctuary with statues of all ten eponymous heroes of the tribes.

As we build the Athenian male social/political structure from family to deme to tribe, we reach the Athenian Boule, the Council of 500, fifty citizens from each tribe who served for a year. The Boule met in the Bouleuterion in the Agora, and it too had its patrons, Zeus Boulaios and Athena Boulaia, at whose altar prayers were offered before each meeting. A prayer opened also the meetings, four times each month, of the Ekklesia, the town meeting of all Athenian citizens. We don't have the content of this prayer itself, but the women of Aristophanes' *Thesmophoriazusae* (lines 295–371) offer a prayer before their "Ekklesia" which is a parody of the prayer of the real Ekklesia. Now that we have investigated the religious roles of women and the festival of Thesmophoria in Chapter V, we are in a position to appreciate both the serious and humorous elements of this Aristophanic prayer. A heraldess – just as the herald in a real Ekklesia – begins the prayer, and the chorus of women continues it:

Heraldess: "Let there be silence. Let there be silence. Pray to Demeter and Kore, the Thesmophoric goddesses, and to Ploutos and Kalligeneia and to Ge Kourotrophos and to Hermes and the Charites that we make this Ekklesia and assembly in the finest and best way, in a way beneficial to the city of the Athenians and successful for us women. And grant that she who does and says the best things concerning the *demos* of Athenian men and that of the women prevail. Pray for these things and good things for yourselves."

Chorus of Women: "We accept what you say and we beseech the race of gods to appear and be pleased (*charis*) by these prayers. Zeus of the great name and you who, with your golden lyre, hold holy Delos, and you, all-powerful, owl-eyed, golden-speared maiden who inhabits our much fought over city, come here. And the girl of many names, animal-slayer, child of golden faced Leto, and you, revered Poseidon of the sea, leaving your fish-filled, current-whirling haunt, and the daughters of Nereus of the sea, and the Nymphs who wander the mountains. And may the golden lyre sound out over our prayers. And, at last, may we, the well-born daughters of the Athenians, hold our Ekklesia."

Heraldess: "Pray to the male and female Olympian deities, and to the male and female Pythian deities, to the male and female Delian deities, and to the other gods. If anyone plots some evil for the *demos* of the women, or if someone gives out information to the Persians or Euripides[1] for the harm of the women, or if someone plans to establish a tyranny or to restore a tyrant, or if someone reported a woman who has brought in a supposititious child, or if a slave woman who is a procuress whispered to her master, or if a slave woman sent on a mission brings back false reports, or if some adulterer deceives by lying and does not give what he promises, or if some old woman gives gifts to an adulterer, or if some concubine accepts gifts and betrays her lover, or if a male or female merchant falsifies the liquid or dry measures, pray that the man and his family perish badly, but pray that the gods give many good things to all of you."

Chorus of Athenian women: "We pray that what we pray for be accomplished for the city and the *demos*, and that those who say the best things win in the debate. But those women who deceive and violate the traditional oaths harmfully for profit, or who seek to change the decrees and law of the state, or who tell our secrets to our enemies or bring back the Persians to our land to cause harm for their own profit, they are impious and treat the city unjustly. Zeus all-powerful, may you bring to pass these things so that the gods may stand by our side even though we are women."

The heraldess in the Ekklesia of women at the Thesmophoria naturally invokes first the deities associated with their festival: Demeter Thesmophoros and Kore, Ploutos, and Kalligeneia. In addition to them she appeals to Ge Kourotrophos (Nurse of the Young), Hermes, and the Charites (Graces). The women themselves then add Zeus, Apollo, Athena, Artemis, Poseidon, the Nereids of the sea, and the Nymphs of the mountains. Some of the women's prayerful requests – the condemnation of adulterers, lying slaves, and cheating merchants – derive from typically Aristophanic humor directed against women, slaves, and merchants, but many of the others are paralleled in actual prayers and oaths made in the legislative and judicial assemblies and reflect deep-seated concerns of Athenians: that those who make the best arguments prevail in the debates, that those who deceive their fellow citizens and violate the traditional oaths, or who seek to change the decrees and law of the state, or who tell secrets to the enemy for their own profit be punished. The fear of tyrants, nearly a century after the ouster of the tyrant Pisistratus, and the fear of the Persians, two generations after their defeat, remain palpable in these prayers. Aristophanes in his comedy and Athenian men in life, in their assemblies and courts, asked the gods to attend to all of these essentially political matters and to punish offenders.

One major concern was that fellow citizens not violate the "traditional oaths," and that is because through these oaths Athenians put under divine supervision critical elements of their political system. The Athenians believed that such oaths "held together their democracy" (Lycurgus, *Leocrates* 79). One such oath was taken by the ephebes, as we saw in Chapter V, and there they swore, among other things, to obey the officials and the laws and to oppose anyone who attempted to destroy them. The members of the Boule swore "to counsel the best things for the city," and the archons had to swear "to rule justly." The jurors of Athens, numbering 6,000 each year, swore the most elaborate oath:

"I will vote in accordance with the laws and decrees of the Athenian people and of the Boule of five hundred. And I will not vote to have a tyrant or an oligarchy. If someone attempts to destroy the power of the Athenian people or if he speaks or brings a vote contrary to this, I will not be persuaded. Nor will I vote for the cancellation of private debts or for the redistribution of Athenian land or houses. I will not bring back those who have been exiled or condemned to death. I will not myself banish, nor will I allow anyone else to banish, the residents here contrary to the established laws and decrees of the Athenian *demos* and Boule. And I will not confirm in office a person in such a way that he holds one office when he is subject to audit for another. . . . Nor will I allow the same man to hold the same office twice or the same man to hold two offices in the same year. And I will not accept bribes because of my jury service, not I myself nor another for me nor in any other way with me knowing of it, not by a trick or by any contrivance. And I am not less than thirty years old. And I will listen to both the prosecutor and the defendant equally, and I will bring my vote on the basis of the issues being prosecuted." The juror is to swear by Zeus, Poseidon, and Demeter, and he is to curse himself and his family to utter destruction if he transgresses any of these things, but he is to pray that if he keeps his oath there may be many good things for him.

(Demosthenes 24.149–51)

In this and the other oaths the Athenians revealed their most immediate political concerns and put themselves under divine sanctions for what they determined was proper civic and legal behavior. If the jurors violated these principles, if they broke this oath, they would suffer the curse they put upon themselves and their families. And there was no place of escape from the curse because the three gods they invoked, Zeus, Poseidon, and Demeter, represented, respectively, the sky, the sea, and the land.

> I could never deem happy a man who is aware that he has disregarded such oaths. For I do not know with what swiftness of foot he might escape the hostility of the gods or any place to which someone might flee, nor do I know any dark spot he might run off to or how he might withdraw to a secure place. For all things everywhere are subject to the gods and they control all things equally.
>
> Clearchus in Xenophon, *Anabasis* 2.5.7

Athens is, of course, justly famous for its democratic institutions, but the gods themselves in Athens were not, on their own initiative, promoters of democracy or supporters of one political group or class of citizens against another. Certain gods did not serve as patrons of the "democratic" or "oligarchic" party or of the rich or poor. In the fifth century there are no surviving prayers or sacrifices to a god to promote "democracy" or "oligarchy," the favored political system of a minority of Athenians. But the Athenians created oaths such as that of the jurors to compel their gods to address their political concerns. By being invoked as witnesses to these oaths, the gods were obliged to enforce obedience and punish perjury – whatever the provisions of the oath. Gods elsewhere in the Greek world supported city-states governed by oligarchs, aristocrats, and even tyrants, but the Athenians by these oaths with their democratic provisions essentially forced their gods to support the democratic principles of their society.

We have focused much of our discussion of state religion on Athens, and as we close it is important to remember that Athens for most of the Classical period was no ordinary Greek city-state. For a good part of the fifth century she was receiving large revenues from allied and later tributary city-states throughout the Aegean, and she was, simply put, incomparably rich. Athens dedicated 1/60 of these revenues to Athena Polias, and with this and other state monies Athens was able to support the most extensive and grandest program of religious festivals known in the Greek world. It was claimed that she had twice as many festivals as other cities, and at least 120 days of the Athenian year featured some religious offering or festival. Furthermore, these offerings and festivals were often made on a scale and at an expense unknown in the Greek world of the time. The Athenians could spend for each Greater Panathenaea and its sacrificial victims, contests and prizes, and gold-bedecked basket carriers the equivalent of millions of dollars, whereas records from other cities suggest for their festivals much more modest expenditures, in the thousands of dollars. So too the Athenian state could spend hundreds of millions of dollars each for a large number of marble temples while most Greek cities had to remain content with temples in only a few sanctuaries, and those being of limestone with, perhaps, a marble veneer. We might attribute the Athenians' unusually grand expenditures on religious cults to a number of things: to the availability of excess capital, to an attempt to amuse and entertain the common people, to their love of country, and even, as Thucydides (2.40.1) has Pericles describe it, to their love of beauty. But it is also perfectly understandable and appropriate in Greek religious terms. As we have seen, the gods are owed a return – as "first fruits" or as tithe – from the gifts they bestow on humans. The greater the gifts, the greater the return owed, and from about 490 to 415 B.C.E. the gods were very generous to the Athenians. The Athenians in this period became militarily, politically, economically, and artistically dominant in the Greek world, and the scale and expense of their religious program reflects this and also their commitment to return a share of their successes to the gods who helped provide them.

We have seen that each city-state would have, to a greater or lesser degree, its own distinctive pantheon of deities serving its needs; its own program of festivals, a few of which were commonly Greek, several of which were unique; its own religious calendar; and, quite certainly, its own collection of heroes tied closely to its own traditions. It could not afford the many expensive temples, statues, and festival productions of Athens, but it had, on a lesser scale, all these same components of religion. It, like Athens and every other city-state, turned to its deities for assistance in the critical needs of fertility of crops, animals, and human beings, of good health, of economic prosperity, of safety in dangers of war and seafaring, and of establishing its national identity and supporting its political and social structures.

NOTE

1. In the *Thesmophoriazusae* Euripides, commonly labeled as a woman-hater by Aristophanic women, tries to sneak into the women's festival.

FURTHER READING

On deities' contributions to military, agricultural, and economic life:

Geagan, D., "Who was Athena?" pp. 145–63 in *Religion in the Ancient World*, ed. M. Dillon, Amsterdam, 1996
Mikalson, J.D., *Herodotus and Religion in the Persian Wars* (Chapel Hill, 2003) and *Athenian Popular Religion* (Chapel Hill, 1983), 18–38
Pritchett, W.K., *The Greek State at War* (Berkeley, 1971–1985), especially volume 3

On religion and Athenian political and social institutions:

Cole, S.G., "Oath Ritual and the Male Community at Athens," pp. 227–48 in *Dêmokratia*, ed. J. Ober and C. Hedrick, Princeton, 1996
Jameson, M.H., "Religion in the Athenian Democracy," pp. 171–95 in *Democracy 2500? Questions and Challenges*, edd. I. Morris and K.A. Raaflaub, Dubuque, 1998
Sourvinou-Inwood, C., "What is *Polis* Religion?" pp. 295–322 in *The Greek City from Homer to Alexander*, edd. O. Murray and S. Price, Oxford, 1990 and "Further Aspects of Polis Religion," *Annali: Istitituto orientale di Napoli: Archeologia e storia antica* 10 (1988), 259–74
Versnel, H.S., "Religion and Democracy," pp. 367–87 in *Die athenische Demokratie im 4. Jahrjundert v. Chr.*, ed. W. Eder, Stuttgart, 1995

VII

Greek Religion and
the Individual

rJrJrJr

We have thus far seen the Greek man, woman, child, and slave in the religious environment of family, village, and state. In this chapter we look more to the personal concerns and beliefs of individuals: how they thought they were to act in religious matters, what constituted piety and impiety for them and how the one might be rewarded and the other punished, and, finally, how they viewed their deaths and afterlife in terms of their religion.

As in most religions, Greeks were "born into" their religion. From earliest childhood on they naturally assimilated the religious practices and beliefs of their families, villages, and city-states. Since, as we have often noted, the deities, cults, and festivals varied somewhat from one city-state to another, the beliefs and practices of an individual would be determined by which city-state he or she happened to be born in. A young Spartan would be acculturated to a religious system in some ways markedly different from that of a young Athenian. But in the Classical period within his or her own city-state there would be for the individual only the one system of deities, cults, practices, rituals, and festivals – with slight variations from village to village, and that system as a whole would provide what the Greeks thought they needed from their deities. Within that city-state there was no competing religious system which would require individuals to choose between systems. What choice was offered was the relatively few "elective" cults such as the Eleusinian Mysteries which were usually additions to, not replacements of, the religious system of one's own city-state.

Xenophon in his defense of Socrates in the *Memorabilia* illustrates well how a Greek was to act in regard to the religion of his city-state. He claimed (1.3.1) that in matters concerning the gods Socrates obviously acted and spoke in the way that the Pythia prescribed to men who were asking how they must act concerning sacrifices or the care of ancestors or any other such thing. For the Pythia responded that they would be acting piously if they acted in accordance with the "custom" of their city.

You see that the god in Delphi, when someone asked him how he might win favor (*charis*) with the gods, answered, "by the 'custom' of the city." And, I suppose, it is the custom everywhere to please the gods to the maximum of one's ability with sacrifices.

Socrates in Xenophon's *Memorabilia* 4.3.16

Socrates is unjust because he does not believe in the gods in which the city believes but introduces other, new spirits. He is unjust also because he corrupts the young men. The punishment is death.

The indictment against Socrates in 399 B.C.E., Diogenes Laertius 2.40

The individual is pious and wins the favor (*charis*) of the gods by follow-ing the traditional customs of his or her own city-state. The customs of one's country determined which deities were to be worshiped, how, where, at what times, with what offerings, and for what purposes. For the Greeks these customs were not the "revealed" instructions of the gods but prac-tices established by their ancestors and carried on for generations.[1] These Greek "ancestral customs" were formulated in general terms, were usually unwritten, and offered guidance, not, like those of the Romans, highly detailed manuals concerning minute ritual detail. It was, for example, an ancestral custom for Greeks to give burial to the dead or not to enter a sanctuary unbathed after sexual intercourse. For Athenians it was their ancestral custom to offer Athena a *peplos* on Hekatombaion 28 at her festival and for girls to "play the bear" at the Brauronia. These ancestral customs were the product of human beings, not gods, and hence were not inalterable. They might be amended or expanded by a state law, and they might be codified in calendars of the year's sacrifices and festivals, but any changes were the subject of great concern and scrutiny and often had to be approved by the Delphic Oracle. In times of national crisis, there was often a call to "reestablish" the ancestral customs in religious matters. The Athenian orator Isocrates, writing in the middle of the fourth century and complaining of current practices, well represents this con-servative view:

Our ancestors did not perform the services and celebrate the rites in an irregular and disorganized fashion. Nor did they send in procession three hundred cattle whenever it struck their fancy, nor did they leave aside the ancestral sacrifices on chance occasions. Nor did they celebrate with great grandeur the new festivals in which a feast was included. . . . They guarded against the elimination of any of the ancestral sacrifices and against the addition of any sacrifices outside the traditional ones. For they thought that piety consisted not in great expenditures, but rather in not changing any of those things that their ancestors had handed down to them. And furthermore, help from the gods occurred for them not in fits and starts and not confusedly, but at the proper time for the working of the land and for the harvest of the produce.

Areopagiticus 29–30

Our ancestors, by making the sacrifices listed on the archaic calendar of Solon, handed down to us the largest and most divinely favored of all Greek cities. Therefore we ought to make the same sacrifices as they did, if for no other reason, then because of the good fortune that resulted from those sacrifices.

An Athenian in 399 B.C.E., in Lysias, *Against Nicomachus* 18

Most Greek religious activities fell under the purview of "ancestral customs," and, as we have seen, with the authority of the Delphic Oracle behind it, obedience to them was the test of an individual's piety and was the means for the individual to win the favor of the gods. These ancestral customs, as Isocrates indicates, included sacrifices to the gods of the state, and an individual who failed to participate in these might well find himself labeled "impious." Funeral rites and later offerings at the tomb were also "ancestral customs," and a relative who neglected them was impious. The Greeks believed that the gods were concerned with such funerary matters, but also with the treatment of one's parents when they were alive. Neglect or maltreatment of living parents was also an impiety.

In Athens some of the ancestral customs were bolstered by formal laws. A law of the seventh-century lawgiver Dracon reportedly bade the Athenians "as a group to honor the gods and local heroes in accordance with the ancestral practices, and in private as best they can, with pious language and with first-fruit offerings of produce and with annual offerings of cakes" (Porphyry, *de Abstinentia* 4.22). A decree enacted by the Ekklesia about 433 B.C.E. ordered that those who "did not respect the divine things" be brought to trial for impiety (Plutarch, *Life of Pericles* 32.2). And there was a fifth-century law that forbade the importation of a "foreign

[There is a story] which, even if it is rather mythical, will still be appropriate for all you younger men to hear. It is said that on Sicily a stream of lava arose from Etna. They say that this lava flowed over the rest of the island and was approaching one of the cities situated there. The other people sought their own safety and rushed off in flight, but one young man, when he saw that his father was too old to flee and was being overtaken by the lava, lifted him up and carried him. And because of the extra burden, I suppose, the young man himself was also caught in the lava. But from this event you ought to see that the divine is well-intentioned towards good men, because, as the story goes, that place was engulfed by lava and only this father and son survived. From them the place still even now is called "The place of the Pious." Those who tried to quicken their retreat by abandoning their parents all perished.

Lycurgus, *Leocrates* 95–6

god" without, presumably, the approval of the Ekklesia (Josephus, *Contra Apionem* 2.267). In the Classical period a few Athenians, including Socrates, were brought to trial for violating such laws, and, as in Socrates' case, the punishments could be very severe, including death or exile.

Murder, too, was an impiety, and, as we saw in Chapter I, brought pollution to the murderer and with that in Athens exclusion from sanctuaries, sacrifices, libations, contests in religious festivals, the marketplace, and even the city itself. A murderer faced punishment through the legal system but also had to undergo ritual purifications of the pollution he had incurred. The polluted person in the city put at risk the whole city's relationship with the gods, and therefore any in the city who hindered the identification and proper conviction and punishment of the murderer could be thought to share in the impiety as well as in the pollution of the murderer himself.

Traitors were considered impious because by treason against their country they also, as the Athenian orator Lycurgus put it, "betray the gods' and heroes' temples, statues, sacred precincts, their honors established in the laws, and the sacrifices handed down by our ancestors" (*Leocrates* 1). A traitor's success could result in the destruction of the deities' sanctuaries and property and the loss of their cults in his city, and that is man's ultimate "dishonoring" of the gods, the ultimate impiety. Traitors and temple-robbers were engaged in analogous activities – the destruction or diminution of a deity's property –, and therefore in Athens the same law dealt with both: "the law applies to the temple-robbers and traitors and states that if anyone betrays the city or steals from the sanctuaries, if he has been tried and convicted in court, he is (to be executed and) not to be buried in Attica and his property is to confiscated" (Xenophon, *Hellenica* 1.7.22).

Suppliants having asylum in a deity's sanctuary were, as we noted in Chapter I, for the time the deity's property, and respect for this asylum was respect for the god. It was a grave impiety, often punished by the gods with death, to violate such asylum by killing suppliants or dragging them from the sanctuary against their will.

A friend one had in another city-state was his *xenos*, and the relationship between the two was termed *xenia*. When the friend visited the city-state of his *xenos*, when, for example, an Athenian visited a Spartan friend in Sparta, he would lodge with and be entertained as a guest by his *xenos* there. In his own city-state he would be the host to his *xenos*. This guest/host relationship, *xenia*, was also a concern of the gods, especially of Zeus Xenios. Violation of the traditions of *xenia*, for example to steal property from one's *xenos* or even worse, as Trojan Paris did to Spartan Menelaus, to take his wife, was a grave impiety which would bring punishment from the gods, as it did to Paris, his family, and his country.

> What god or deity listens to you when you are a perjurer and deceive *xenoi*?
>
> Medea to Jason, in Euripides, *Medea* 1391–2

The adherence to an oath taken with gods as witnesses, such as the Jurors' Oath we saw in Chapter VI, is in one sense a show of respect for the power of the deities named. Most such oaths included a curse that the divine witnesses punish the oath-taker and his family if the oath was broken, and the one who violated the oath, the perjurer, would implicitly be expressing the view that the divine witnesses would not or could not punish him in the manner specified in the curse. This was disrespect of the gods, and it, too, was an impiety. Average Athenians would rarely if ever commit impieties such as murder or robbing sanctuaries or violating asylum and *xenia*, but oaths were so commonly used in the Athenian legal system, in commercial transactions, and in everyday life that quite probably here Athenians and other Greeks faced most often a stark choice between financial or social gains and personal piety.

> When an oath has been added, a man is more
> careful, for he guards against two things,
> the criticism of his friends and committing a transgression
> against the gods.
>
> Sophocles, frag. 472 [Radt]

Since there were no trials or legal punishments for perjury itself, except as false testimony in court, the temptation to casual perjury, that is, to casual impiety, must have been strong. That may be why ancient writers so often emphasize in their discussions of personal piety the importance of keeping one's oaths and sometimes made the keeping of oaths a proof of an individual's piety in general.

> Be pious in matters concerning the gods not only by sacrificing but also by remaining true to your oaths. The former is an indication of a ready supply of money, but the latter is an indication of goodness of character. Always honor the divine, but especially in association with your city. For thus you will seem at the same time to be sacrificing and to be following the laws of the city.
>
> Isocrates, to Demonicus, a young Cyprian (1.12–13)

The historical writings and the orations from classical Greece offer occasional instances of real individuals committing the impieties we have described, and the sinners are regularly punished by the legal system or by the gods themselves. Athenian tragedies, however, provide the most vivid and compelling accounts of individuals caught in the nexus of impiety and punishment. These tragedies are set in the courts of kings, in heroic times almost a thousand years before the time of their performance, but they reflect many of the religious concerns and practices of fifth-century Athenians. In Sophocles' *Antigone* we see Creon denying burial rites to his nephew Polynices, and the play examines this action from several different angles. In the end, of course, Creon suffers terribly. The title character of Euripides' *Hippolytus* shows disrespect for Aphrodite and pays the penalty, as does Pentheus for his disrespect of Dionysus in Euripides' *Bacchae*. Aeschylus' trilogy *Oresteia* offers violation of *xenia*, destruction of altars, and, especially, the murder of kin, all gross impieties. Sophocles' *Oedipus Tyrannus* opens with the pollution of the city of Thebes from Oedipus' killing of his father Laius. Asylum in a sanctuary and threats to it are features of the *Suppliant Women* of Aeschylus and *Heraclidai* of Euripides, and are also central to the denouement of Euripides' *Ion*. Almost every Athenian tragedy offers at least one moment of actual or intended impiety, and in virtually every case the individual who violates "ancestral religious customs" or commits other impieties suffers. But these plays are not simple morality plays showing only that sinners are punished. Each places the impious actions into morally complicated human and social situations, and a careful reading of tragedy will give a deeper understanding of how Athenians in the fifth century imagined that the gods regarded and punished the impieties of human beings. But in reading these tragedies and other poetic genres such as epic and comedy, one should be aware of how the religion and deities they present differ in some important respects from the religion that the Greeks themselves practiced. The gods of tragedy are, for example, more personally and directly involved with the royal characters of these plays, some of whom are their children, grandchildren, or lovers. The gods of tragedy are more often blamed for causing evils of life – including death – which in real life were most often attributed to fate, fortune, or a nameless *daimon*. The impieties committed in tragedies are also often very heinous, and some characters, like Pentheus in the *Bacchae*, directly challenge the "honor" and authority of a god. And, of course, the punishments tragic sinners receive are usually very harsh, involving not just the sinner but his family and city as well. Finally, there is in Greek epic and tragedy often expressed the view that the gods should be "just" by human standards, but we do not find the morality of the gods an issue in the sources for popular religion. In these and other ways the religion and gods of tragedy in particular differ from that of practiced religion, and one needs to take these differences into account and also the differing views of the individual poets as one attempts to understand Greek religious beliefs.

A late author claimed that the "first elements of just behavior are those concerning the gods, the fatherland and parents, and the dead. Of these piety consists." "Impiety," he said, "is error concerning the gods or concerning the dead, or concerning parents and the fatherland" ([Aristotle] *Virtues and Vices* 1250b2 and 1251a2). These summary accounts provide a reasonably accurate and comprehensive synopsis of those areas in which Greeks believed piety and impiety were involved. Maintenance of oaths, respect for the rights of asylum and *xenia*, observance of ancestral customs and law in cult matters and tendance of the dead, loyalty to one's country, and proper care of one's living parents were all elements of the pious life. The reward for pious behavior was to maintain the favor (*charis*) of the gods, a favor which might result in material success and favorable opportunities for the pious individual. The individual who violated oaths, mistreated hosts or those having asylum, violated traditional cult practices in sacrifices and the tendance of the dead, or committed a number of other impious acts incurred the hostility of the gods. The individual who betrayed his country or neglected his living parents incurred this same hostility. This divine antagonism would affect the individual's welfare in all those areas of life in which the gods intervened – in fertility of one's crops, animals, family, and self, in economic prosperity, in health, and in personal safety at sea and war. It might also adversely affect innocent

> Respect and fear the gods. This keeps a man
> from doing or saying impious things.
>> Theognis, lines 1179–80, to his friend Cyrnus

> Let no one wish to be unjust and
> let no one sail with perjurers.
> I, a god, speak to mortals.
>> Castor, one of the two sailor-saving Dioscuri,
>> as *deus ex machina* in Euripides, *Electra* 1354–6

people around the sinner. A Greek proverb, for example, warned against sailing on the same ship as an impious man. Specific types of punishments were associated with certain types of impious behavior, and an individual might be condemned to death by a law court or lose his right to be buried in Attica. Sometimes the gods themselves did more than withhold their favor. They might inflict a punishment obvious to all. The Athenian dithyrambic poet Cinesias and his friends in the late fifth century had mocked certain religious traditions, and he himself had defecated on statues of the goddess Hecate. A speaker in a courtroom oration composed by Lysias (frag. 73 [Thalheim]) describes the punishment which the gods imposed upon Cinesias:

> Each of the others perished as you would expect such men to, but the gods put Cinesias, who was known to very many people, into such a condition that his enemies preferred that he live rather than die. The gods made him an example for other men, so that they might see that the gods do not put off the punishment of those who are excessively insolent towards divine matters upon their children, but they destroy miserably the sinners themselves by afflicting them with greater and harsher misfortunes and diseases than other men suffer. All of us by nature share in death and disease, but to continue in such a bad state so long and to be unable every day to end one's life by death befalls only those who have committed such sins as Cinesias has.

One prefers not to close a discussion of these aspects of ancient Greek religion with the portrait of a man notoriously and exceptionally impious, and fortunately we have for comparison to the impious Cinesias the Athenian statesman and general Nicias who was recognized in his own time and in later antiquity for his exemplary piety. A contemporary of the poet

Cinesias, Nicias in 421 B.C.E. helped negotiate a treaty, the Peace of Nicias, that brought a long period of relative peace in the midst of the Peloponnesian War between Athens and its allies and Sparta and its allies. In 415 he was chosen, despite his own reservations and objections, to lead the ill-fated Sicilian expedition that the Athenians undertook to extend their empire to the west. Plutarch in his *Life of Nicias* reports that Nicias sacrificed to the gods every day and kept a seer in his house to consult on public affairs and his own business operations (4.2). He was a very wealthy man and performed the religious duties assigned to him with an expense and beauty previously unknown (3.2). He seems particularly devoted to Delian Apollo. In 417 he financed and made lavish arrangements for the chorus which the Athenians annually sent to Delos to hymn the god, he dedicated a bronze palm tree there, and he also gave to Delian Apollo an expensive tract of income-producing land to endow annual sacrifices and feasts. As the Delians performed these sacrifices, they were to ask "many good things from the gods for Nicias" (3.4–6). In Plutarch's time, five centuries later, two of Nicias' private dedications were still standing in Athens, a gilded statue of Athena on the Acropolis and a temple in the sanctuary of Dionysus (3.3). Plutarch (4.1) notes that these public religious services and dedications were surely intended to win political favor with the people, but they also reflected the personal piety of the man.

As a general, too, Nicias exemplified piety. In a battle with the Corinthians in 425 he gave up claim to a military victory in order to recover and bury the bodies of the two Athenian soldiers (6.5–6), and at Syracuse he prevented his men from sacking and desecrating a sanctuary of Zeus Olympios. Despite the gold and silver there, he thought no benefit would result and that he would bear the responsibility for the impiety (16.6). Thucydides has Nicias say in his final days, "In my life I have performed what is traditional towards the gods and what is just and without reproach towards men. In return my hopes for the future are still bold" (7.77.2–3). Nicias' final days, however, belied those hopes, as he and his army in Syracuse were defeated and captured, and many of them, including Nicias himself, were killed. An eclipse of the full moon had occurred, and Nicias heeded his seer's advice and his army's inclination to delay an evacuation for twenty-seven days, until the next full moon. The delay cost the army any chance of escape, and Nicias was later criticized by some for excessive dependence on omens and seers (Thucydides 7.50.4 and especially Plutarch, *Life of Nicias* 23.1–6). The tragic death of the pious Nicias brought troubling thoughts to the minds of his men, as reported by Plutarch (26.6): "They were disheartened in their expectations from the gods when they reasoned that a man who was god-loved and famous for his many and great services to the gods was suffering a fortune no fairer than that of the worst and most lowly men in the army." The life and fate of Nicias reflect both the ideals and the occasional grim realities of the ancient Greek religion as it was actually practiced. Many a sailor who had prayed to Poseidon for safety no doubt perished at sea. In real life some pious men and women met bad ends, while in the works of Greek literature they rarely do.

In general terms the Greeks believed that piety was a necessary, though by no means sufficient, cause of personal prosperity. The vast majority of Athenians would have agreed both with Antiphon (6.5) when he claimed that "a man who acts impiously and transgresses against the gods would deprive himself of the very hopes which are the greatest good men have," and with Isocrates (*Antidosis* 281–2) when he exhorted all the Greeks "to think that those who get more from the gods both now and in the future are those who are most pious and most diligent in their tendance of the gods."

Death and the Afterlife

The rewards for piety and punishments for impiety were thought to be, almost exclusively, in this life, and that introduces the question of the Greeks' expectations of the afterlife. For many modern students of the Greeks, conceptions of the Greek afterlife have been shaped by the famous account of Odysseus' encounter with the dead in Book 11 of Homer's *Odyssey*. There souls of the dead, insubstantial, without strength and "sense," flit around Hades. At an entrance to the underworld Odysseus holds back with his sword the throngs of souls, but is able to converse with those he wishes by giving them some of his blood offering. He consults the long-dead seer Teiresias about his plans for his return to Ithaca. He talks extensively with his dead mother and then with a number of women famous in Greek mythology, among them Alcmene, Heracles' mother, and Leda, the mother of Castor and Polydeuces. Agamemnon, too, drank of the blood and told Odysseus of his shameful murder at the hands of Aegisthus and Clytemnestra. Odysseus interviews Achilles, too, gives him news of current events on earth and of his son, and hears from him his famous assessment of the underworld:

> "O shining Odysseus, never try to console me for dying.
> I would rather follow the plow as thrall to another
> man, one with no land allotted him and not much to live on,
> than be a king over all the perished dead."
>
> *Odyssey* 11.488–91 (Lattimore translation)

Odysseus also sees the punishments of three great "sinners" of antiquity: Tityus, with vultures eternally attacking his liver, for assaulting Leto, Zeus' paramour and the mother of Apollo and Artemis; Tantalus, eternally tantalized by water and food that just escape his reach; and Sisyphus, eternally trying to roll his rock up the hill. From other sources we learn that Tantalus tested the perspicacity of the gods by serving to them his son Pelops as the meat for a banquet, and that Sisyphus, the consummate trickster, tried, with temporary success, a number of means to escape the god Thanatus (Death).

This picture of the underworld, with masses of insubstantial souls fluttering about, with the great heroes and heroines of the past being able to be restored to consciousness, with the eternal punishment of notorious sinners who wronged the gods, was then elaborated or remodeled by later Greek poets and even philosophers. Homer's account was also a major source for Virgil's compelling description of the underworld in Book 6 of the *Aeneid*. The conception of the underlife that arises from these various accounts is quite naturally taken by many to be what the Greeks themselves believed awaited them after death, but in fact it appears to be largely a poetic fantasy with little if any correlation to what Greeks of the Classical period themselves expected.

To judge from the non-poetic sources, Greeks foresaw no meaningful existence after death. We might expect to find in the afterlife rewards for piety and punishments for impiety, but, outside of poetry, the Greeks express no such expectations. The Greek gods and heroes we have described throughout our account were deities of the living. They demonstrated their favor (*charis*) to humans only when they were alive or to their families after their deaths. The immortal, ouranic Greek gods wanted nothing to do with death, the dead, and the underworld, an aspect of the Greek gods poignantly reflected in Euripides' *Hippolytus* when Hippolyus' patroness Artemis must withdraw at the time of his death (lines 1437–8). So, too, impieties committed against these gods were punished during life, and, if not then, the Greeks thought the punishment of the impieties would fall upon the family and descendants of the sinner. In their strongest oaths the Greeks cursed, if they violated the oath, themselves and their families to destruction. They never cursed themselves to punishment in the afterlife.

If Greeks had strong expectations of good or evil in the afterlife, we might well expect to find them expressed on their tombstones. Thousands upon thousands of inscribed tombstones survive, and very rarely, and then only formulaically or uncertainly, is there any such expression. Most tombstones give only the decedent's name, with, for a male, his father's name, with her husband's or father's name for a female. The few more extensive epitaphs list the individual's virtues in this life, lament his or her death, and describe the sorrow of surviving relatives.

> Philostratus, son of Philoxenus,
> your grandfather's name you bore,
> but to your parents "Chatterbox,"
> once their joy, now mourned by all,
> by a *daimon* you were carried off."
>
> *IG* II² 12974

> Had you, by fortune's escort, attained maturity,
> we all foresaw in you, Macareus, a great man,
> a master of the tragic art among the Greeks.
> But now, in death, your reputation does remain
>   for temperance and virtue.
>
> *IG* II² 6626

Such epitaphs perhaps cannot be taken to prove that the Greeks did not believe in an afterlife, but they do indicate, as do other sources, that at the time of the death of their loved ones their thought was focused primarily on this world, not on the next. Those epitaphs which do mention the afterlife speak in vague terms of the soul being with Persephone and Pluto, as in the following:

> Your virtue left behind many monuments,
> in Greece and in the minds of men,
> of the kind of man you were, Nicobolus,
> when, mourned by friends, you left the sun's bright light
> and descended to the house of Persephone.
>
> *IG* II² 6004

> It is an easy thing to praise good men.
> Abundant eulogies are quickly found.
> Now, in the chamber of Persephone,
>   the chamber shared by all,
> you, Dionysius, enjoy such praise.
> Your body, Dionysius, lies here,
> but your immortal soul is now possessed
>   by the dispenser shared by all.
> In death you left behind undying grief
> for your friends, your mother, and your sisters.
>
> *IG* II² 11169

The strongest assertions of rewards in the afterlife in these epitaphs are conditioned by uncertainty:

> Melitta, daughter of Apollodorus.
> Here lies beneath the earth Hippostrate's good nurse.
> And how Hippostrate now longs for you!
> I loved you so, dear nurse,
> and now, for all my life,
> I'll honor you, though you lie below.
> If the good receive a prize in the underworld,
> you now, I know, enjoy first place with Pluto and Persephone.
>
> *IG* II² 7873

> Your virtue, Nicoptoleme, endures
> undying in your husband's memory.
> If piety finds favor with Persephone,
> fortune, through death, grants this reward to you.
>
> *IG* II² 6551

The house and chamber of Persephone and Pluto were familiar features of the underworld since Homer, and they do occur on some of these longer epitaphs, but none of the other literary features of the underworld such as the river Acheron, the ferryman Charon, or the dog Cerberus appears. Most of the longer epitaphs were in verse form, and the references to Persephone and Pluto in these epitaphs may be merely reflections of a poetic tradition with little or no basis in contemporary religious belief. The best evidence for ancient Greek practiced religion indicates that most Greeks did *not* expect a meaningful afterlife of conscious souls receiving rewards or punishments for their religious deeds during their lives. That, like their belief that "the gods help those who help themselves," may have contributed to the Greeks' extraordinary vitality in this life in the Classical period.

There are, however, in Greek beliefs about the afterlife more variety and more contradictions than in other aspects of their religion. Food and drink offerings, as we have seen, were made annually at the tombs of the dead, and this presumes that the dead have consciousness and appetite, or at least that people believed this when these "ancestral customs" were first established. The Greeks, like most societies, even many Christian societies, had a rich store of ghost stories, of mysterious underworld figures such as the Lamia that harass the living and can be put off only by magic rituals, and of curses on the living directed to the dead. There were also tales of the vengeance of the dead and of spirits that accomplished this revenge. The presumed *modus operandi* of such avenging spirits in the legal system is described in this speech composed as an exercise for a hypothetical murder trial by the Athenian Antiphon (4.1.3–4):

> The one who has died, since he is deprived of those things which the god gave him, naturally leaves behind as the vengeance of god the hostility of the avenging spirits. Those who unjustly judge the case or unjustly testify, by joining in the impiety of the one doing these things, bring this hostility of the avenging spirits, a defilement which was not originally theirs, into their own houses. And if we, while professedly seeking vengeance for the dead, should prosecute innocent men because of some personal hatred, we will have as terrible avenging spirits against us the avengers of the dead for whom we have not sought vengeance.

In Athens such avenging spirits of the dead were not introduced into real courtroom speeches, nor were the other tales of ghosts and underworld figures said, in other contexts, to cause death, misery, and madness. Such stories were certainly told in classical Athens, and amulets, evil-eyes, and other magical means were employed against these fearful figures, but they are very much matters of private practice, outside and perhaps beneath the notice of the traditional religious system of the city. For that reason, perhaps, they were not thought respectable points and arguments to raise in a public legal trial before one's peers.

Plato in the *Republic* (1.330d–331b) has the aged, wealthy Cephalus worrying about the possible punishments after death:

> When the thought of his own death approaches a man, he feels fear and concern about things about which he did not before. The stories that are told about the things in Hades, that the man who acted unjustly in this world must pay the penalty there, are laughed at until this time, but then the fear that they may be true racks his soul. And either because of the weakness of old age or because he is now closer to Hades, he himself sees these things more clearly and is filled with suspicion and terror. Then a man does his accounts and examines whether he has committed any injustice against anyone. The man who discovers unjust acts in his life wakes up from sleep frequently like children and is terrified and lives with a bad hope for the future. But the man who knows of no unjust acts which he has committed always has a hope that is sweet and, as Pindar says, a good "nurse of his old age." In a charming way Pindar said this, Socrates, that if a man lives his life in a just and holy manner,
>
> > Sweet hope, which guides man's roving thought,
> > a nurse of his old age,
> > attends and nourishes his heart.

It is remarkable how well Pindar puts this. In this respect I consider the possession of wealth most valuable, nor for every man, but for the man who is good and decent. For the possession of wealth contributes much to not deceiving and cheating anyone involuntarily and to going to the afterlife not owing sacrifices to a god or money to a man.

As in the rest of their religion, the Greeks had no revelation from the gods or canonical statements by priests as to what they could expect in the afterlife. They had descriptions of forms of it in their poetry, they had various visions of it from their philosophers, and they had promises of it in a few of the religious cults of their world. What Cephalus wished to have, in the face of death, was "sweet hope" about the afterlife, and we have seen in Chapter IV that the Eleusinian Mysteries offered to its initiates, perhaps through a special connection with Kore, Queen of the Dead, "sweeter hopes about the end of life and all eternity." The *Hymn to Demeter* promised to initiates that

> Whoever on this earth has seen these (mysteries) is blessed,
> but he who has no part in the holy rites has
> another lot as he wastes away in dank darkness.

And, finally, Aristophanes in the *Frogs* (lines 154–8) portrays Eleusinian-type initiates enjoying eternal light, music, and dancing in the afterlife, an afterlife which would answer well to Cephalus' "sweet hope."

There were thus various alternate views to the common expectation of a meaningless, almost non-existent existence of the soul after death, views expressed privately, in poetry and philosophy, and also, most importantly for our purposes, in cult. Although we have no information as to what specifically the Eleusinian Mysteries promised in the afterlife to its initiates, it was the mystery cult that in the Classical period reached the greatest number of Athenians and non-Athenians. It was, moreover, an "elective" cult, one in which one chose, or chose not, to participate and to be initiated, and we find promises of a blessed afterlife associated exclusively with such elective cults.

The great majority of an Athenian's or other Greek's religious life was devoted to the cults of his family, village, and state, and participation in them was required by tradition or, in some cases, by state law. Beyond these an Athenian might choose to join a cult association, virtually a club, devoted to a local hero, or he might join other Athenians in supporting, through a private association, a new, state-approved deity such as Asclepius. Usually such elective cults, like that of Asclepius and the Eleusinian Mysteries, were compatible with the traditional cults, but a few, most notably the esoteric cults which took as sacred texts the hymns and poems attributed to the legendary poet Orpheus, set themselves in opposition to traditional cults and offered their own promises for a blessed afterlife. Such cults, sometimes devoted to an Orphic Dionysos, were scattered here and there in the Greek world, had their own theology and cosmology and strict dietary, dress, and behavioral restrictions. If one followed their prescriptions, one was assured of special guidance in traversing the perils of the underworld and finding eternal bliss. Others, the non-initiates, were to wallow eternally in a sea of mud. Such cults and the few itinerant priests promoting similar doctrines were always on the fringe of classical Greek life and were treated as oddities, but they offered to a small minority of Greeks the possibility of escaping the bleak afterlife that most Greeks foresaw for themselves.

Mainstream Greek religion offered little to its devotees in terms of the afterlife, but much to them during their life on earth. We return, for one last time, to the benefits that the favor of the gods granted to its pious worshipers: fertility of their crops, animals, and themselves; economic prosperity; good health; and safety in the dangers of war and seafaring. In addition, as Thucydides has Pericles say in his famous Funeral Oration (2.38.1), for the Athenians "the competitions and sacrifices throughout the year" provided many respites for the mind from their labors. Religious festivals had solemn moments of hymn, sacrifice, and prayer in honor of the deities, but they also offered the delights of feasting, drinking, singing, and dancing with friends and fellow citizens. Many provided the pleasures of athletic competitions, others featured in their choral competitions the beautiful and yet edifying productions of dithyrambs, tragedies, and comedies. And, finally, the Greek inclination to give to their gods only what was beautiful filled their cities and villages, the richer ones more than the poorer ones, with temples, statues, and dedications of unsurpassed beauty. Most of what we think of as characteristically Greek in architecture, sculpture, mythology, lyric poetry, tragedy, and comedy owed its origins and, especially in the Classical period, its development to the religious institutions and practices of the Greek people. The cultural environment in which the Greek individual lived, whether in Athens or Sparta or Thebes, was significantly determined by his religion and that of his ancestors.

NOTE

1. An exception here, as we have seen in Chapter IV, is the rituals of the Mysteries at Eleusis. They were taught to the Eleusinians by Demeter.

FURTHER READING

On religion of the individual:

Dover, K.J., *Greek Popular Morality* (Berkeley, 1974)
Hermann, G., *Ritualized Friendship* (Cambridge, 1987)
Mikalson, J.D., *Athenian Popular Religion* (Chapel Hill, 1983)
Rudhardt, J., *Notions fondamentales de la pensée religieuse et actes constitutifs du cult dans la Grèce classique* (Geneva, 1958)

On religion and tragedy:

Mikalson, J.D., *Honor Thy Gods: Popular Religion in Greek Tragedy* (Chapel Hill, 1991)

On the piety of Nicias:

Mikalson, 1991, pp. 162–4
Powell, C.A., "Religion and the Sicilian Expedition," *Historia* 28 (1979), 15–31
Zaidman, L.B., *Le commerce des dieux* (Paris, 2001), 131–44

On death and the afterlife:

Garland, R., *The Greek Way of Death*, second edition (Ithaca, 2001)
Mikalson, 1983, pp. 74–82
Vermeule, E., *Aspects of Death in Early Greek Art and Poetry* (Berkeley, 1979)

On alternative views of the dead and afterlife:

Parker, R., "Early Orphism," pp. 483–510 in *The Greek World*, ed. A. Powell (London, 1995)
Johnston, S.I., *Restless Dead* (Berkeley, 1999)

VIII

Greek Religion in the Hellenistic Period

ᛁᛁᛁᛁ

From Mycenaen times there had been established Greek settlements, then cities, on the coastlines of the Black Sea and on the Aegean shores of Asia Minor, Syria, and Egypt. From the residents of these Greek cities and colonies, and from traders, pirates, travelers, and historians such as Herodotus the Greeks of the Classical period had acquired some knowledge of the native peoples and religions of these areas. The Greeks of these areas largely continued the religious cults and practices they had brought with them from their homelands in mainland Greece. They seldom extended their reach far inland and only occasionally took into their Greek pantheon a deity and cult of the local population. The campaigns and conquests of Alexander the Great, from 334 until his death in 323, opened up to the Greeks territories far, far inland, in Asia Minor and the Levant, in Mesopotamia, Iran, and Afghanistan, in central Asia, Pakistan, and even India. Alexander's successors, after a series of wars and accommodations, established three great kingdoms from some of the regions in which Alexander campaigned: Ptolemy created the first and most stable in Egypt; by 300 Seleucus controlled Syria and much of Asia Minor; and the family of Antigonus finally assumed control of Macedon, Alexander's homeland, and much of Greece. Later a separate dynasty, that of Attalus, established firm and lasting control over Pergamum and much of Asia Minor.

With the death of Alexander and the establishment of these very large kingdoms begins the Hellenistic Age, an age dominated politically, militarily, and even culturally by these great kings and their descendants, an age that came to an end when, in 31 B.C.E., at the battle of Actium the victory of Octavian (soon to be known as Caesar Augustus) over Antony and Cleopatra completed Rome's victory over these kingdoms and Rome henceforth exercised its political and military control over these areas. This is a immensely complex and dynamic period, and for Greeks significant

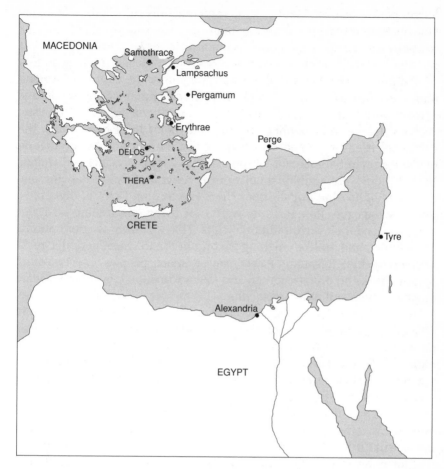

Map VIII.1   Map of Hellenistic sites discussed in the text.

changes, always within the context of underlying continuity, may be seen in the areas of national and international politics, warfare, trade and commerce, art, literature, and, most relevant for us, in religion.

In the Hellenistic period many Greeks, no doubt often the most enterprising ones, left their home city-states for the opportunities presented by the new kingdoms in Asia Minor and Egypt. They went as mercenary soldiers, as traders and merchants, as staff for the royal courts, and even as actors, poets, teachers, and scholars at the new cultural centers such as Alexandria and Pergamum. Some went as settlers to the many new cities founded by the Hellenistic dynasts. Similarly, native peoples of these areas, Syrians, Egyptians, and others, now moved more freely about the Mediterranean, and this meant that the Greeks were more broadly and for longer periods exposed to the deities and religious cults of these peoples. One notable "mixing pot" for these many cultures was the island of Delos, the birthplace of Apollo and Artemis but also, in the late Hellenistic period, a major port and trading center almost dead center in the Aegean Sea. By the mid-second century the island was under the control of Athens, and many of Delos' native Greek cults were maintained: of Apollo and Artemis and their family, of Zeus Polieus and Athena Polias, of Dionysus, Hermes, Pan, and Asclepius, and of their major local hero Anius. But this small island now had also major cults, with extensive sanctuaries, of the Egyptian Sarapis and Isis and of the Syrian Atargatis and Hadad. By 100 there were additional cults of the Assyrian Ba'al of Babylon and of Astarte of Ascalon in Palestine. There was also on Delos at this time a Jewish synagogue. Romans, too, were now living and trading on Delos and practiced their own traditional cults. This was truly an international community, and, unlike anything we find in the Classical period, Greeks of different cities, Egyptians, Palestinians, Romans, peoples of several other nationalities, and even freedmen and slaves worshiped together in a wide range of Greek and non-Greek cults.

The effects, however, of this new cosmopolitan movement were felt quite differently in different areas of the Greek world. During the early Hellenistic period, when Athens' political and economic development was being repressed by Macedonian kings, Athenians seem almost untouched by the new religious currents. After 168 some Athenians did experience life on Delos and brought back home with them a few foreign cults but none that won a significant following. Until the Roman devastation of Athens in 86 B.C.E., Athenian state religion remained, at least in outward form, much what it had been at the end of the Classical period. The same is true for many of the old, mainland cities of Greece such as Corinth and Sparta. But by geography and national concerns the Greek cities of Asia Minor, some now many centuries old, were more exposed to these new influences, and we see them already in the late third century adding new, non-Greek deities to their pantheon.

Two of the new deities, Sarapis and Isis, are of particular interest because in the late Hellenistic and Roman periods their cults became very widespread and, eventually, competed with Christianity. Isis had been a major pan-Egyptian deity for millennia, with particular concern for the annual flooding of the Nile River and the fertility of crops that resulted from that. Herodotus in the fifth century in his description of Egypt (2.59.2 and 156.5) naturally identified her with the Greek Demeter. The mythology of the Isis cult had her intensely mourning the death of her brother and husband Osiris and, through that mourning, reviving him, much as Demeter mourned for and eventually won the (partial) return of her daughter Kore from the underworld. The early Ptolemies, kings of Egypt, Macedonians themselves, wished to blend the traditions of the native Egyptians, their Macedonian soldiers, and the many Greek settlers, and they transformed and hellenized Osiris, renamed him Sarapis, and made him into the patron of their dynasty. Ptolemy I Soter had an Egyptian priest, Manetho, and two Athenians, the Eumolpid Timotheus and Demetrius of Phaleron, develop mythology, ritual, and liturgical hymns for Sarapis, and his cult statue was Greek, not Egyptian, in form. The result was a god who was ruler of the underworld and the husband of Isis and who gave bounty and prosperity and healed, much like Asclepius, the sick and injured through incubation and dreams in his sanctuaries. It is not surprising, then, that the Sarapis cult caught on with the Greeks. His cult was founded on Delos by an Egyptian priest from Memphis and soon become one of the major sanctuaries on the island. In Athens Sarapis first appeared in 215/4, worshiped by non-Athenians, but by 158/7 an Athenian was serving as his priest on Delos.

On the very eve of the Hellenistic period, before 332/1, the Athenians allowed Egyptians, probably merchants, to purchase land for a sanctuary for Isis in Piraeus, a sanctuary intended only for Egyptian worshipers (*IG* II² 337). This was the type of privilege that the Athenians granted also to the Thracians for their goddess Bendis and to the Citians of Cyprus for their Aphrodite Ourania (Of the Sky). There is no further evidence for this cult of Isis in Piraeus, and we first have Athenians worshiping Isis *in Athens* in 133/2 (*SEG* 24.225). In her developing Greek tradition Isis' "motherhood," like that of Demeter's, was emphasized more than her "wifehood," but other Egyptian elements of her cult, including the giving of life, protection of the family, healing, and saving, particularly from the dangers of the sea, were prominent too. On Delos she was praised as "just," "savior," and "good," and was linked with such Greek goddesses and personifications as Aphrodite, Mother of the Gods, Nemesis, Nike, and Hygieia. The spread of her cult was facilitated by a number of very unGreek elements: the goddess' own commands to her devotees, usually in dreams, to found new cult centers; the propagandizing and proselytizing efforts of her priests and devotees; the existence of standardized, if not canonical and identical, liturgical texts which mixed together Greek and Egyptian elements; and, perhaps, an appeal initially aimed at under-privileged and disadvantaged social groups. By the end of the Hellenistic period Isis, usually with Sarapis, had sanctuaries and devotees in virtu-ally all Greek cities everywhere, and her devotees were identifying her in long *aretologies* (lists of "virtues," *aretai* in Greek) with many of the Greek goddesses and were crediting her with power over and protection of virtually all aspects of human life and even with the initial structuring of the cosmos and all elements in it. Unlike a Greek god or goddess, Isis alone

The Syrians call You: Astarte, Artemis, Nanaia,
The Lycian tribes call You: Leto, the lady,
The Thracians also name You as Mother of the gods,
And the Greeks (call You): Hera of the Great Throne, Aphrodite,
Hestia the goodly, Rheia, and Demeter.
Deathless Savior, many-named, mightiest Isis
Saving from war cities and all their citizens:
Men, their wives, possessions and children.
As many as are bound fast in prison, in the power of death,
As many as are in pain through long, anguished, sleepless nights,
All who are wanderers in a foreign land,
And as many as sail on the Great Sea in winter
When men may be destroyed and their ships wrecked and sunk,
All these are saved if they pray that You be present to help.

> First Hymn to Isis, by Isidorus, lines 18–22, 26–34, second or first
> century, B.C.E., from Egypt (translation of V.F. Vanderlip, *The
> Four Greek Hymns of Isidorus and the Cult of Isis*
> (Toronto, 1972), 18–19)

now could, for her devotees, fulfill virtually all their religious needs. Of all the gods we have encountered, Isis alone opens the way to concepts of monotheism for her worshipers – she can be thought of as the goddess who encompasses and incorporates all other deities and their powers.

Isis, Sarapis, and, importantly, Asclepius became major figures of cult throughout much of the Greek world in the late Hellenistic period, and they share the characteristics that they show maternal/paternal concern for their worshipers and that they were largely free, unlike the various Zeuses and Athenas, from the military, political, and nationalistic concerns of the individual city-states. The physician-god Asclepius was Greek, but non-political. Although Sarapis and Isis were strongly identified in Egypt with the political structure and ruling dynasts, their cults abroad seem largely free of such political ties. The exotic Egyptian features of their cults and myths appealed to the long and deep respect Greeks had for Egyptian traditions. They attracted individuals, promising personal health, safety, and welfare, and stood outside, or alongside, the established national cults. Unlike traditional Greek gods, their cults were easily transplanted to new areas. This was usually carried out by individuals but won approval and later even financial support from state authorities. In each new locality cults of Isis, Sarapis, and Asclepius would be among the "elective" cults which an individual could choose, or not choose, to participate in. Initially, at least, they were private rather than civic religious cults.

After his astounding military triumphs, in 324/3, the year before his death, Alexander let it be known that he wished for himself "divine honors." Different Greek states reacted differently to the news. The Athenians, many of them long and bitter opponents of the Macedonians, debated the issue in their Ekklesia, and, despite considerable opposition, voted him those honors, in the fear, it was said, that by "begrudging Alexander heaven they might, because of him, lose their land" (Val. Max. 7.2, ext. 13). The Spartans reportedly responded laconically, "If Alexander wishes to be a god, let him be a god." In Athens the death of Alexander the next year brought with it the end of his cult and the prosecution of the man who had proposed it. But some Greek cities in Asia Minor had benefited immensely from the campaigns of Alexander, and many seem willingly and eagerly to have established a cult for the man who almost superhumanly had freed them from the centuries-long Persian threat and brought them security and prosperity. In the Greek tradition one might expect these cities to have worshiped Alexander as a cultic hero, but such heroes, as we saw in Chapter II, were locally bound and often malignant figures. Alexander had ranged widely throughout the Greek and non-Greek world, and to many what he had done was good. The divine honors given to Alexander and, eventually, to the Macedonian kings who succeeded him were usually those of gods – altars, sacrifices, priests, statues, and festivals.[1] In the cities that Alexander, Seleucus, Antigonus, Ptolemy, and their successors most benefited these cults lived long through the Greek and Roman periods. They appear to be genuine expressions of gratitude and respect for their power, because these kings could now determine, by careful choice or whim, the safety, prosperity, food supply, welfare, and even existence of these cities. These "ruler cults" were, again, simply added to a city's pantheon and religious calendar. The introduction of the divine cult of rulers in the Hellenistic period is often viewed as a indicator of the debasement of Greeks and of Greek religion, but it perhaps may better be seen as a recognition in these cities that these supremely powerful kings were now providing to their Greek subjects what Greeks traditionally asked of their gods: peace, protection against foreign enemies, food, economic prosperity, and personal safety. These Greeks were acknowledging in their traditional ways new powers that determined critical elements in their lives that were no longer in their own control.

The Macedonian kings – Alexander's ancestors in Macedonia, Alexander himself, and after him his successors throughout their kingdoms – were philhellenes, and they adopted and promoted, sometimes in new festivals, sometimes in secular settings, the athletic and music contests and the productions of tragedy and comedy that had, in the Classical period, been central elements of the religious festivals of individual cities. It is in this period that much of Greek art and poetry was separated from its religious context. Secular portrait sculpture, for example, became widespread, and tragedy, comedy, and lyric poetry were now often presented as entertainment at royal banquets. Religious historians may lament the secularization of these elements of Greek culture, but the Macedonian love for things Greek also assured the survival of the old and development of the new. Ptolemy III Euergetes, for example, saved for us what we have of the works of Aeschylus, Sophocles, and Euripides because he gathered from Athens texts of them for his library at Alexandria. The Ptolemies also financially supported Greek poets composing innovative adaptations of earlier poetic genres such as epics and hymns.

Alexander's expeditions and the wars and policies of his successors brought changes to religious traditions and practices, but the extent of these changes varied greatly for Greeks living in different parts of the Hellenistic world and in different kinds of cities. Here we survey four quite different cities and see the different kind of religious environment that each had in the Hellenistic period.

Athens

In the Hellenistic world the traditional cults of family, village, and state continued to be practiced as they had been for centuries. In Athens Athena was still worshiped at the Panathenaia and Dionysus was celebrated with dramatic productions at the City Dionysia throughout the Hellenistic period. These were, however, turbulent and violent times for cities which challenged Macedonian authority or were caught up in hostilities between the rival kings. Alexander himself in 335, after its revolt, destroyed Thebes and enslaved its inhabitants. In 201 the Athenians became entangled with Philip V, king of Macedonia, a man widely known for his desecration of sanctuaries and tombs in enemy land. Philip unsuccessfully attacked the city of Athens and Eleusis, but then turned his wrath on the Attic countryside. The Roman historian Livy (31.26.9–12) reports the damage:

> Although Philip had previously pillaged by destroying the tombs around the city, now, so that he might leave nothing unviolated, he ordered that the sanctuaries of the gods which the Athenians had consecrated in the countryside be destroyed and burned. And the Attic countryside, which was exceptionally well ornamented by such works because of the abundance of local marble and the talents of the craftsmen, provided much material for this madness. And Philip did not think it enough only to destroy the sanctuaries and overturn the statues; he ordered that even the individual blocks of stone be broken so that they might not form a pile of undamaged blocks.

It was only by the intervention of Attalus I of Pergamum and the Romans that the city and Eleusis were spared the same desecrations. Athens itself was saved, but the rich religious life of the Attic villages appears to have come to an end.

For reasons of tradition, geography, and political, social, and economic repression Athens was relatively unaffected by the new religious currents of the Hellenistic period, but an Athenian citizen transported from mid-fifth century to mid-second century would have seen some changes. Family religious cults and practices no doubt remained virtually the same, and the calendar of state festivals and sacrifices was little changed. The sanctuaries in the villages, though, had been ruthlessly destroyed fifty years earlier by Philip V of Macedon, and the now relatively impoverished Athenians did not have the resources to restore them. Our demesman of Erchia would still belong to the same tribe, Aegeis, and would participate in annual sacrifices to Aegeus. But a demesman of Ikarion, the deme named after Icarius, the favorite of Dionysus, would now no longer belong to the tribe of Aegeus with the Erchians but would have been assigned to that of Attalus I and would annually make offerings to this new hero who rescued Athens from Philip V fifty years earlier. There was a major new festival, the Ptolemaia, instituted in 224, in honor of Ptolemy III Euergetes, with the usual apparatus of a procession and athletic contests for young Athenian men. Many of the traditional festivals remained much the same, but now, for example, at the City Dionysia the tragedies would include some revivals of plays of the old masters, especially Euripides, as well as new plays written for the occasion. Now, too, the plays were acted by professional troupes rather than by common fellow citizens, and prizes were awarded to the best actors as well as to the best plays. Increasingly throughout the period major festivals, once financed entirely by state and cult revenues, were subsidized by wealthy individuals, either individually or by subscription. Similarly, priests were now expected to contribute to cover some costs of the cults of the deities they served. The positions of authority in Athenian state religion were becoming increasingly plutocratic, and just before the Roman attack in 86 were in the hands of a very few, very wealthy families. The classical Athenian in Hellenistic Athens would have seen some remodeled religious buildings such as the Theater of Dionysus and a small, new temple of Apollo Patroös in the Agora. The Olympieion of Zeus Olympios, built scarcely above the foundations by the tyrant Pisistratus in the sixth century and left in that state by the classical, democratic Athenians, was now half-finished, thanks to the Seleucid king Antiochos IV, an abnormally, even irrationally strong devotee of the god. On entering the second-century Athenian Acropolis a fifth-century Athenian would have been struck by the hundreds of portrait sculptures erected there as dedications. In the Classical period most statues on the Acropolis represented Athena herself, but in the Hellenistic period it was no longer the fashion to dedicate such statues of the goddess. Now worshipers erected statues of themselves, their families, or, especially, of their daughters who had served the goddess as *arrephoroi*. In the Classical period Greek religion seems more to have been a corporate enterprise, of the village and the state, with individual participants somewhat concealed behind the communal unit. But in Athens and throughout the Hellenistic world it was now the fashion more for individual families to assert their contributions to state religion in the form of statues of themselves, other dedications, and inscriptions recording their contributions. The major sanctuaries at Athens and elsewhere were now filled with statues of men, women, and children, not of gods and goddesses.

Delos

If our Athenian were one of the dozens who took up residence on Delos each year, he might well find himself administering, as the priest for a year, the sanctuary of Sarapis. There he would find, in addition to Sarapis, the Egyptian deities Isis, Anubis, and Harpocrates. Their cult, on Delos, seems to have featured healing and, what was particularly important for the port of Delos, the protection of sailors. In the Delian Sarapeum there were also dedications to Ammon, Bubastis, Osiris (all Egyptian deities), and to Zeus Ourios (Of the Favoring Wind), Demeter Eleusinia, Kore, Hermes, Heracles, Apallaxikakos (Warder Off of Evil), Asclepius, Hygieia, the Dioscuri, and even Apollo, and this collection of dedications *in one sanctuary* indicates how completely Greek and Egyptian cult figures had been mixed together here. Our Athenian priest's cult personnel would, too, have been unusual, more Egyptian than Greek, with, in addition to the usual Greek "key-bearer" and "basket-carriers," a subpriest, an "attendant," lamp-bearers, and an aretologist to sing of the virtues of the deities. The worshipers of Sarapis, hundreds of them, bore mostly Greek names, a few of them Athenians but many of them not even Greek, and there were also some Romans, freedmen, and slaves. Athenian priests serving this cult and other, non-Greek cults on Delos seemingly took to their new roles, often erecting new altars and buildings or setting up dedications, usually portrait statues of themselves or their families. But the Athenian priest of Sarapis might, another year, assume a completely different priesthood, perhaps that of the very traditional Delian Apollo. Interestingly, when these same Athenians who held priesthoods on Delos returned to Athens, they did not bring with them these exotic cults. Rather, they resumed participation and leadership in the traditional Athenian cults. There was not yet in the Hellenistic period what appears in some cults in the Roman period, exclusive dedication by individual Greeks to one deity. Rather, for individuals this was an increasingly polytheistic world, and Greeks tended more to participate in the cults of that part of the world where they happened, for the time being, to reside. A classical Athenian knew by report of most of these foreign deities, but what we find in mid-second century B.C.E. Delos, the mix of Greek and non-Greek deities honored in one sanctuary, the many nationalities and even slaves worshiping together, and the later Athenian state financial support of such Delian cults, would have shocked him.

Erythrae

Delos, because of its function as an international port and its unusual history, was exceptional in its mix of foreign and Greek residents and cults, as, in turn, Athens was probably exceptional in its adherence to traditional cults and slowness to adopt foreign deities. More characteristic of the period is the Ionian city of Erythrae on the north coast of Asia Minor, a city with no special claim to fame in the Classical or Hellenistic period, a city just trying to survive the dangers of the Macedonian kings and their armies threatening their land. From one inscription of the early Hellenistic period (ca. 300–260) we know of fifty-four cults there, and from a later sacred calendar (ca. 188–150) and various dedications other deities and ritual details may be added. Among the fifty-four cults are such familiar figures as Athena Polias on their Acropolis and Athena Nike; Zeus Olympios, Agoraios, and Boulaios; Hera Teleia; Apollo Delphinios and Pythios; Artemis Aithopia (Of Brightness), similar to Artemis Brauronia of Athens; Demeter and Kore; Ares, Enyalius, and Enyo; several Aphrodites, including Pontia (Of the Sea) and Strateia (of the Army); Dionysus Baccheus, with "ecstatic" cult rituals and a theater; Asclepius; and Poseidon Asphaleios, Hippios, and, new to us but known elsewhere in Greece, Phytalmios (Of Human Birth). Heracles was the most important god at Erythrae. His image was on their coins, his statue had its own cult myth (Pausanias 7.5.5–8), and along with Athena as a warrior god he protected the city, especially its acropolis, walls, and gates. He even kept worms from the vines. The Erythraeans continued to worship heroes, including their eponymous founder Erythrus, Achilles, and a batch of other named and nameless heroes.

These Erythraean cults, though there were variations in rituals and divine epithets and functions from those in Athens – as we would expect –, give unmistakable evidence, paralleled throughout the Greek world at this time,

Figure VIII.1   The head of Heracles on a silver four-drachma ($400) coin of Erythrae, from about 375–350 B.C.E. Courtesy of the Trustees of the British Museum, inv. no. BMC Erythrae 42.

that in the Hellenistic cities traditional cults were strongly maintained in their traditional forms.

But there are new elements as well. Erythrae, as did several cities in Asia Minor, met the new challenges of financing state cults not by individual contributions or subscriptions as at Athens, but by auctioning off the priesthoods of these gods to the highest bidder. The priest, for a considerable sum, would lease the priesthood from the state and in return would receive the skins and other portions of victims sacrificed, exemptions from some taxes, and special privileges such as preferred seating in the theater. Some new cults were added. Alexander the Great had given this city independence from Persian control and freed it from Persian tribute in 334/3, and for this the Erythraeans were grateful. Their prophetess, in the tradition of their local Sibyl, was among the first to claim Alexander's descent from Zeus, and they gave him, during his lifetime, a cult which, unlike in Athens, lasted throughout the Hellenistic period well into Roman times. It was of critical importance to its survival for Erythrae to remain on good terms with the Hellenistic kings who succeeded Alexander, and so understandably they established a cult and festival of Seleucus I Nicator when he secured control of the area in 281 and a cult of his son Antiochus I Soter when he confirmed the autonomy of the city and defended them against the Galatians. In 188, in their great reorganization of the area, the Romans made Erythrae a "free and tax-free city," and the Erythraeans responded with a cult and festival of the goddess Roma. When Rome's Sibylline books were burned in the temple of Jupiter Capitolinus in 83 B.C.E.,

> Over the libations sing of Seleucus, son of dark haired Apollo.
> Apollo of the golden lyre himself begot him.
> Opening of an Erythrean hymn to Seleucus I Nicator who claimed
> Apollo as his father. *IE* 205 B, 74–5, after 281 B.C.E.

the Romans sent to Erythrae and brought back about a thousand verses of the Erythraean Sibyl to reestablish their collection. Sarapis and Isis, favorites of the Ptolemies, arrived in Erythrae about the time they came to Athens, by the end of the second century, but at Erythrae they were warmly received with a state, not private cult. By this same century the Erythraeans, like many other Greek states, had in their state pantheon a few abstract deities such as Eirene (Peace), Homonoia (Concord), Arete (Virtue), and Nike (Victory), all probably referring to national, not personal, life. Such personifications had been a regular feature of Greek poetry since Hesiod's time in the seventh century, but this treatment of them as cult deities with altars, priests, and sacrifices is a new development of the late Classical and Hellenistic periods. In Athens it had begun with a state altar and statue of Eirene dedicated in 375/4 after a major military victory and with an altar and temple of Agathe Tyche (Good Fortune) in 335. Instead of personalized deities like Athena Nike who provide to the state the benefits designated, we now have the benefits themselves deified and worshiped. But, of course, in this very polytheistic world their cults could stand beside those of the established gods, without replacing or challenging them. They, like Hellenistic kings, could simply be added to the religious calendar. Erythrae, with its preponderance of traditional cults, with its gratitude and respect toward Alexander and his successors expressed in cult, and with its introduction of the Egyptian deities and of the occasional new personified deity, probably represents the more usual religious environment of a Hellenistic Greek city, between the extremes of multinational Delos and conservative Athens.

Alexandria

Our last example, which offers another, quite radically different type of city in the Hellenistic period, is Alexandria, a new city founded in Egyptian territory near the Canobic mouth of the Nile by Alexander the Great in 331 B.C.E. Settlers included Macedonians, Athenians and many other Greeks, native Egyptians, other peoples from the surrounding areas, and, by the third century, a large community of Jews. Ptolemy I Soter made it his residence and the capitol of Egypt, and his dynasty was to rule there until the death of Antony's Cleopatra in 30 B.C.E. Alexander laid out the walls and streets of the city, indicating which gods were to have sanctuaries and where these sanctuaries were to be built. These were to be for Greek gods, with one notable addition, the Egyptian Isis (Arrian, *Anabasis of Alexander* 3.1.5). Who these Greek gods were is not known, but when Ptolemy I divided Alexandria into demes, at least fifteen of them took their names from the names or epithets of Greek deities, including Athena, Apollo, Hermes, Heracles, Hephaestus, Castor and Polydeuces, and Demeter. The name of one Alexandrian deme, Sunium, must refer to the Athenian cult of Poseidon at Sunium that we came to know in Chapter I! Only four of the demes were named after deities with Egyptian connections: Zeus Ammon, Isis, the Nile, and Sarapis. Most intriguing is the deme Eleusis, a suburb of Alexandria and a cult center of Demeter, founded, probably, by the philathenian Ptolemy I Soter with the help of his Athenian Eumolpid expert Timotheus. Demeter and Kore were worshiped in Alexandria, Demeter bore the epithet Thesmophoros, and there was held in Alexandrian Eleusis a festival of Demeter with musical and perhaps theatrical contests. There is, however, no indication that Eleusinian-type mysteries were held there.

Reigns of Selected Ptolemies in Egypt

Ptolemy I Soter	323–282
Ptolemy II Philadephus	282–246
Ptolemy III Euergetes	246–221
Ptolemy IV Philopator	221–205
Ptolemy XII Auletes	80–51
Cleopatra VII	51–30

Some of the other deities after whom these demes were named were worshiped in Alexandria, and these include Zeus, Poseidon, the Dioscuri, Hermes and Heracles, and, especially, Dionysus. The formal oath of the city was sworn by Zeus, Hera, and Poseidon; the Ptolemies placed a statue of Zeus Soter on the top of the immense lighthouse on the island of Pharos to guide ships to the harbor; Poseidon and the Dioscuri, both protectors of sailors, had temples in Alexandria; and Hermes and Heracles were associated with the gymnasia. The Ptolemies also patronized the cults of other Greek deities. Ptolemy I made the Greek Muses whom we encountered in Chapter II the patrons of his new literary, philosophical, and scientific research center, and he called the whole complex the

Mouseion (Museum). But it was Dionysus who won particular favor with the Ptolemies. Early in the reign of Ptolemy II Philadelphus a massive procession featuring Dionysus and his train was held in the streets of Alexandria. Ptolemy IV Philopator also apparently renamed an Alexandrian tribe Dionysia and its eight demes after the members of Dionysus' family. Dionysus was claimed by the Ptolemies as a divine ancestor, but those aspects of Dionysus they featured in cult were wine, revelry, drama, and luxury. Ptolemy IV seems especially to have promoted his cult with new festivals and sacrifices. The close association of the Ptolemies with Dionysus lasted to the end of their dynasty, closing with the final Dionysiac revels of Antony and Cleopatra.

In the very center of this new city Ptolemy placed the tomb of Alexander, in the Classical tradition a place appropriate for him as the founder of the city but also, now in the Hellenistic period, appropriate for him as the first in a line of divine rulers, a new tradition which the Ptolemies would promote for their own benefit as they assumed the role of the divine ruler for Greeks and of the pharaoh for the Egyptian population. We will return to the Ptolemaic ruler cult, but this cult of Alexander concludes our brief survey of apparently purely Greek religious elements of Alexandria, and we can see that, initially at least, there was a very strong presence of Greek gods and religious traditions, as one would expect in a city dominated by Greek settlers and designed by philhellenic rulers.

The Isis for whom Alexander took special concern was, unlike most Egyptian deities, worshiped throughout Egypt, and by giving her a place among the gods in his new city Alexander was accommodating the large native Egyptian population he envisioned for his city. It was not Isis, however, but the new Sarapis who was to be featured in Alexandria itself. The Ptolemies, as we have seen, hellenized the Egyptian god Sarapis to be the patron of their dynasty. Ptolemy I built a sanctuary of Sarapis, and Ptolemy III Euergetes developed it into a monumental cult center. Some Ptolemies, now as deities, shared sanctuaries with Sarapis and Isis. As it turned out, it was primarily the Greeks who worshiped Sarapis in Alexandria, building a number of private shrines and making numerous dedications. Apparently the native Egyptians remained largely devoted to their purely Egyptian cults, including Isis. In the power struggle, as it were, between the married couple, the worship of Sarapis and Ptolemaic support for it seems to have climaxed in the third century, and after that the more Egyptian Isis came to the fore in Alexandria and elsewhere in the Greek world.

In the Hellenistic period Athenians and residents on Delos, as we have seen, gave to the Ptolemies ruler cult, with altars, sacrifices, priests, and festivals. But these places, like many others, were mere offshoots of the

Ptolemaic cult. Alexandria was its epicenter, because it was there that the Ptolemies created for themselves these cults. Ptolemy I Soter gave formal and enduring status to the cult of Alexander the Great at Alexandria, with a sanctuary and a priest. Ptolemy II Philadelphus proclaimed his father the "savior" (Soter) god in 280, one year after his death, and instituted a major quadrennial festival with games, the Ptolemaieia, in his honor. The games of the Ptolemaieia were explicitly intended to match the splendor of the Olympic Games. About ten years after his accession Ptolemy II declared himself and his wife/sister Arsinoe deities, the Theoi Adelphoi (Brother-Sister Gods). After Arsinoe's death in 270 he created a separate cult, with its own priestess, for her. Ptolemy III Euergetes and his wife Berenice appear as gods, the Theoi Euergetai (Benefactor Gods), just four years after their accession, in 243/2. And so it went on, with ever more Ptolemaic deities and ever more complicated relationships between their cults. These Ptolemaic deities had priests and priestesses, elaborate temples, sacrifices, and, sometimes, festivals. This particular form of the ruler cult seemed directed primarily at Greeks, but in the background lay the divinity of the pharaohs whom the Ptolemies were, for the Egyptian population, replacing. Even the very Greek names Soter, Philadelphus, Euergetes, and Philopator, fully intelligible in the Greek context of the Ptolemies, were chosen to fit also into traditional Egyptian conceptions of the pharaoh's responsibilities and relationships to Osiris, Isis, and Horus. As time went on the Ptolemaic "deities" were associated more and more with established Greek and Egyptian deities, first by taking on their epithets, as Arsinoe did Teleia from Hera Teleia (Of Marriage); then by becoming partners in cult, as, for example, Arsinoe and Aphrodite as protectresses of sailors in one sanctuary; and finally by simply becoming the deity or a new incarnation of the deity, as Ptolemy XII Auletes identified himself as the "new" Dionysus and his daughter Cleopatra as the "new" Isis. Isis and Aphrodite were favored by the Ptolemaic queens, but Dionysus had the place of favor with the kings, and this, too, has its basis in both Greek and Egyptian tradition. The Greek side of Ptolemaic Dionysus we have seen, but since as early as Herodotus (2.42.2 and 144.2) the name of Dionysus was given to Osiris, and the son of Osiris was Horus, the embodiment and protector of the living pharaoh. By calling himself the "new" Dionysus, Ptolemy XII was declaring himself, for the Egyptian audience, the "new" Osiris. In ruler cult, as apparently in the rest of the religious life of Ptolemaic Alexandria, what began as a strongly Greek-dominated tradition gradually incorporated more and more native Egyptian elements as time passed.

Few non-Greek, non-Egyptian deities are attested for Alexandria in the Hellenistic period, but they include the important Zeus Hypsistos (Highest) = Jahweh of the Jewish community. Ptolemy I had brought 30,000 Jewish

colonists to Egypt, and by the mid-second century Jews held important roles in the Ptolemaic administration. The Jews were concentrated in
one quarter of the city, and they represent the earliest Jewish community
among the Hellenistic cities. These Jews spoke Greek and were highly
Hellenized, and it was at this time and place that the Torah was translated
into Greek as the Septuagint, the completion of which the Jews celebrated
with a festival that became annual. The Jews of Alexandria were able
to accommodate themselves to the ruler cult of the Ptolemies by making
their dedications in synagogues to Zeus Hypsistos "on behalf" of the
ruling Ptolemy and his wife, not "to" them, a formula which, in fact, was
common in all dedications of the Hellenistic period in Alexandria.

In Alexandria we have now, as a first in the Greek world, a major city
in which all citizens and residents apparently were *not* expected, as a
matter of course, to be worshiping the same deities in common sacrifices
and festivals. For the Greeks there was an Eleusis, a Demeter Eleusinia, and
the festival Eleusinia. For Egyptians there was Isis to fulfill many of the
same functions. For the Greek sailors there was a Poseidon, for Egyptian
sailors Isis Pelagia (Of the Sea). Greeks took up the Sarapis cult promoted
by the Ptolemies, whereas the Egyptians seem to have preferred Isis and
their traditional deities. All, of course, paid due homage to the Ptolemaic
deities, but within their own traditions. Also, because the Greeks, Egyptians,
and Ptolemies all promoted identifications of Egyptian gods with Greek
gods, the situation must have been immensely complex. The living deity,
the "new" Dionysus Ptolemy XII must have meant quite different things
to the Greek, Egyptian, and, of course, Jewish communities of Alexandria
in the first half of first century B.C.E.

The cult structures of most Greek cities, like Athens and Erythrae,
were inherited from Archaic and Classical times and remained even in
the Hellenistic period a fairly unified and coherent whole in which all the
citizenry and, now, many of the non-citizen residents participated. The
new, Hellenistic cults on Delos were a haphazard collection, reflecting
the nationalities and concerns of the sailors and merchants who traded
there. With Alexandria, however, as probably with most of the many cities
newly founded by the Hellenistic kings, the cult structure was planned,
but multifarious, with Greek, Egyptian, Jewish, and other cults introduced
to suit the needs of the multinational citizenry and residents. We have in
Alexandria, for the first time, different religious and national communities
all practicing their own religions in one very large city, sharing in some
areas, being exclusive in others – a concept familiar to us but alien to the
classical Greek world and to much of the Hellenistic Greek world as well.
All of this we should see in good part as the result of the Hellenistic practice
of bringing together separate nationalities to create one new city.

The religious cults of the cities we have described give some sense of the quite different civic religious environments in which Greek individuals of the period lived. We are fortunate to have also a rather extensive record of the religious life of one individual of these times, Artemidorus, son of Apollonius, of the city Perge in Pamphylia on the south coast of Asia Minor. Artemidorus was one of those Greeks who took advantage of the new freedoms of the Hellenistic period to move about the Greek world. In him we have one of our best recorded examples of how an individual responded to the religious environment of his times, roughly the last half of the third century and the first half of the second century B.C.E. In the reign of Ptolemy III Euergetes (246–21) Artemidorus sailed west across the Aegean from his homeland and took up residence on Thera, an island about 110 kilometers south of Delos. Thera is now known as Santorini and is famous for its mystic beauty and for the volcanic eruption which created this landscape and brought an end to the Minoan settlement there in the seventeenth century. In the Hellenistic period, however, it was, much like Erythrae, a small city-state with no special claims to fame. For his good services Artemidorus was made a citizen of Thera and lived out there his life of ninety-three years. Thera was at the time a possession of the Ptolemaic kingdom, and Artemidorus, obviously a wealthy man, embraced the royal cult by building temples for Ptolemy I Soter, Ptolemy II Philadelphus, and Ptolemy III Euergetes, the last, at least, in association with the people of Thera.[2] Of more interest is the large, new sanctuary he had carved out of a rocky hillside, close to the city center of Thera. First, advised by a dream, he established for his adopted city an altar of Homonoia (Concord), quite likely after a period of internal political strife. He then put, at the flanks of this altar, altars of the Samothracian Theoi Megaloi (Great Gods) and the Dioscuri. The mysteries of the Theoi Megaloi on Samothrace, in which Artemidorus had probably participated, promised, among other things, safety at sea, and such too was the role of the Dioscuri. The aid of both sets of gods would be welcome in the port and naval station of Thera. To the left of this central complex Artemidorus had carved in rock three dedications: an eagle

Of Homonoia.
Artemidorus, son of Apollonius.
from Perge, on the basis of a dream.
Artemidorus from the homeland of Perge on the basis of a dream established here for the city an immortal altar of Homonoia.
Inscription on altar of Homonoia (*IG* XII.3.Supplement 1336)

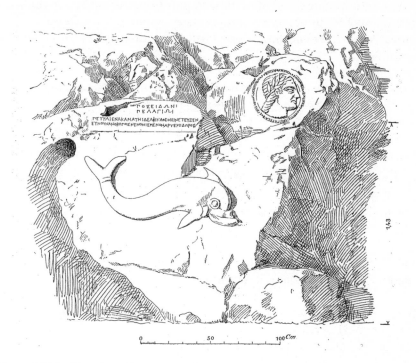

Figure VIII.2 Drawing of a section of Artemidorus' rockcut sanctuary on Thera (*IG* XII.3, Supplement, p. 296). The dolphin represents Poseidon Pelasgios. The head is of Artemidorus. The inscription (#1347) above the dolphin reads, "To Poseidon Pelasgios. On this hard rock Artemidorus fashioned for the gods the dolphin which is thought kindly to human beings." Around Artemidorus' head is the inscription (#1348), "A memorial for Thera. As long as the stars of the sky arise and the earth's surface remains, the name of Artemidorus is not lost."

for Zeus Olympios, a lion for Apollo Stephanophoros (Crown Wearer), and a dolphin for Poseidon Pelasgios (Of the Sea). In the inscriptions accompanying these dedications, Artemidorus makes it clear that they are intended for both the gods and the city. To the right of the altar of Homonoia, cut like steps into the rock, are statue bases for Hecate, whom, Artemidorus tells us, "the rural people honor" and for Priapus, who himself says in his epigram that he, from Lampsacus, a city on the Hellespont, "has come to Thera bringing imperishable wealth." The Heroïssae, perhaps local heroines, are honored too, with an altar, because "they bring new crops each year."

Two inscriptions which were found apart from the sanctuary, probably at the site of his tomb, reveal something more about Artemidorus and his times. At the very end of his long life Artemidorus dedicated an altar to Artemis:

> To Artemis Soteira of Perge.
> Artemidorus, son of Apollonius, of Perge.
> Artemis prophesied for Artemidorus ninety years of life,
> and Pronoia (Forethought) added another three to it.
>   (*IG* XII.3.Supplement, 1350)

Artemidorus, by the erection of this altar, created in his adopted country a cult of the Artemis Soteira (Savior) of his old homeland. We see here the transplantation of a cult from one city to another, from Perge to Thera.[3] The cult is brought to Thera by an old devotee of the goddess, a goddess who had prophesied a life of ninety years for him. Near his life's end Artemidorus erected this altar of a goddess new to Thera as a memorial of and perhaps in gratitude for Artemidorus' and Artemis' long relationship, a relationship suggested even in Artemidorus' name (Gift of Artemis). And we know that the Theraeans maintained this cult for at least the next century.

A second altar at this same site bears this epigram:

> The prophetess of the god in Delphi sent an oracle,
> indicating that Artemidorus was an immortal, divine hero.
>   (*IG* XII.3.Supplement, 1349)

Here, as could happen only in the Hellenistic age and later, Artemidorus, an ordinary mortal, has become one of those deities whose worship, honor, and sanctuaries he has so richly developed on Thera. The Theraeans, after giving him citizenship, after awarding him crowns of ivy for his good services, must have, after his death, sent to Delphi to ask whether they should treat their great benefactor as a cultic hero. And Apollo responded: "Yes, Artemidorus was an 'immortal, divine hero.' " Presumably, from this time forth, the Theraeans would make annual offerings to their new hero, Artemidorus.

Most Greeks even in the Hellenistic period would have remained in their homelands, and for them we can imagine a religious life very much like that we described for Athens or Erythrae, very similar in deities, rituals, and festivals to that of the Classical period, with the appearance of occasional new deities such as Isis and Sarapis, and with the appearance, welcome or not, of the ruler cults of the Macedonian kings. But Artemidorus was one of the many entrepreneurs of the period, looking for new opportunities on an island more in the center of the renewed life of the Aegean. Unlike in the Classical period, he could be welcomed into the religious community of Thera, and in turn he embraced the ruler cults and deities of his new homeland. As a rich individual Artemidorus could build new sanctuaries, altars, and even temples for state deities, and this too, if not an entirely new feature of the Hellenistic period, is one now quite common. And his name, not that of the city, is explicitly associated with each new foundation and contributes to his reputation. He greatly enhanced the cult of the Ptolemies, and for his own sanctuary he turned first to Homonoia, political Concord, a personified deity of the type now becoming fashionable. He then gave due honor to some traditional gods of the city, Zeus Olympios, Apollo Stephanophoros, and Poseidon Pelasgius. The other deities look to be more of personal and perhaps professional interest to Artemidorus. The Dioscuri protected sailors and merchants, and so did the Theoi Megaloi into whose mysteries Artemidorus may well have been initiated on Samothrace. Artemidorus added to these "saving gods" deities who promised agricultural prosperity, Hecate, Priapus from Lampsacus, and the Heroïssae. And, near the end of his life, he paid honor to a deity of his homeland, Artemis Soteira of Perge. Despite the obvious personal preferences he revealed in this very Hellenistic mix of gods he included, Artemidorus intended his new creations as public sanctuaries, open to worship for all Theraean citizens and residents.

Of all these deities it is conceivable that Artemidorus first introduced to Thera Homonoia, the Theoi Megaloi, Priapus, and, of course, Artemis Soteira, and the example of Artemidorus alone helps to explain the variety and movement of deities and the expansion of local pantheons so characteristic of the Hellenistic period. Finally, Artemidorus himself, with the warrant of the Delphic oracle, was heroized, and this reflects the increasing trend in the Hellenistic period to grant to benefactors of the state heroic or divine status. As we saw in Chapter II, in the Classical period primarily legendary figures such as Theseus or Ajax or else founders of colonies received such status. Only rarely then were ordinary humans heroized for outstanding athletic or military accomplishments. Beginning with the Macedonian kings, great benefactors to the state could be given divine honors, usually as gods, and this led, already in Artemidorus' time, to lesser benefactors being heroized. It is in this context that Artemidorus, after decades of illustrious service to the Theraeans and their deities, became himself a divine hero.

In Hellenistic Athens, Delos, Erythrae, Alexandria, and, thanks in part to Artemidorus, in Thera some new gods and new types of gods have appeared, gods like people are now moving more freely from city to city, and peoples of different countries and nationalities and their gods now mix much more freely together in worship, but, importantly, the human needs these old and new gods fulfill, in providing safety, fertility, health, and national and personal prosperity, remain much what they had been in the Classical period.

NOTES

1. When the Athenians finally decided to give "divine honors" to royal benefactors, they made them eponyms of new tribes added to Cleisthenes' original ten: Antigonus I and his son Demetrius in 307/6, Ptolemy III in 224, and Attalus I in 200. The eponyms of the original ten tribes were heroes, not gods.
2. The relevant epigraphical texts for this and the following discussion are *IG* XII.3, 464 and *IG* XII.3.Supplement, 1333–48.
3. On the site and prominence of the cult of Artemis Soteira at Perge, see L. Robert, *Hellenica* 5 (1948), 64–9. Her cult was later to be found also on Rhodes and at Halicarnassus and Naucratis.

FURTHER READING

On various religious aspects of the Hellenistic Age in general:

Bringmann, K., "The King as Benefactor: Some Remarks on Ideal Kingship in the Age of Hellenism," pp. 7–24 in *Images and Ideologies: Self-Definition in the Hellenistic World*, ed. A. Bulloch, E.S. Gruen, A.A. Long, and A. Stewart (Berkeley, 1993)
Chamoux, F., *Hellenistic Civilization* (Oxford, 2003), pp. 323–52
Mikalson, J.D., *Religion in Hellenistic Athens* (Berkeley, 1998), pp. 315–23 and "Greek Religion in the Hellenistic Period," forthcoming in *The Cambridge Companion to the Hellenistic Period*, G.R. Bugh, editor
Nilsson, M.P., *Geschichte der Griechischen Religion*, vol. 2, second edition (Munich, 1961), pp. 1–309
Stewart, Z., "La Religione," pp. 503–616 in *Storia e civiltà dei Greci*, vol. 8, ed. R. Bianchi Bandinelli (Milan, 1979)

On religion in Hellenistic Athens and Delos:

Mikalson, J.D., *Religion in Hellenistic Athens* (Berkeley, 1998)

On Isis and Sarapis:

Fraser, P.M., *Ptolemaic Alexandria*, 3 volumes (Oxford, 1972), especially Vol. 1, pp. 246–76
Merkelbach, R., *Isis regina – Zeus Sarapis* (Stuttgart and Leipzig, 1995)

On religion and cults in Erythrae:

Graf, F., *Nordionische Kulte* (Rome, 1985), 147–375

On Alexandria and its religious cults:

Fraser, J.M. *Ptolemaic Alexandria*, 3 volumes (Oxford, 1972), especially Vol. 1, pp. 189–301

Koenen, L., "The Ptolemaic King as a Religious Figure," pp. 25–115 in *Images and Ideologies: Self-Definition in the Hellenistic World*, ed. A. Bulloch, E.S. Gruen, A.A. Long, and A. Stewart (Berkeley, 1993)

Lewis, N., *Greeks in Ptolemaic Egypt* (Oxford, 1986)

Stambaugh, J.E., *Sarapis under the Early Ptolemies* (Leiden, 1972)

On Artemidorus, his sanctuary, and Hellenistic features of his religious life:

Graf, F., "Bemerkungen zur bürgerlichen Religiosität im Zeitalter des Hellenismus," pp. 103–14 in *Stadtbild und Bürgerbild im Hellenismus*, ed. M. Wörrle and P. Zanker (Munich, 1995) = *Vestigia* 47

Index

DATE			